The Rational Animal

ALSO BY DOUGLAS T. KENRICK

Sex, Murder, and the Meaning of Life:
A Psychologist Investigates How Evolution, Cognition, and Complexity
Are Revolutionizing Our View of Human Nature (2011)

The Rational
Animal

HOW EVOLUTION MADE US
SMARTER THAN WE THINK

Douglas T. Kenrick
and Vladas Griskevicius

BASIC BOOKS
A Member of the Perseus Books Group
New York

Designed by Jeff Williams

Library of Congress Cataloging-in-Publication Data

Kenrick, Douglas T.
The rational animal : how evolution made us smarter than we think / Douglas T. Kenrick and Vladas Griskevicius.
pages cm
Includes bibliographical references and index.
ISBN 978-0-465-03242-6 (hardcover)—ISBN 978-0-465-04097-1 (e-book) 1. Reasoning (Psychology) 2. Decision making. 3. Evolutionary psychology. I. Griskevicius, Vladas. II. Title.

BF442.K46 2013

153—dc23

2013008954

DOUG:
For my sons, Dave and Liam,
who taught me a deeper lesson about rationality.

For my wife, Carol, who puts up with my irrationality.

For my mother-in-law, Jean Luce, who contributed the most
rational portion of Liam's nature and who nurtures us all.

VLAD:
For my strong-willed father, who always finishes what he starts.

For my self-sacrificing mother, who prefers that
I not refer to people as animals.

For my nurturing wife, who liked the bit about
diamond-encrusted grillz.

For my curious children, who are confused about why
daddy's name is next to a picture of an ape.

BUT WAIT, THAT'S NOT ALL!
DOUG AND VLAD:
For Bob Cialdini, our mentor and guru.

Contents

Introduction: Cadillacs, Communists, and Pink Bubble Gum   ix

Why did Elvis gold-plate the hubcaps on his Cadillac?

1: Rationality, Irrationality, and the Dead Kennedys   1

*What do testosterone-crazed skateboarders have in common
with Wall Street bankers?*

2: The Seven Subselves   23

*Did Martin Luther King Jr. have a multiple personality
disorder? Do you?*

3: Home Economics Versus Wall Street Economics   51

*Why did Walt Disney play by different rules
than his successors?*

4: Smoke Detectors in the Mind   75

Why is it dangerous to seek the truth?

5: Modern Cavemen   95

*How can illiterate jungle dwellers pass a test that tricks
Harvard philosophers?*

6: Living Fast and Dying Young   117

*Why do people who go from rags to riches often end up
in bankruptcy court?*

7: Gold Porsches and Green Peacocks   143

*Do people buy a gold Porsche and a green Toyota Prius
for the same reason?*

8: Sexual Economics: His and Hers   161

When is a gain for the goose a loss for the gander?

9: Deep Rationality Parasites   185

How do snake oil salesmen exploit deep rationality?

Conclusion: Mementos from Our Tour   207

What's in it for moi?

Acknowledgments   217

Notes   221

References   235

Index   255

Introduction

Cadillacs, Communists, and Pink Bubble Gum

It has been said that man is a rational animal. All my life
I have been searching for evidence which could support this.

—BERTRAND RUSSELL

ARE YOUR DECISIONS rational or irrational?

Let's begin with a few quick questions. Would you do any of the following:

- You're a young fellow with some rhythm who grew up poor in Mississippi. Would you spend $785,400 on a Cadillac with gold-plated hubcaps and forty coats of paint custom-made from pearls, oriental fish scales, and diamond dust?

- You're a British woman living as an unemployed single mother. You've been writing in your spare time, though, and your books have begun to sell like wildfire. Would you give away your hard-earned money?

- You're an immigrant from a poor Communist country, where you once stood in line for four hours to buy your first banana.

Just after you first land in America on a Pan Am jumbo jet, you are taken to a giant supermarket full of unimaginably delicious and nutritious goods. If your rich American relative offered you the opportunity to choose any one item to buy, would you purchase a pack of bubble gum?

- You're a college professor who has carefully protected his paltry retirement savings by putting them into safe bond accounts. You have watched the stock market running up wildly for several years, and there are rumors among financial experts that the bubble is about to burst. Would you choose that exact moment to take half of your already scarce retirement nest egg and put it into risky stocks?

- You're a wealthy Indian man in the state of Patiala with the legal right to marry as many women as you like. You have ninety wives already. Would you say enough is enough, or would you instead start looking for bride number ninety-one?

- You're a New Yorker working long hours as superintendent of an apartment building on East Eighty-sixth Street in Manhattan. Would you spend all of your savings on lottery tickets?

If you didn't answer yes to these questions, meet the folks who did:

- Elvis Presley, the King of Rock 'n' Roll, who didn't just buy the gaudiest Cadillac of all time but purchased over one hundred of them.

- J. K. Rowling, author of the Harry Potter books, who gave away much of her hard-earned money, including writing one check for $15 million.

- Vlad Griskevicius (one author of the book you now hold in your hands), whose first decision as a newly minted capitalist was to buy a pack of Bubblicious pink watermelon bubble gum. And as for that banana he stood in line for four hours to buy back in the old country, he ate it with the peel still on, thinking it would be downright stupid to throw away any part of so desirable a delicacy.

- Doug Kenrick (the other author of the book in your hands), who, after watching his own retirement account grow sluggishly while the stock market shot up, transferred a large portion of those funds into the stock market in 2001, just in time to participate in a couple of historically unprecedented crashes in stock values. Unless this book makes the *New York Times* best seller's list, he's now planning to retire some time after his seventy-ninth birthday, probably to a small hut in rural Ecuador.

- Rajinder Singh, Sixth Maharajah of the Indian state of Patiala, who not only married a ninety-first wife, but didn't stop saying "I do" until he hit bride number 365.

- New York building superintendent Ray Otero, who not only squandered his savings, but continues to spend $30,000 a year on lottery tickets—without hitting a big win yet.

Some of these decisions, involving gold-plated hubcaps, $15 million donations, ninety-first wives, and $30,000 lottery budgets, might seem disconnected from normal people's everyday decisions, which are more likely to involve whether to dine at Taco Bell or Pizza Hut. Yet the decisions made by the King of Rock 'n' Roll and the Maharajah of Patiala actually have a lot in common with those we all make every day. Even seemingly absurd choices often mask deeper questions of profound significance about how people make decisions.

THE RATIONAL ANIMAL

Lurking behind those seemingly silly decisions about Bubblicious bubble gum, bags of lottery tickets, and diamond-dusted Cadillacs is a profoundly important question. It is a question philosophers have pondered for centuries, and one that is central to economics, psychology, and our daily lives: What are the underlying reasons for people's choices?

Great thinkers from Aristotle and Descartes to Bertrand Russell and Oscar Wilde have all debated whether people are "rational animals." Philosophers, scientists, and pundits alike have focused on one side of the coin, vigorously arguing whether humans are or are not "rational." But the controversy has mostly overlooked the other side of the coin—the "animal" within the so-called rational animal. This book is about that creature.

In the great debate about whether human decisions are rational or irrational, economists and psychologists have been obsessed over the surface features of our decisions—whether a person's particular choice in a particular situation achieves that person's goal. For example, does the decision to buy a $2 lottery ticket or a shiny new car make a person richer or happier? But to fully understand our decisions, we must dig below the surface and connect our present choices to the evolutionary past. To understand how people make decisions, we ask a fundamental question neglected by traditional views: Why did the brain evolve to make the choices that it does?

Asking this question transforms the way we think about human decisions. New scientific findings are revealing that our decision making, rather than being either rational or irrational, is characterized by *deep rationality*. Our choices today reflect a deep-seated evolutionary wisdom, honed by our ancestors' past successes and failures. This book explores how the choices made in the modern world—by you, me, and Elvis Presley—are rooted in a finely orchestrated set of ancestral mechanisms that often operate outside our conscious awareness.

THIS NEW way of thinking is based on two insights at the center of this book:

Insight 1: Human decision making serves evolutionary goals.

The traditional way of thinking about human behavior is based almost completely on a consideration of people's surface goals—getting a decent bargain on a pair of dress shoes, for example, or picking a fine restaurant for a date next Saturday. But humans, like all animals, evolved to make choices in ways that promote deeper evolutionary purposes. Once we start looking at modern choices through this ancestral lens, many decisions that appear foolish and irrational at the surface level turn out to be smart and adaptive at a deeper evolutionary level.

Insight 2: Human decision making is designed to achieve several very different evolutionary goals.

Economists and psychologists have often assumed that humans seek a single broad goal: to feel good or to maximize benefits. In actuality, all humans pursue several very different evolutionary goals, such as acquiring a mate, protecting themselves from danger, and attaining status. This is an important distinction. Depending on which evolutionary goal they currently have in mind, consciously or subconsciously, people will have very different biases and make very different choices.

These deceptively simple insights represent a profound departure from earlier views of decision making. They imply that our choices, like those made by Elvis Presley and Maharajah Rajinder Singh, are often subconsciously guided by deeper evolutionary goals. And they suggest something even more radical: that there's more than one you making decisions. Although it feels as if there is just one single self inside your head, your mind actually contains several different *subselves*, each with a specific evolutionary goal and a completely different set of priorities. You make decisions differently when your goal is wooing an attractive mate versus fending off the bad guys or climbing upward in the local status hierarchy. Although the divided nature of your mind often leads you to appear inconsistent and irrational, many of your choices are, at a deeper evolutionary level, even more rational than the great philosophers ever imagined.

A ROUGH MAP OF THE TERRITORY

In the pages ahead we journey into the depths of the ancestral mind.

Each chapter begins with a visit to a mysterious corner of human decision making. Why do three out of four professional football players go bankrupt? How did such a large group of otherwise shrewd and intelligent investors allow Bernard Madoff to swindle them out of millions and millions of dollars? To solve each puzzle, we go beneath the surface and look at the newest scientific findings, letting you peek under the hood to examine the evidence for yourself. Along the way, you'll discover the intimate connections between ovulating strippers, Wall Street financiers, testosterone-crazed skateboarders, Elvis Presley, and you.

Here's how our behind-the-scenes tour is organized. In Chapter 1 ("Rationality, Irrationality, and the Dead Kennedys"), we introduce the idea of deep rationality by comparing an eminently rational man, Joseph Patrick Kennedy, with his famously irrational descendants. In Chapter 2 ("The Seven Subselves"), we more properly introduce you to your subselves and consider whether you and Martin Luther King Jr. are hypocrites or just victims of a common form of multiple personality disorder. In Chapter 3 ("Home Economics Versus Wall Street Economics"), we examine how each subself negotiates with other people, exploring some nasty problems that arose when the Walt Disney Company stopped being a family business.

In Chapter 4 ("Smoke Detectors in the Mind"), we take a closer look at the biases and mistakes each of your subselves is prone to make, and try to understand why the people in one African nation chose to starve rather than accept help. In Chapter 5 ("Modern Cavemen"), we investigate how understanding our subselves can help us make better decisions, asking why uneducated members of tribes deep in the Amazon can solve logical problems that stump students at Harvard.

In Chapter 6 ("Living Fast and Dying Young"), we examine how the subselves change across the lifespan and try to understand why many people who go from rags to riches later go bankrupt. In Chapter 7 ("Gold Porsches and Green Peacocks"), we ask whether people might buy a shiny gold Cadillac and a dull green Toyota Prius for some of the very same reasons, even if they're not consciously aware of them. In Chapter 8 ("Sexual Economics: His and Hers"), we probe more deeply into the ways that men's and women's subselves differ and try to figure out why in some societies men pay several years' income for the company of a woman, while in others a woman's family pays an immense dowry to buy her the company of a man.

In Chapter 9 ("Deep Rationality Parasites"), we explore the dark side of the story—how our otherwise deeply rational tendencies can open us up to exploitation by clever parasites in the modern world, many of whom are hiding behind respectable business suits and sincere smiles. Finally, we wave good-bye and send you off with a few colorful postcards, each inscribed with an important takeaway message from our journey to the decision-making centers of the mind.

YOUR TOUR GUIDES

Your tour guides will be Doug Kenrick and Vlad Griskevicius. In some ways, it's amazing that the two of us ended up on the same boat. Doug grew up in a junkie-infested New York neighborhood and seemed destined to join his male relatives in the state prison at Sing Sing. Vlad was born in Lithuania when it was still part of the Soviet Union, in a region more likely to produce potato farmers than college professors. But Doug managed to avoid a life of crime and instead became an evolutionary psychologist who has conducted hundreds of scientific studies on topics ranging from sex and murder to love and altruism. Vlad slipped out from behind the Iron Curtain and, after delighting in the joys of watermelon-flavored bubble gum, went on to study economics and social psychology among the capitalists. He is now a professor of marketing, conducting research and teaching courses on consumer behavior, advertising, and decision making. The two of us shared a brilliant mentor, Bob Cialdini, and we've collaborated with a group of highly creative colleagues, many of whom have contributed greatly to the scientific revolution we describe in this book.

Most of the findings we'll describe have been reported in scientific journals, and a few of those discoveries have been reported more widely in the media. But the big picture, connecting our own colleagues' research findings with work by other psychologists, economists, decision scientists, biologists, and anthropologists, has yet to be filled in. In this book, we try to paint that wider canvas in a colorful way, showing why an intimate familiarity with our inner rational animal matters to business leaders and working stiffs, to armchair economists and their real-world counterparts, to politicians and their constituents, to teachers and those of us who still have a lot to learn.

1

Rationality, Irrationality, and the Dead Kennedys

JOSEPH PATRICK KENNEDY was a shining example of a rational economic man. At age twenty-five, he became America's youngest bank president, bragging to a newspaper reporter, "I want to be a millionaire by the age of thirty-five." That was quite an aspiration in 1915, when the average yearly income was barely $1,000, and a loaf of bread cost nine cents. Kennedy made good on his lofty goal, though, becoming a Wall Street trader and turning a profit of $650,000 on a single transaction in 1922. Kennedy's good fortunes continued even when the stock market took its infamous nosedive (he had sold off his holdings just in time). His impeccable sense of timing struck again in 1933, when he arranged a lucrative contract with Dewar's to import liquor into the United States—just as Prohibition was about to end. And as the Hollywood movie industry was hitting the big time, he co-founded RKO pictures, with assets of over $80 million.

Joe Kennedy also exhibited keen rational self-interest in his personal life. After having an affair with the beautiful movie star Gloria Swanson, he jilted the actress when her movie went grossly over budget, and left her holding the tab. Later in life, he turned his ambitions from money to political power, becoming the American ambassador to

England and plotting to have his eldest son become president of the United States.

But the luck of this particular Irishman did not pass on to his descendants. His handsome and charming eldest son, Joseph Jr., the one he hoped would someday become president, was killed at age twenty-nine during a World War II bombing mission. His beautiful daughter Kathleen seemed to be living a charmed life when she married William Cavendish, heir to the Duke of Devonshire. But she was widowed only four months later when Cavendish was killed in action; then she herself died in a plane crash in 1948. Joseph's second son, John, was elected president, then famously assassinated in Dallas on November 22, 1963. His third son, Robert, was shot down during his own campaign for the presidency in 1968. And his youngest son, Teddy, narrowly escaped death in 1969 when he drove his car off a bridge on Chappaquiddick Island, drowning his passenger, Mary Jo Kopechne.

The next generation of Kennedys seemed to fare even worse. In 1984, Joseph's grandson David died of a drug overdose in a Miami hotel. David's brother Michael perished in a skiing accident in 1997. And in 1999, John F. Kennedy Jr., the strikingly handsome son of the former president, met a tragic end when the plane he was piloting crashed into the cold night waters off Long Island. At this point in the story, you should be able to hear that spooky organ music playing in the background. It was enough to lead one former *New York Times* editor to write a book called *The Curse of the Kennedys*.

How is it that Joe Kennedy could lead a life of charmed decisions, whereas his descendants seemed magnetically drawn to ill-fated choices? The mystery of the Kennedy family vividly exemplifies a much broader question: Are people's decisions rational or irrational? Experts have been sharply divided on this question. Some assert that our choices are eminently rational. But others argue that our decisions are frequently irrational—and occasionally even tragically moronic.

In this book, we offer a third view, based on emerging scientific evidence that connects human behavior with that of the rest of the animal kingdom. Although human decisions often appear foolish, they are, if you probe beneath the surface, often deeply rational.

To see under the veneer, though, we need to radically reframe how we think about the human mind. Rather than asking whether the mind is good at solving modern problems such as investing on Wall Street or acing the SATs, we should instead ask how it solves the central problems our ancestors faced over hundreds of thousands of years. By looking at modern behavior through a wider-angled evolutionary lens, we can gain a fresh perspective on how people make decisions. This new way of thinking transforms how we think about rationality and reveals the surprising, hidden wisdom behind seemingly senseless decisions—including ones made by the Kennedys, your coworkers, your family members, and your stockbroker.

As we'll discover, a deeper understanding of the Kennedys' fortunes and misfortunes reveals something fundamental about us, about our friends and neighbors, and about the nature of human nature. Let's take a closer look at the choices of Joe Kennedy and his descendants, as viewed through the eyes of three very different kinds of scientists.

RATIONAL MAN: PEOPLE AS ECONS

One explanation for the Kennedy clan's fortunes and misfortunes is grounded in the classic view that dominated our understanding of decision making for over a century: rational economics. You are familiar with this view if you've taken a class in business or economics or merely perused the financial pages of the newspaper. This perspective is caricatured in the movie *Wall Street,* in which the coldly calculating Gordon Gecko proclaims, "Greed is good!" and high roller Roger Barnes asks the classic question, "What's in it for *moi?*"

Rational economists view people as, well, rational. To get a better feel for the rational economist, imagine someone in a finely cut business suit seated in front of a computer, with a stock market ticker flashing overhead. Poring over mountains of data, our prototypical rational economist crunches numbers and scribbles mathematical equations on scraps of paper between triple-espresso coffee breaks. Although rational economists in the real world are a diverse lot and don't all wear suits to jobs on Wall Street, they share a commitment to analyzing decisions in terms of rational self-interest. Any decision—be it to encourage one's older versus younger child to run for president, to import liquor or to go into showbiz, or to frolic with a Hollywood starlet or dump her—boils down to the question: What's it worth to me?

According to this view, we make decisions like ultrarational "Econs." Like Joe Kennedy or Gordon Gecko, the average person is good at knowing which choices will best serve his or her self-interest. Like Joseph Kennedy did in deciding to sell his stock holdings or end his relationship with Gloria Swanson, we base our choices on the best available information. Of course, we can't predict the future with certainty, and random, unexpected events do happen. Those random events average out statistically, but as in the case of stock market and airplane crashes, an otherwise well-reasoned choice sometimes turns out to have been unfortunate. From the classic rational economic perspective, the tragic succession of deaths among the second and third generation of Kennedys is not some mystical curse but more like a string of unlucky bets—nothing more magical than random bad luck.

IRRATIONAL MAN: PEOPLE AS MORONS

But there is a very different explanation for the Kennedy family's calamities. Maybe Joe Kennedy's descendants were cursed not with bad luck but with bad judgment. "The Curse of the Kennedys," argued *New York Times* columnist Sandy Grady, stems from "their code of macho daring that crosses into recklessness." That certainly applied to the very first tragedy—the death of Joe Jr. The eldest Kennedy son had already flown enough bombing missions to qualify for a discharge, when he daringly volunteered to fly a plane full of explosives directly at a heavily fortified German cannon site. The same rash judgment style was shown by grandson Michael, who died playing football while recklessly zooming down a tree-filled mountain slope on a pair of skis. And when Teddy's car plunged off the Chappaquiddick bridge, random bad luck also had a little help from an evening of heavy partying and a dose of bad judgment.

This bad judgment theory of the Kennedy curse fits well with what is currently the most popular view of decision making—that our judgments and decisions are often flawed and irrational.

Consider the following situation:

Person A is waiting in line to see a movie. When he gets to the ticket window, he is told that he is the millionth customer and wins $100.

Person B is waiting in line at a different theater. The man in front of him gets to the ticket window and is told he's the millionth customer and wins $1,000. Person B receives $150 for being the person right after the millionth customer.

Would you rather be Person A or Person B?

Unless you're allergic to money (like the people who get a rash when they touch the nickel in coins), a rational economist would expect any sensible person to choose Person B, who makes off with $50 more than Person A. But in fact, most people would rather be Person A, making the irrational choice to pass up an extra $50, just to avoid the bad feeling they might have from being so close to getting $1,000.

This irrational bias is known as *loss aversion*—the tendency for people to focus more on losses than they do on gains. This bias was discovered by Nobel Prize winner Daniel Kahneman and his colleague Amos Tversky, two pioneers in the field of behavioral economics, the marriage of economics and experimental psychology. Behavioral economists are rigorous scientists who typically work in a laboratory, conducting experiments on people's behavior. Although rigorous, the prototypical behavioral economist also has a sense of humor and loves to root out human foibles, point a spotlight at them, and have a good chuckle over our shared irrationalities. Imagine someone in a white lab coat but wearing a Rolling Stones T-shirt underneath—the one with the big red tongue hanging out.

From the behavioral economist's perspective, our brains are rather flawed contraptions. In contrast to the rational economist's view, which sees the mind as a polished Rolls Royce with a purring V-12 engine and a state-of-the-art navigation system, the mind looks to a behavioral economist more like a rusty Yugo schlepping along on three cylinders with a compass sticker to help navigate. Behavioral economists have demonstrated in countless studies that our overworked brains are often incapable of making the logical choices expected by rational economists. While people might aspire to be rational, everyday choices made by us folks down in the real world simply do not adhere to the cold, hard principles of rational economics.

There are enough books and scientific articles exposing our mental flaws to fill up an entire library. If you look up "list of cognitive biases" on Wikipedia, you will find ninety-seven different mental defects identified so far. Since you may need a good chuckle as you wait in your broken-down Yugo for the AAA truck, let's check out a few of our comical faults.

First take a gander at the *gambler's fallacy,* an irrational tendency to think that past events influence future probabilities. This fallacy shows up when people flip a coin and get heads five times in a row, then guess that the next flip has an especially high chance of coming up tails. That's silly, of course, since the next flip still has a 50 percent chance of landing heads or tails, no matter what happened earlier. In John Irving's novel *The World According to Garp,* the hero, Garp, makes this error when he decides to buy a house right after a small plane crashes into it, reasoning that the chances of another plane hitting the house have just dropped to zero. And when one of our wives was expecting a third child after having two girls in a row, several people were confident that she was "due" to have a boy.

And then there's the *hindsight bias,* the irrational tendency to react to new information with the feeling that "I knew it all along." Before presidential elections, people are moderately confident that their candidate is going to win. But a few months later, when the count is in, those who supported a Mitt Romney or a John Kerry say they knew all along that he was going to lose!

Our brains are further riddled with biases like the *clustering illusion,* the tendency to see patterns where none exist, as when people are convinced a basketball player's string of three-pointers is evidence of a "hot hand," even though statistics reveal it's merely a random streak of luck. Here's one you can try at home: flip a coin twenty times, record the sequence of heads and tails, and then ask one of your buddies if he can see "the pattern." If your friends are like most people, they will quickly see a meaningful pattern in the sequence, even though it is random.

The gambler's fallacy, hindsight bias, and the clustering illusion are merely the tip of the irrationality iceberg. There's also the base-rate fallacy, the false-consensus illusion, the conjunction fallacy, the Barnum effect, the pseudocertainty effect, the ultimate-attribution error, the ostrich effect, and about ninety others. Based on all the evidence of mental errors, behavioral economists have disagreed strongly with traditional depictions of people as rational, computer-like Econs. From the behavioral economist's perspective, you don't have to be a Kennedy to make bad decisions. Hundreds of studies have demonstrated how people's decisions are often simple-minded, irrational, and self-defeating, even when those people are so-called experts. All these inherent mental deficiencies suggest that, rather than being ultrarational Econs, we real people are often more like thickheaded morons.

DEEP RATIONALITY: HUMANS AS ANIMALS

But are people really bumbling morons, persistently making foolish decisions that go against their self-interest? A closer look at the Kennedy clan suggests that their decisions weren't quite so foolish after all. Despite all the tragedies that transpired during the half century between the two plane crashes that claimed the lives of Joe Jr. and John Jr., the Kennedy clan has hardly been cursed. After the Chappaquiddick incident, Teddy Kennedy went on to become the fourth-longest-serving senator in US history and a powerful force on the world political stage, right up until his death at the ripe old age of seventy-seven. And the next generation of Kennedys includes US representatives, lieutenant governors, highly successful businessmen, film producers, and philanthropists. These descendants are similarly cursed with abundant wealth, opportunity, and social connections to other rich and powerful people. So despite occasional bad judgments, Joe Kennedy's descendants seem to have made plenty of good decisions as well.

Although the Kennedys may not be ultrarational Econs, they are certainly not morons. The same goes for the rest of us. Although some of our particular decisions are annoyingly ill informed, we manage to get by reasonably well. And the decisions of our sometimes feckless parents and their uneducated and uncouth predecessors were, at the very least, good enough that we are now here to talk about them. The fact that you are calmly reading a book instead of scouring the forest for morsels of food and worrying about deadly predators is a testament to our sophisticated brains. *Homo sapiens* is the most successful member of the great ape family and arguably the most successful species on the planet, possessing an enormously powerful brain that has allowed humans to thrive in an incredible range of environments. How could it be, then, that modern science has declared the most inventive organism on our planet an irrational fool?

The debates about whether human decisions are rational or irrational have been handicapped by a crucial limitation: they have largely ignored the fact that humans are part of the animal kingdom. By focusing only on our exalted species and ignoring our place in nature, we have missed the forest for the trees. But by panning out with our cameras, to see where *Homo sapiens* is situated in the context of other primates, other mammals, and other members of the animal kingdom, we can get a new perspective on ourselves.

This wide-angle view is the one adopted by our third scientist: the evolutionary psychologist. Trained in experimental psychology, anthropology, and evolutionary biology, the evolutionary psychologist looks at the big picture, examining the commonalities and differences between animals and humans from all corners of the globe. Picture someone in a khaki shirt and sporting a pair of binoculars, with a copy of Darwin's *Origin of Species* jutting out of a tattered backpack. Of course, all evolutionary psychologists don't fit this stereotype (some wear suits and work in marketing departments), but they do all share that important connection to Darwin's ideas, which inspires them to think about human beings in the same way evolutionary biologists think about other animals.

Biologists assume that all animals have brains designed to maximize evolutionary success, which they call "fitness." Evolutionary psychologists apply this same presumption to the human animal. This doesn't mean people are always consciously wondering: How does this choice improve my reproductive success? But it does mean that, as in the case of all other animals, natural selection has endowed modern humans with brains designed to make decisions in ways that consistently enhanced our ancestors' odds of passing their genes to the next generation. The decisions made by you, me, and the Kennedys are informed by an underlying wisdom developed over millennia, during which our ancestors successfully solved the problems of existence and exchange. This means that our modern skulls house Stone Age brains, designed to operate in the environments inhabited by our ancestors and to make decisions in ways that solved the types of problems those ancestors regularly confronted.

From the evolutionary psychologist's perspective, the classic rational economists and the modern behavioral economists got the story partly right but also partly wrong. Behavioral economists are right that our decision making is biased in ways that sometimes lead us to make silly choices. But this does not mean that our decisions are typically foolish. And rational economists are correct that our decisions are profoundly rational and smart, just not in the way they have long presumed.

LOSS AVERSION IN MONKEYS AND MEN

Which would produce a stronger emotional reaction: finding $50 on the street or discovering that a $50 bill was missing from your wallet? If you're like most people, you'll be more affected by losing money. Although people are reasonably happy to find money, they are really upset to lose it. This is the idea behind loss aversion: people are more psychologically moved by a loss than by an equal-sized gain. To an economist, loss aversion is irrational because $50 is worth exactly $50, whether it's coming or going. But is loss aversion all that foolish? Let's consider it from an evolutionary perspective.

Until recently, it was presumed that only humans were "irrationally" loss averse. But new evidence suggests loss aversion may run much deeper in our evolutionary lineage. In a series of experiments, Venkat Lakshminarayanan, Keith Chen, and Laurie Santos at Yale University gave capuchin monkeys tokens they could use to "purchase" tasty apple slices. Despite never having taken Econ 101, the monkeys quickly learned how to use the tokens as money. But the researchers then threw in a clever twist: they gave the monkeys a choice between buying apple slices from two different people. Person 1 always showed one apple slice and gave it to the monkey in exchange for a token. Person 2, on the other hand, always showed the monkey two apple slices but gave only one of the slices for a token. From an economic perspective, both were offering the exact same deal: one apple slice for one token. But by first offering two, then only delivering one, Person 2 focused the monkeys on what they were losing—the second apple slice. The monkeys strongly preferred dealing with Person 1, even though Person 2 was offering, from an economic perspective, the exact same deal. Just like humans, monkeys hate to feel like they're losing out.

Would human (and monkey) brains come prewired to be loss averse if this bias led our ancestors to persistently make bad decisions? Probably not. It makes more sense that our brain arrives with a built-in bias because this bias has historically led to decisions that enhance fitness. Natural selection is a pretty efficient process, so if a behavior is found widely in humans and other species, it's a better starting guess to presume it is adaptive rather than to assume it's merely dumb.

When considered in terms of evolutionary success, many of the seemingly irrational choices that people make do not seem so foolish after all. Most animals, including our ancestors and modern-day capuchin monkeys, lived very close to the margin of survival. Paleontologists who study early human civilizations have uncovered evidence that our ancestors faced frequent periods of drought and freezing. When you are living on the verge of starvation, a slight downturn in your food reserves makes a lot more difference than a slight upturn. Anthropologists who study people still living in hunter-gatherer and simple horticultural societies have discovered that they regularly make choices designed to produce not the best opportunity for obtaining a hyperabundant supply of food but, instead, the least danger of ending up with an insufficient supply. In other words, people everywhere have a strong motivation to avoid falling below the level that will feed themselves and their families. If our ancestors hadn't agonized over losses and instead had taken too many chances in going after the big gains, they'd have been more likely to lose out and never become anyone's ancestor.

Although we may not be living under the same conditions as our Ice Age progenitors, we did inherit our brains from them. So to understand how we behave in the modern world, it is essential to look at the broader picture. Evolutionary psychologists try to pull together the different threads, to interweave the diverse findings from psychology and economics with those from anthropology and biology. When we look at the deeper logic of decisions across the entire animal kingdom, it becomes clear that decision making in all critters, including us, is geared to promote deep-seated evolutionary goals. This is important because it suggests that many of our decision biases, errors, and misjudgments might not be design flaws; instead, they may be design features.

PROXIMATE VERSUS ULTIMATE
REASONS FOR BEHAVIOR

Imagine you have a friend who just spent $5 on a triple-chocolate fudge brownie, and you want to know the reason behind her purchase. So you ask her, "Why did you buy that?" She might simply respond, "I was hungry." If she were feeling more analytical, she might mention that she loves the taste of chocolate and couldn't resist the delectable scent of a freshly baked brownie.

Your friend's explanations for her behavior refer to something biologists call *proximate causes*. The word "proximate" here is related to the word "proximity." These causes point to relatively up-close and immediately present influences—to what I am presently feeling or thinking, for example.

Proximate causes are important, but they tell only the surface part of the story. They don't address the deeper question: Why do brownies taste good in the first place? This deeper inquiry seeks what biologists call an *ultimate cause*. Ultimate explanations go below the surface, focusing not on the immediate triggers of a behavior but on their evolutionary function. They ask what purpose a certain tendency would have served for our ancestors. In the brownie case, we humans have brains that light up whenever we see, smell, or eat foods that are rich in sugars and fats. These brownie-appreciation mechanisms exist because an attraction to calorie-dense foods helped our ancestors store energy and survive in an environment in which nutritious foods were often scarce. This is the ultimate reason why most humans are attracted more to fatty and sugary brownies than to much healthier, low-calorie, fat-free kale. Whereas the proximate reason your friend shelled out $5 for a triple-chocolate fudge brownie may be that she liked its pleasant aroma, the ultimate reason is that a preference for sugary and fatty foods helped solve the critical evolutionary challenge of survival.

Economists and psychologists of all stripes have typically been concerned only with proximate reasons for human behavior. At the proximate level, people behave one way rather than another because they want to feel good. People strive to experience pleasure, happiness, or satisfaction and to avoid pain, sadness, or frustration. Economists characterize all proximate goals as providing "utility." If you ask an economist why a person has done something, the answer is always utility. For example, when I decide to blow $200 for dinner at Café Sydney in Australia, I have concluded that the utility I'll get from the stunning views of Sydney Harbor, the artfully presented and delicately spiced fusion cuisine, and the fine bottle of Hunter Valley Semillon is greater than the utility I'd get from spending $10 twenty times at McDonald's.

If you delve into the massive scientific literature on decision making, you will discover mostly proximate explanations for human choices. But the entire other half of the story—the ultimate reasons for behavior—is conspicuously missing.

It can be easy to overlook the ultimate reasons for behavior. They are often difficult to see, especially if you don't even realize there is something more going on beneath the surface. In some cases, the link between proximate and ultimate reasons for behavior is readily apparent. In the case of the brownie, a proximate explanation, such as "I was starving," connects obviously to the ultimate goal of obtaining calories to survive, and the conscious link is not hard to make. But often the links between proximate and ultimate reasons are not so clear. Consider the question of why birds migrate each year. The proximate reason is because days get shorter; day length is the immediate cue triggering the bird's motivation to begin its journey. But the ultimate reason for bird migration has nothing to do with day length. Instead, it has to do with the fact that the best food and mating sites change with the seasons.

When an oriole decides to make his annual trek from Baltimore, Maryland, to Bogota, Colombia, the bird does not need to be aware of the connections between day length, seasons, survival, and mating. Likewise, it's a safe bet that we bird-watching hominids are usually un-aware of most of the connections between the proximate triggers for our decisions and the ultimate evolutionary reasons behind them. To make decisions right here and now, you don't need to understand how your choices connect to your ancestors' success, any more than you need to know the history of the automobile or the principles of the combustion engine to turn the ignition key and drive to the supermar-ket. But just because you're not always aware of the ultimate reasons for your behavior, that doesn't mean they're not influencing your choices at a subconscious level.

THE SUBCONSCIOUS INFLUENCE OF THE OVULATORY CYCLE

Imagine you're a woman shopping online for clothing. Do you think you will buy different outfits on days when your body's physiology makes you more likely to become pregnant?

A woman's ability to become pregnant depends on her menstrual cycle, which in humans typically spans about four weeks. A woman can become pregnant during roughly one week of the cycle, known as the *ovulatory phase*. Whereas female chimpanzees advertise their ovulatory phase with a bright red swollen rump, for humans the signals are not so obvious. Without specific education or equipment, most college-age women do not even know when they themselves are ovulating. But if a woman is unaware that she is ovulating, does that mean it can't influ-ence her behavior?

To dig a little deeper, marketing professor Kristina Durante and her research team recruited women who were not on hormonal contraception. When the women arrived for the study, they were given a urine test, which involved a trip to the restroom to pee on a stick. Although the women were told this test was a measure of their general health, the actual purpose was to determine whether they were experiencing the hormonal surge associated with ovulation. Ovulating and nonovulating women were then sent on an online shopping spree—to a website designed to look like The Gap or Old Navy. The virtual store had over one hundred clothing items and fashion accessories, including pants, skirts, shirts, shoes, handbags, and purses. But the products were strategically preselected. Half the items were sexier, flashier, and more alluring, while the other half were more conservative and demure. Even though none of the women in the study knew whether or not they were ovulating, those in the fertile phase of their cycle chose sexier and more revealing clothing—shorter skirts, higher heels, and sheerer blouses that revealed a lot of skin.

It turns out that ovulation alters women's behavior even when they aren't wearing any clothing at all. In another study, Geoffrey Miller, Josh Tybur, and Brent Jordan recruited a rather unusual team of research assistants—eighteen women who made their living as professional lap dancers in "gentlemen's clubs." The women recorded their tips over a sixty-day period, during which the researchers monitored each woman's phase in her cycle. When the dancers were least fertile, they made an average of $185 per five-hour shift. But when they were ovulating, they made almost twice as much: $335. The researchers speculated that ovulation subconsciously led the women to act sexier, leading an invisible change in the women's hormonal condition to have a very visible economic effect.

If you were to ask a woman who is currently ovulating why she chooses to buy a sexy dress, she might offer a proximate explanation, such as "I'm feeling adventurous" or "I'm in a party mood today." Such explanations are useful for understanding what's going on at the surface, but they say nothing about why ovulation leads women to feel more adventurous in the first place. At a deeper, ultimate level, the reason why ovulation alters women's behavior goes well beyond their current mood.

Throughout evolutionary history, women's behavior has had the largest reproductive consequences during the brief monthly window when they are ovulating, and can therefore become pregnant. In other mammals, ovulation is known to alter female behavior in ways to maximize reproductive opportunities during the fertile phase (think about those red rumps on our chimpanzee cousins). An ovulating woman's hormones appear to do likewise, altering her decisions to maximize her mating opportunities at the precise time of the month when doing so would have mattered most to her ancestors.

The proximate reason why ovulation leads a woman to dress and behave in a more alluring manner might be that she feels more adventurous at this time. But the ultimate reason is that ovulation promotes behavior designed to make women more appealing to the opposite sex. This suggests that women feel more adventurous and flirtatious during the particular time when pregnancy is most likely because such feelings would have produced behavior that best served their ancestors' reproductive interests. Whether we're trying to figure out why hungry people eat brownies or why ovulating women buy sexy dresses, it is useful to know the ultimate, not just the proximate, reasons for these behaviors.

An ultimate explanation does not contradict a proximate explanation. It would be senseless to argue whether a person bought a brownie because she was hungry (a proximate reason) or because sugary and fatty foods helped her ancestors solve the evolutionary challenge of survival (an ultimate reason). Instead, the two levels of explanation complement one another. A proximate explanation explains what's happening on the surface; an ultimate explanation explains what's going on at a deeper, evolutionary level.

Why should you care about the ultimate causes of people's choices? For one thing, proximate explanations by themselves provide an incomplete and often unsatisfying understanding of human behavior. For example, an economist might observe a number of ovulating women buying sexy dresses and infer that sexy outfits must be especially desirable to women at that particular phase of the menstrual cycle. But this fact alone tells us nothing about why. In fact, most traditional scientists would have had no reason to even begin investigating whether women's purchasing decisions change depending on their ovulatory cycle. And even if they stumbled upon the relationship, they might conclude that acting sexy during ovulation is irrational, since at the surface level modern female shoppers or exotic dancers may have absolutely no conscious interest in getting pregnant. To fully understand what's actually going on, we need to go below the surface.

Looking below the surface—at the ultimate reasons underlying our behaviors—provides valuable insight into decisions that might otherwise seem strange. Behavioral economists, for instance, have identified myriad decision errors, biases, and distortions. But they have simply provided a laundry list of blunders without offering a theory of the underlying causes for why people make these mistakes. Evolutionary psychology, on the other hand, provides a theory of mistakes. As we describe in this book, this adaptive theory of mistakes not only helps us appreciate the hidden wisdom of our otherwise senseless decisions but allows us to predict in advance what particular mistakes people will make—and when.

THE KENNEDYS AND THE BIOLOGY OF RISK

Let's reconsider the curse of the Kennedys in light of the distinction between surface-level explanations and their deeper evolutionary causes. On the surface, Joe Kennedy's descendants made a lot of choices that seemed rather foolish. The willingness to make hazardous choices started with Joe Kennedy himself. He got to be the youngest bank president by going way out on a limb—he borrowed lots of money and went head-to-head with Boston's powerful financiers in a deal that could have turned out quite badly. In fact, not all of Joe Kennedy's risks paid off. A few years before pulling off his famous $650,000 Wall Street win, he lost most of his assets by following a bad tip on a stock that later plunged to half its value. And while he was a student at Harvard, he took other risks as well. Despite the antialcohol laws, Kennedy supplied plentiful booze at parties. And his liquor business continued to flow during Prohibition, leading later commentators to speculate that he had some shady connections with the underworld. (Mobster Frank Costello claimed to have done business with Joe Kennedy before the Irishman moved on to more legitimate enterprises.)

Joe Kennedy took chances in the sexual department as well. He had affairs with many women, not just Hollywood starlet Gloria Swanson, despite his prominence in Boston's Roman Catholic establishment. Joe's descendants were notorious for risky decisions when it came to women and sex. JFK infamously used his Secret Service agents to cover for him when he snuck beautiful women into the White House. And to make bad judgment worse, one of the president's mistresses was a friend of Mafia don Sam Giancana—a fact Republicans later leaked to the press. Later, Joe's grandson Michael Kennedy narrowly avoided going to jail for statutory rape after an affair with a teenage babysitter, and another Kennedy grandchild, William Kennedy Smith, was accused of sexual assault by several different women and prosecuted for rape in one case. And what was Teddy, a married man, doing in that car with Mary Jo Kopechne in the first place?

What does all this risky behavior have to do with evolutionary biology? A lot, it turns out. Beneath the surface of seemingly ill-advised choices is a deeper link between men's risk taking and reproductive success. Women in societies all around the world are attracted to ambitious men who are willing to take risks to become successful (we'll talk more about women's psychology in Chapter 8, "Sexual Economics: His and Hers").

This doesn't mean that a man's risky choice will always lead to reproductive success. Risk, after all, is inherently risky. But the link between risk and mating does suggest that men are not likely to take risks haphazardly. Instead, men should be prone to making riskier choices specifically when their behavior could lead to a reproductive opportunity. To see how this works, let's go Down Under.

At a skateboard park in Queensland, Australia, psychologists Richard Ronay and William von Hippel offered ninety-six young male skaters $20 to perform two tricks on their speedy little land-surfing devices. The researchers asked skaters to choose one easy trick and a more difficult stunt they were working on but could only complete successfully about half the time. A male researcher filmed the skateboarders as they practiced their two tricks. Midway through filming, though, a highly attractive eighteen-year-old female strutted onto the scene. To verify that young blokes found her good-looking, the researchers asked twenty other guys to rate her attractiveness. Not only did she score as a knockout, but the ratings were, as the researchers noted, "corroborated by many informal comments and phone number requests from the skateboarders."

With the attractive young woman looking on, each skateboarder demonstrated his tricks a few more times, then donated a sample of saliva to the researchers, who later analyzed it for the amount of the hormone testosterone.

The researchers found that the beautiful woman caused the young skaters to throw caution to the wind. Taking more chances led to a lot more crash landings, but it also led to more successes on the difficult tricks—the kind of daring stunts that a young woman who enjoys the punk musical stylings of the Dead Kennedys might find impressive. But this boost in riskiness was accompanied by two additional findings that reveal something deeper about the evolutionary biology of risk.

First, the guys' testosterone levels automatically shot up when the beautiful woman was watching. Having more testosterone flowing through their veins tends to inspire men to move faster and more recklessly. In fact, the boost in risk taking was found primarily among those fellows whose testosterone levels zoomed up the most.

Second, the researchers gave the men a test tapping the functioning of the ventral medial prefrontal cortex, an area of the brain that cranks into high gear when we need to assess rewards and punishments. When the beautiful woman was watching, guys did worse on the test, suggesting that boosts in testosterone may have shut down this brain area, normally involved in making careful judgments. These findings make evolutionary sense to the extent that successfully showing off to a beautiful woman enhances a man's chances of attracting her as a mate. To show off, though, a bloke needs to be willing to throw caution to the wind—to take his foot off the brakes and hit the gas—and take some otherwise foolish risks.

The skateboarders didn't consciously decide to take more risks when the woman was watching. Instead, unconscious ancestral mechanisms made this decision for them, by flooding their bodies with testosterone specifically when a woman could observe their behavior.

Evolution has honed male biology to be attuned to reproductive opportunities, like the presence of an attractive woman. From the perspective of a fellow's genes, though, it would be especially nice if, before he risked his neck, he could somehow ascertain that the woman watching him was currently capable of becoming pregnant. But is that even possible?

In a laboratory at Florida State University, psychologists Saul Miller and Jon Maner investigated this precise possibility by observing men as they played a game of blackjack. In case you don't hang out in casinos, blackjack is a card game in which you can choose to play it safe (by declining any new cards once you get to sixteen or higher) or to take risks (by deciding to take a new card and risk the possibility of "busting" by going over twenty-one). As the men played blackjack, the researchers had a young woman observe them.

Just like the Aussie skateboarders, the Floridian fellows took more risks when the woman was watching. But this study raised the stakes. Over the course of the experiment, the researchers kept track of where the female research assistant was in her ovulatory cycle. Although she had been carefully instructed to dress and act identically every single day, her presence had a different effect on men's play on the days she was ovulating. When she was most fertile, the fellows took the most risks.

How did the men know she was ovulating? They didn't, at least not in any way they could consciously identify. But their bodies knew. In a follow-up study, the researchers found that merely exposing men to the subtle scent of an ovulating woman's T-shirt instantly caused men's testosterone levels to shoot up.

Armed with an understanding of the intimate connections between men's risk-taking biology and reproductive success, let's return to the saga of the Kennedys. The family's penchant for risk occasionally led to bad judgments, unfortunate outcomes, and even a few dead Kennedys. Risk always involves trade-offs. Taking hazardous chances can lead to death, but it can also lead to payoffs like money and status. At a deeper level, though, the Kennedy men's risk taking paid off in the most valuable currency in the evolutionary realm—reproductive success. Recall that women in all societies around the world are attracted to ambitious men willing to take risks to become successful. Although taking these kinds of risks led some of Joe Kennedy's descendants to perish, his genes have flourished. In the course of only a few generations, the genes of this one Irishman have thrived—producing twenty-nine grandchildren and over sixty great-grandchildren. And as we noted before, those descendants themselves continue to live rich and successful, if occasionally risky, lives.

THE ULTIMATE QUESTION

So, are people rational or irrational? If we look only at the surface, many of our choices appear rather foolish. Most of us would choose to be the person in the movie-ticket line who lucked into $100 instead of the one who won $150 but didn't win $1,000. It's not economically rational to say, "No thanks. I prefer not to have an extra free fifty bucks." The many superficially worrisome tendencies of the human mind lead some of us to seriously doubt whether people are rational Econs and to consider instead that they are all dim-witted morons.

Well, we beg to differ. Rather than Econs or morons, we are rational animals. Yes, decision making is biased, and yes, individual decisions are sometimes rather moronic. But underneath all those biases and misjudgments is an exceptionally wise ancestral system of decision making. To understand how people make decisions, we must first ask why the brain evolved to make the particular choices that it does. By connecting the story of human behavior with that of the rest of the animal kingdom, we come to see that our brains are designed to make choices in ways that enhanced our ancestors' fitness.

BUT THERE'S a twist in the plot! Just because evolutionary forces guide our behavior does not mean that you or I or Joe Kennedy's newest great-grandson is driven to achieve just one single evolutionary goal of "maximizing fitness." Just as it is too simple to say that people seek utility, it is too simple to say that people seek fitness. Instead, as we discuss next, human decision making is designed to achieve a set of very different evolutionary goals. In investigating how people meet these evolutionary goals, scientists have discovered something important: solutions to these different problems often require us to make decisions in different—and sometimes completely incompatible—ways. We are, in fact, inconsistent by design. To see why this has profound implications for your decisions, let's make a stop in Alabama and take a look at several puzzling decisions made by Martin Luther King Jr.

2

The Seven Subselves

ON SEPTEMBER 28, 1962, Martin Luther King Jr. was sitting peacefully on a convention stage in Birmingham, Alabama, when a man in the audience casually walked onstage and approached him. Suddenly, the man began punching Dr. King in the face. King was knocked over by the first blow, but even as the civil rights leader fell, his attacker continued throwing a brutal barrage of punches. Although King had been advocating nonviolent protests against racial discrimination, no one would have blamed him if he had gotten violently angry at his assailant, a white supremacist later revealed to be on a mission from the American Nazi Party. Instead, King chose a different course of action. He stood back up, gazed into his attacker's face with a look of transcendent calm, and dropped his arms defenselessly, "like a newborn baby," according to one observer. As others jumped to his defense, King pleaded with them, "Don't touch him. Don't touch him. We have to pray for him."

This incident is one of many that demonstrated King's commitment to moral principles. Ordained as a Baptist minister, Reverend King devoted himself to embodying and promoting the ideals of decency, integrity, and virtue. His commitment to nonviolence was steadfast and consistent, extending well beyond issues of civil rights for African Americans. He spoke out against the war in Vietnam, for example, even though it cost him the support of powerful allies such as

President Lyndon Johnson. On other occasions, his commitment to nonviolent protests against civil rights landed him in jail.

Yet Dr. King's unwavering commitment to moral principles did not extend to the realm of extramarital affairs. King's friend and fellow civil rights leader Ralph Abernathy admitted that the iconic religious leader, despite being a married man with four young children, was a "womanizer." Besides having an ongoing affair with a woman he saw frequently, King allegedly also engaged in numerous short-term liaisons with other women while he was traveling. According to biographer David Garrow, King's promiscuity caused him to feel extreme guilt. But that guilt was not enough to alter his behavior. When faced with temptations of the flesh, Dr. King repeatedly put aside his higher moral values.

Did King's moral lapses result from an occasional breakdown in the operation of the otherwise rational man inside his head? Or might there be another explanation for his behavioral inconsistencies? We argue that Martin Luther King Jr. suffered from a common form of multiple personality disorder. Even without reexamining the evidence from his biographies or consulting a single psychiatrist, we believe we can diagnose King as having at least seven personalities.

In fact, when we say King had a "common" form of multiple personality disorder, we are understating the case. Multiple personalities are not just common; they are universal. Without knowing a single thing about the particulars of your life, we argue that you also have at least seven personalities. Although it feels as if there is just one single self inside your head, at a deeper evolutionary level, you have a multiplicity of selves. And worse yet, each of these selves is like a little dictator who completely changes your priorities and preferences when he or she takes charge. This is important because it means that the same person will make different choices depending on which self is currently at the helm.

SELVES WITHIN THE SELF

A famous clinical case study of multiple personality disorder was turned into the movie *The Three Faces of Eve,* in which the central character switches between the timid and self-effacing "Eve White" and the dangerously fun-loving and flirtatious "Eve Black." The real-life character depicted in this movie was Chris Sizemore, whose psychiatrists claimed had not just three but twenty different personalities. While the majority of people do not suffer from the clinical version of multiple personality disorder, each normal person does have multiple selves.

At first blush, it might seem shockingly counterintuitive to claim that there is not one single you running the show inside your head. But an overwhelming body of scientific evidence supports the idea of multiple selves. Some of the earliest research came from a classic series of studies on "split-brain" patients, conducted in the 1960s by Michael Gazzaniga and Roger W. Sperry. Gazzaniga and Sperry studied people whose left and right cerebral hemispheres had been surgically separated (as a treatment for epilepsy). For these people the verbal left side of the brain could not communicate with the nonverbal right side. If the researchers showed an image (a picture of a spoon, for example) to the subject's verbal left brain (by flashing it into the right half of the visual field), the person was able to name it. But if the same image was flashed into the left half of the visual field (thus appearing only to the nonverbal right brain), the person could point to a spoon to indicate that it was the object in the image, but was unable to name it. This work, which became a cornerstone of modern neuroscience and eventually won a Nobel Prize, began to challenge the idea of a unified consciousness. It showed that our conscious experiences can be very different depending on which part of the brain is currently active and processing incoming information.

In the intervening fifty years, many other findings—from human and animal neuropsychology, biology, and studies of learning and memory—have revealed that there is not one single executive system inside your head but a conglomeration of separate systems, running different subprograms to deal with different problems. Reviewing the evidence in his book *Why Everyone (Else) Is a Hypocrite,* University of Pennsylvania psychologist Rob Kurzban points out that the mind's different systems (or modules) sometimes disagree with each other, which can lead us to behave inconsistently. This means that it's not just Martin Luther King Jr. who's a hypocrite—you, your neighbors, and the guy with the split brain pointing at a spoon are all hypocrites. According to Kurzban, the nature of our divided mind suggests that there is no "I"; instead, each of us is a "we."

Despite the mounting evidence for multiple selves, the idea that each one of us has a single unitary self remains intuitively compelling and widespread. For rational economists, the number-crunching business whizzes we met in the last chapter, a cornerstone assumption about human behavior is that people have stable preferences. If you choose to put cream and sugar in your coffee on Tuesday in Birmingham, Alabama, you are also likely to choose cream and sugar with your coffee in Memphis, Tennessee, on Wednesday.

This assumption about stable preferences is pervasive in business and psychology. Advertisers, for instance, look to pitch particular products to matching market segments. They don't place ads for Harley-Davidson motorcycles in church periodicals. Financial advisors categorize their clients according to various investment risk-tolerance profiles and avoid recommending highly risky and volatile stock opportunities to librarians. Personnel officers try to match the right person for the right job and steer clear of placing artistic coffeehouse types in the accounting department. In all of this, there is a presumption that a given consumer, investor, or job applicant will be the same tomorrow as today, the same in an hour as now, and the same in another building as in this one.

But what if each one of us is really several different people?

If each of us actually has multiple people living in our heads, this has radical implications for the way we think about behavior. Instead of having just one self, we are really a collection of selves—a group of *subselves*. Like different personalities, each of your subselves has peculiar quirks and preferences. And each comes out only when you are in a particular situation. At any one time, only one subself is in charge, which is the current you at that moment.

If we are a multiplicity of subselves, this suggests that even though we feel like we are the same person all the time, we might actually change who we are depending on where we are, what we're doing, and who else is around. To see how this might work, let's take a closer look at a study showing how the same person will respond very differently to an advertisement, depending on which subself is currently in the driver's seat. After that, we'll more formally introduce whichever one of your subselves is reading this book to the other people living inside your head.

PRIMED FOR PERSUASION

Before proceeding with our program, we'd like to take a moment for a brief word from our sponsor—the Nouvelle Breton Café. The Nouvelle Breton provides a completely unique experience, as noted by a reviewer for the *Los Angeles Times:* "It is truly a one-of-a-kind place that has yet to be discovered by others." Gina Polizzi from *Pacific Food News* calls it "a unique place off the beaten path." If you're looking for a great dining experience different from any other, look no further than the Nouvelle Breton Café.

Given that description, would you go out of your way to dine at the Nouvelle Breton Café?

What if you'd instead seen an ad emphasizing that this café was the most popular restaurant in the area, noting that over 1 million people have eaten there, and stating that "if you want to know why everyone gathers here for a great dining experience, come join them at the Nouvelle Breton Café."

Here's a more general question for your inner marketing consultant: Which of the two ads do you think would be more effective, the first (emphasizing that the restaurant is unique) or the second (emphasizing that the restaurant is popular)? If you considered this question from a traditional market-segmentation perspective, you might guess that the answer would depend on the type of person seeing the ad. One type of person—the conforming, yes-man sort—might be attracted to going where millions have gone before, eagerly following the masses. But another type of person—the rebellious, independent sort—might be turned off by lemminglike conformity, preferring something unique and off the beaten path. Different people are, well, different. Some people have one set of preferences, while others have another.

But the idea of multiple subselves suggests something radically different: that the same ad might be effective or ineffective depending on which person inside your head is currently viewing the ad. This means that even for the same individual, an ad might be appealing to one subself and repulsive to another.

Working with our colleagues Noah Goldstein, Chad Mortensen, Bob Cialdini, and Jill Sundie, we initially tested this idea by asking people to view advertisements promoting products ranging from restaurants and museums to the city of Las Vegas. Before anyone saw the ads, however, we first activated, or primed, one of two different subselves inside people's heads. The idea was to put people in a situation they might experience when watching television. Ads on TV don't just appear at random; they pop up during particular programs, perhaps an uplifting romantic comedy or a frightening police crime drama. The type of program a person is watching might naturally bring out one of his or her different subselves. Is it possible that the you watching a romantic comedy depicting flirtatious, sexy characters might be different from the you watching a thriller depicting violent killers in our midst? If so, these two yous might have entirely different responses to the exact same marketing appeal.

To test this possibility, some people in the study viewed a clip from the hair-raising classic *The Shining*, in which Jack Nicholson plays a madman chasing his family members around an isolated and deserted hotel with an ax. A few minutes into the clip, at an especially scary moment, we went to commercial, showing people several ads. Some of the ads included a message informing viewers about the popularity and high demand for each product (for example, "visited by over a million people a year"). Other times people saw the same ads, but the ads didn't mention anything about popularity or high demand.

When people viewed the ads in between segments of a scary program, they found the products more attractive when the ad emphasized the product's popularity. Adding the message "visited by over a million people a year" to a museum ad, for example, boosted people's desire to visit that museum. People became especially receptive to messages about following the crowd after watching a frightening movie clip. Like wildebeests in the presence of a leopard, people who are feeling threatened want to be part of a larger group.

In fact, the people who had been viewing the scary film weren't simply drawn to follow the masses; they actively avoided products and experiences that would make them stand out from the crowd. We know this because some of the ads in the study included a message emphasizing the uniqueness of the product (think "limited edition"). After watching the scary movie, people rated unique products as less attractive. Adding a message about standing out from the crowd to the museum ad actually led people to avoid the museum. Despite its being the exact same museum as shown in the other versions of the ad, an art gallery presented as unique and different wasn't the kind of place people wanted to visit while they were feeling defensive. When people watched a scary movie, then, they were attracted to products that were common and popular and avoided those that were different and unique.

But people's preferences changed drastically if they instead watched a romantic movie. Before seeing the same commercials, a second group of people watched a clip from the romantic film *Before Sunrise*, which portrays an attractive man and woman (Ethan Hawke and Julie Delpy) falling in love as they travel by train through the most picturesque cities in Europe. This film clip brought out a very different subself, leading viewers to experience erotic and loving feelings. Unlike people who saw the scary movie clip, the people in a romantic frame of mind were most affected by ads that emphasized a product's uniqueness. Now, when they saw the message about standing out from the crowd in the museum advertisement, they were especially drawn to it. Like animals on the prowl for a mate, people primed for romance want to stick out from the crowd. By contrast, including information about the popularity of the product repelled the romance-minded subjects. Adding the message "visited by over a million people" made the museum seem blasé and commonplace, leading people with a romantic mind-set to avoid the destination.

Rather than showing that some people are inherently disposed to be conformists while others are inherently disposed to be unique, the study found that the same person will sometimes want to conform and at other times seek to be unique. When the situation elicited a person's romantic subself, he or she craved uniqueness and avoided conformity. But when the situation elicited a person's vigilant subself, he or she now craved conformity and actively avoided opportunities to be unique. From the perspective that you have a single unitary self—that you have only one personality—shifting between conformist and rebellious tendencies seems inconsistent and even hypocritical. But from a multiple-subselves perspective, the behavior is logical and consistent since, in different situations, you follow the deeply rational preferences of your different subselves.

So given that there are multiple subselves living in your head, the next question is, how many?

HOW MANY SUBSELVES ARE THERE?

When people talk about evolutionary success, they often think only about survival and reproduction. But it is a gross oversimplification to assume that this is the whole story. Although surviving and reproducing are important challenges, humans had to surmount a number of distinct challenges to achieve evolutionary success. At a base level, our ancestors, like other animals, needed nourishment and shelter. But because humans are intensely social animals, they also faced a recurring set of crucial social evolutionary challenges. These evolutionary challenges include (1) evading physical harm, (2) avoiding disease, (3) making friends, (4) gaining status, (5) attracting a mate, (6) keeping that mate, and (7) caring for family.

The humans who became our ancestors were those who protected themselves from enemies and predators, avoided infection and disease, got along with the other people in their tribe, and gained the respect of their fellow tribe members. They also successfully attracted a mate, established a partnership with that person (perhaps for the rest of their lives), and, if all went well, cared for their needy and relatively helpless offspring. Those humans who succeeded in solving these critical challenges enhanced their fitness and became our ancestors. Those who were less successful at solving these challenges failed to become anyone's ancestors.

Each evolutionary challenge is unique. The things a person does to successfully charm a date are different from the things one does to avoid a predator or care for a baby. Solving these different problems required our ancestors to make decisions in different—and sometimes completely incompatible—ways. What is effective when you are taking care of a child, for example, is different than what is effective when you are negotiating a business deal with distant acquaintances.

The evolutionary result of our ancestors' continually having to solve different problems is that the mind has different psychological systems for meeting each challenge. Just as it is more efficient to have different brain systems for analyzing color, sound, and taste, it is more efficient to have different psychological systems for attracting a mate, evading physical harm, and managing each of the other challenges.

You can think of these different psychological systems as our subselves, where each is an executive vice president in charge of reaching a different evolutionary goal. Depending on which evolutionary goal is currently on your mind, consciously or subconsciously, a different subself will guide your decisions.

To understand how the different subselves work, think of the brain as analogous to a computer. Like a computer, your brain receives input and produces output. Someone pressing a button or shouting a voice command generates input for a computer. Your senses—what you see, hear, touch, smell, and feel—provide the input for your brain. The critical part is what happens after the input arrives. For computers, pressing a particular button on a keypad will lead to a different output, depending on which software program is currently running. For example, pressing the button with the equal sign is going to produce a different result if you do it in Word versus in Excel. Word will show you an "=" character; Excel will presume that you're beginning to type in a mathematical formula.

Computers have different software programs specialized to solve different challenges, such as the different tasks that arise at the office. For instance, your computer solves the challenges of writing documents, creating numerical spreadsheets, and designing slideshow presentations with different software programs (such as Word, Excel, and PowerPoint). Each software program is designed to solve a specific problem. Just as computers have different software programs to solve challenges faced at the office, the brain has different programs—the subselves—to solve the social challenges perennially faced by our ancestors. At any given point, your brain is running a different subself program, depending on whether you're consciously or subconsciously trying to make a friend, seduce a date, impress your boss, avoid an aggressive panhandler on a dark street, or teach your child how to read.

Just as a computer will process the same input differently depending on which software program is currently running, the brain will process the same input (a pat on the arm or an ad for a unique museum) differently depending on which subself is currently activated. For example, researchers at the University of Groningen observed activity in men's brains when the men believed they were being touched either by an attractive female research assistant or by a male. Even though it was, in reality, always the same person doing the touching, different areas of the brain lit up when men thought a woman was touching them versus a man.

The notion that the brain has different programs for managing different evolutionary goals has vast implications for how people make decisions. Not only will the subselves determine how people interpret the same information, but what a person likes, dislikes, and chooses will depend on which subself is currently running the show.

MEET THE SUBSELVES

Let's meet each of our seven subselves. It might be tempting to think of the subselves as seven crazy dwarfs living inside your head. But instead, think of them as like a council of ancestral elders, with a different wise man or woman in charge of a specific evolutionary problem. Each elder has hundreds of thousands of years of experience—the accumulated wisdom of our ancestors—with successfully solving their assigned problem. So when you confront an important decision in the real world, your mind's council wisely defers to the elder most evolutionarily adept at handling the situation. To see how each subself might deal with a given situation, let's consider how each subself thinks, what triggers it to take charge, and the nature of the specific evolutionary challenge it confronts.

Self-Protection Subself: The Night Watchman

Although human beings can be helpful to others, they have always posed a danger to one another as well. Criminologists examining skull fragments from earlier human societies and anthropologists studying other cultures around the globe have discovered that homicide is not something invented in modern American society. On the contrary, our ancestors lived in groups with homicide rates that make Detroit or inner-city Los Angeles look tame by comparison. And even when the bad guys weren't out to kill you, they often tried to steal your belongings, carry off your spouse or child, or burn down your village. Our ancestors had to successfully avoid threats posed by other predatory individuals.

Threats of violence have hardly disappeared in the modern world. In the United States in 2008, there were over 16,000 reported murders and 830,000 aggravated assaults. And every day the news highlights yet another story of mass violence flaring up in yet another spot around the world. Everyday citizens (as well as gangsters and soldiers) go to great lengths to try to insulate themselves from such violence by investing in motion sensors, infrared detectors, guard dogs, and burglar alarms for their homes—not to mention paying hundreds of dollars in annual fees to have those systems monitored day and night. The wealthier live in gated communities and hire night watchmen; the less well-off invest in multiple locks for their doors and bars for their windows.

Some people take a more active role in their self-defense, buying firearms that range from the smaller-scale Glock 17C pistol with night sites ($542 plus shipping, in case you're wondering) to a Barrett .50-caliber semiautomatic sniper rifle (available online for $11,699, complete with ten-round magazine, scope, and monopod). Though you may not have invested in your own firearms, you have, if you pay taxes, likely bought a few for the national military. The 2011 US budget included $60 billion for "protection" and another $964 billion for "defense." With a population of 311 million people, that averages out to $3,294.60 spent by every man, woman, and child for government protection. That does not include the additional taxes you pay to support your local police, incidentally.

Along with our colleagues, we've conducted a great deal of research on the self-protection subself. We find that your paranoid inner self can be primed not only by real or perceived physical danger but also by angry expressions on the faces of strangers, thoughts about members of other races and religions, scary movies, or the local evening news broadcast, which often starts with a gruesome crime. And speaking of the night-watchman aspect, simply being in a dark room can activate your self-protection subself.

In the advertising study mentioned earlier, the self-protection subself motivated people to want to blend in with the crowd, and it led them to be particularly swayed by the opinions of others. In another study, we asked people whether they preferred a Mercedes-Benz or BMW. When the self-protection subself was activated, people chose the same brand that the majority of others preferred, regardless of which brand it was. If they learned that most other people preferred the Beamer, that's what they wanted. If others liked the Benz, then the Benz was their top choice.

Activating our inner night watchman makes us vigilant. It leads us to ask questions like, Is that band of nasty-looking guys who just walked over the hill going to steal something from me or burn down my hut? In studies conducted with Jon Maner, Vaughn Becker, and some of our other colleagues, we have found that activating the self-protection subself leads people to see men from other groups as angry, even when their expressions are perfectly neutral. This natural proclivity toward vigilance and paranoia inclines people to invest resources to avoid weakness or vulnerability, while placing high value on attaining strength or associating themselves with a powerful numerical majority. Above all, the self-protection subself wants to be safe from any potential physical danger.

Disease-Avoidance Subself: The Compulsive Hypochondriac

Biologists estimate that infectious diseases carried by other humans played a critical role in human evolution. In the 1300s, the bubonic plague killed up to 50 percent of the populations of Europe, Asia, and Africa. Two centuries later, descendants of those Europeans who survived the plague traveled to the Americas, carrying along diseases such as smallpox, measles, and typhoid, which killed over 75 percent of the population of Mexico. More recently, the 1918 Spanish flu killed between 40 and 100 million people worldwide.

Modern humans have developed technologies to control several diseases and to limit their spread—from smearing sanitary wipes over the handles of supermarket carts to pasteurizing milk and sterilizing medical implements, for example. But beware! All those people you pass on the street are transporting contagious and sometimes virulent microorganisms, lurking in wait for any moment of contact, which could provide an opportunity for those potentially life-threatening microbes to jump from that stranger onto you. The World Health Organization estimates that every year, infectious diseases, including influenza, tuberculosis, and AIDS, take the lives of 15 million people (that's more than the total population of every man, woman, and child living in New York City; Boston; Philadelphia; Washington, DC; Chicago; Miami; and Seattle combined).

One result of this ever-present threat has been the evolution of a highly sophisticated biological immune system—an array of bodily defenses designed to defend against the threat of disease. Another is the evolution of our disease-avoidance subself, or what psychologist Mark Schaller calls a "behavioral immune system"—a set of prophylactic psychological mechanisms designed to help us avoid infection in the first place.

The disease-avoidance subself is activated by things like the sound of other people sneezing and coughing, the sight of skin lesions, and foul smells. This subself can even be primed by thinking about people from exotic faraway places such as Sri Lanka and Ethiopia as opposed to Hawaii or London. This makes some sense given that we are unlikely to have resistance to exotic diseases carried by people from those exotic places, any of whom might be an unwitting smuggler of some disease that could be fatal to us.

When our inner compulsive hypochondriac has been primed, we act in ways designed to thwart pathogen transmission. Because other humans can carry diseases, this subself leads people to avoid contact by becoming more introverted and less tolerant of foreigners—folks from exotic places that might harbor even more exotic microbes. Research by Carlos Navarrete and Dan Fessler finds that women become particularly afraid of foreigners in the first trimester of pregnancy, the precise time when developing fetuses are most susceptible to serious problems if mom catches a disease. Above all, the disease-avoidance subself wants to be safe from anything associated with pathogens.

Affiliation Subself: The Team Player

Other people bring threats and disease, but they are also the source of the most important benefits in our lives. To be evolutionarily successful, our ancient ancestors needed to get along with other folks. Anthropologists who study hunter-gatherer groups (of the sort our ancestors evolved in) have found that making friends and forming alliances are essential to evolutionary success. For example, anthropologists Kim Hill and Magdalena Hurtado went deep into the rain forests of South America to study a group called the Aché, carefully recording which members of the tribe shared food with one another. They found that in such groups friends provide a natural insurance policy against starvation. Without refrigeration, one family cannot eat a whole pig, but a group of families sharing their catches can pool their risk and stand a better chance of making it through tough times.

Friends don't just share food; they also teach one another valuable skills, like how to fish, cook, and build a hut. Friends team up to move things that are too big for one person to carry, and they provide safety in numbers when the bad guys come around.

The need for friends and allies didn't end when our predecessors moved out of the bush and took up residence in the big city. We modern urbanites still invest heavily in building and maintaining our friendships. As we write this book, for example, Facebook has already passed 1 billion active users, who devote endless hours to passing on clever newspaper articles or new songs, reading about their friends' children's accomplishments, and choosing the correct comment ("Oh, how cute! You must be so proud, Jenny!"). And let's not forget the time, energy, and money invested in iPhones and other devices people use to text friends while driving home in heavy traffic or to share a picture of their cat's lunch with their 300 closest companions. The majority of our graduate students spend over $1,000 a year on their iPhones, despite having annual incomes in the $15,000 range. Even in the modern era, friends provide more than just digital support. We need them when we want to move a couch, when our car breaks down and we need a ride, if we'd like a place to crash while driving across the country, or if we could use some advice about how to raise a child.

The affiliation subself is triggered by anything that cues friendship, like when your old college roommate sends a Christmas card, when you're thinking about inviting a neighbor for dinner, or when your coworker picks up the tab for lunch. This subself is also active when friendships are threatened. If you're feeling lonely, rejected, or exploited, the affiliation subself takes the helm. When the inner team player is primed, people spend more money on products that connect them with other people (like a wristband sporting their university logo) rather than on products normally consumed alone (like a box of Oreo cookies). This subself also spurs us to do things that we might not like but that a friend enjoys, like smiling happily through a painfully silly movie that our friend thinks is brilliant ("Umm, no, I can't understand why the critics panned *Junior* either. What could be more hilarious than Arnold Schwarzenegger playing a pregnant gynecologist?"). Above all, the affiliation subself wants to be liked and treated as a friend.

Status Subself: The Go-Getter

Besides dealing with the challenge of getting along with their fellow group members, our ancestors also needed to manage the very different challenge of gaining and maintaining status within their groups. Getting some respect from others has always brought a host of benefits, and this arrangement didn't start with human beings. Dominant baboons get first crack at food and the best spot at the watering hole, and dominant male chimps get to mate with the most desirable females. Stanford biologist Robert Sapolsky, who followed the same baboon troop for several years, found that high-status animals show fewer signs of physiological stress than their group mates at the bottom of the totem pole.

The benefits of status continue to apply in the modern world, where the boss gets the big corner office, a special parking spot for his Lexus, a first-class seat on the plane, and an expense account to dine in the best restaurants. As a consequence, people go to great lengths to impress others with their status, shelling out inordinate amounts of money for Gucci shoes, Armani suits, Rolex watches, BMWs, and $500 dinners at The French Laundry. What economist Robert Frank calls "luxury fever" infects purchases at all levels, including $300 shoes, $10,000 outdoor grills, $20,000 Sub-Zero freezers, and $2 million McMansions, not to mention personal jets and supersized yachts. Back in the middle-class suburbs, teenagers, who are in a critical phase of establishing their position in the status hierarchy, often pressure their parents to pay more than twice as much as necessary for shoes, pants, and backpacks so as not to lose face by sporting last year's fashions.

Other animals gain and maintain status mainly by force—by being willing and able to carry out acts of aggression against other members of their groups. This is sometimes true for humans as well, as in the case of gang leaders and military dictators. But as anthropological psychologists Joe Henrich and Francisco Gil-White observed, humans can also achieve status through prestige, by earning others' respect without using force or power. In the modern world, a person can gain status by having access to desirable information and the ability to use it in ways that make him or her desirable to others. Think of Bill Gates, Stephen Hawking, or Mother Teresa, each of whom might lose a fight with the guy who cuts the lawn but nevertheless earned enough prestige to make the world turn with the snap of a finger.

The status subself is attuned to where we stand in the hierarchy and who is above and below us. When the inner go-getter is in charge, we are prone to place special value on being associated with successful others and to regard other people's disrespect as especially costly. When we activated this subself in one of our studies, we found that a seemingly trivial insult could spark an aggressive outburst. For instance, if someone spills some water on you without apologizing, the status subself is quick to trigger a fistfight (for men) and vengeful attempts to exclude the offender from social groups (for women). Above all, the status subself wants to be respected and needs to have reason to respect others.

Mate-Acquisition Subself: The Swinging Single

Making friends, evading all the slings and arrows of marauding bad guys, and dodging billions of deadly bacteria and viruses will count for naught (at least in evolutionary terms) if a person does not manage to find someone willing to help transport his or her genes into the next generation. Finding a mate can be difficult, and some percentage of each generation fails to become anyone's ancestor. But we know for certain that every one of your ancestors, and ours, got this step right.

Deciding who might make a good potential partner is not enough, of course. You need to attract that person's interest in you. If the person is highly desirable, other members of your own sex may be in the running as potential suitors, so you need to stand out from the competition. Hence, people spend lavishly on clothing, salon treatments, and gym memberships and devote time and energy to visiting local singles' bars, churches, parks, Laundromats, concerts, and other public gathering places, in the hopes of meeting Mr. or Mrs. Right (or sometimes just Mr. or Ms. Right Now).

In the book *The Mating Mind*, Geoffrey Miller argues that many behaviors that appear quite innocent are in fact attempts to demonstrate one's value as a mate. These include playing music, writing poetry, and even volunteering at the local charity.

The mate acquisition subself is primed by real or imagined potential mates. When we see sexy ads, read a romantic story, or even touch lingerie, our inner swinging single is quick to take charge. This subself is attuned to information about whether another person might make a good romantic partner, to our own allure to potential mates, and to what we might do to make ourselves more irresistible. In the advertising study mentioned earlier, this subself led people to want to be unique and get themselves noticed. For example, activating this subself led men to choose the opposite brand from what the majority of others preferred. If they learned that most other people preferred the

BMW, they instead wanted the Benz. But if others liked the Benz, they wanted the BMW.

The his and her versions of the mate-acquisition subself are somewhat different (as we will discuss in Chapter 8 on sexual economics). But for both men and women, the mate-acquisition subself seeks to behave in ways that make them more desirable to potential romantic partners.

Mate-Retention Subself: The Good Spouse

For 95 percent of all mammals, the mating game is a short-term affair: the females choose the most dominant or attractive local male, stand in line to receive his genes, and don't worry about the fact that other females are waiting in the same queue. But for humans, gibbons, and a few other furry, warm-blooded species, females and males join forces to help care for the offspring. Although relatively rare among mammals, this sort of two-parent care is found elsewhere in the animal kingdom. It is common in birds, for example, whose newborn offspring are often very helpless and cannot survive without care from two parents. Consider those adorable waddling penguins, whose eggs would freeze if the male didn't take his turn standing on them. Unlike most other infant mammals, human babies are more like fledgling birds: they are born helpless and physically immature and require immense care for many years.

Some biologists believe that our large brains led us to develop a social system in which both partners help raise children. Because large brains require large fetus heads that need to squeeze into the world as soon as possible through painfully small openings, human babies are born early, well before they can fend for themselves. Whatever their evolutionary roots, bonds between men and women are universal across human societies. Hence, human mating involves another set of problems beyond acquiring a mate—getting along with that mate, sometimes for years, sometimes for decades, and sometimes till death do you part.

The problems of keeping a mate, as some of us have learned, are very different from those involved in finding one in the first place.

There are potential conflicts over sharing resources and child care, as well as the dangers of other people trying to steal one's partner away. Lots of time, effort, and money go into maintaining relationships, from Valentine's Day dinners and expensive gifts for Christmas, birthdays, and anniversaries, to business opportunities lost by partners taking expensive plane flights for romantic getaways or visits with in-laws living in the backwoods of Kentucky.

The mate-retention subself is tuned in to information about whether your partner seems to be content or miserable, while also scanning the social horizon for potential interlopers who might be in the market to make your partner happier. This subself is activated by cues that celebrate or threaten a long-term relationship. If you're reminiscing about the good times you've shared, if you notice that an anniversary is coming up, or if you catch an opposite-sex person eyeing your partner, the mate-retention subself takes the helm. Whereas priming the mate-acquisition subself leads people to pay more attention to attractive members of the opposite sex, priming the mate-retention subself leads people to pay more attention to attractive members of their own sex, who can represent a threat to their relationships. Above all, the mate-retention subself seeks to ensure that a long-term romantic relationship is going smoothly.

Kin-Care Subself: The Nurturing Parent

The evolutionary reason human parents are inclined to bond with one another is quite simple: it is good for their offspring. Studies of traditional societies have revealed that children without both parents are less likely to survive, and if they do, they don't fare as well as those with two investing parents.

In traditional societies, parents provide not only food, shelter, and protection but also knowledge—about how to find food, treat one's friends, avoid being eaten by lions or ambushed by the bad guys downriver, and all the sundry problems faced in solving the other fundamental ancestral challenges. In the modern world, people still expend immense amounts of time, energy, and financial resources in raising their children. The costs of bringing up Junior go well beyond food and a bed to sleep in—the tab includes all those diapers, baby bottles, sippie cups, toddler clothes, babysitters, doctor visits, health insurance policies, toys, bigger clothes, bigger toys, summer camps, bicycles, and college tuition. In the United States, it costs, on average, between $205,960 and $475,680 to raise just one child (throw in a couple hundred thousand extra if Junior manages to get into an elite private college). As if that's not enough, parents may then be asked to cough up for a big, fancy wedding and a honeymoon, which may result in grandchildren and the opportunity to spend hundreds of hours babysitting, to shell out still more money for gifts, and to help with everyday expenses.

The kin-care subself not only takes command when you are around your own children but may come into play even when you see someone else's adorable baby or hear a child crying off in the distance. Note that this is not the subself that leads us to have children (the mate-acquisition subself takes care of that by motivating us to have sex). Instead, the kin-care subself motivates us to help out our offspring, younger siblings, cousins, nieces, nephews, or grandchildren. In the modern world, the kin-care system can also motivate giving to helpless strangers, such as starving children in Africa, or even taking care of puppies and kittens. Above all, the kin-care subself seeks to ensure that vulnerable youngsters in need receive proper care and attention.

REMEMBERING THE SEVEN SUBSELVES BY CLIMBING THE DEVELOPMENTAL PYRAMID

If you've ever taken a psychology course, you may remember Abraham Maslow's famous pyramid of needs. Maslow pointed out that different human needs become relevant at different phases of our lives, with the lower levels of the pyramid lighting up at earlier ages than the higher steps. Each of our subselves is in charge of one fundamental evolutionary need that neatly fits into a modified version of the pyramid (see Figure 2.1). This pyramid also serves as a way to help remember the seven subselves. Envision each of your own subselves coming online as

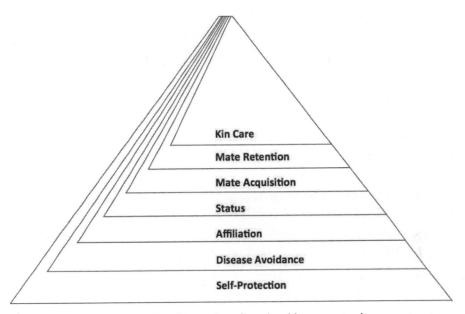

Figure 2.1. A hierarchy of evolved human needs

you moved through toddlerhood and adolescence to your current ripe old age.

Your self-protection subself arrived on the scene around age one, when you became wary of strangers and began clutching fearfully at your mother's skirt hem if someone outside the family approached you. Your disease-avoidance subself clicked into action a bit later, when you started spitting out strange and novel foods with a look of utter disgust. As is obvious from the way they scornfully reject mommy's carefully prepared meal or scream bloody murder at friendly old ladies who dare to greet them, little toddlers don't give a hoot about public opinion. Not until your preschool years did your affiliation subself make its appearance, when you moved beyond parallel play and started seeking out new little friends.

Before we have friends, we are oblivious to whether we do or don't "get no respect." But somewhere around the first or second grade, the status subself comes out of dormancy, and we begin to take umbrage if we're dissed by the other little kiddies.

For the first decade of our lives, we couldn't care less about our romantic lives. But then the mate-acquisition subself is rudely awoken by a surge of hormones. Suddenly we begin obsessing over whether those formerly uninteresting creatures on the other side of the playground might or might not be interested in dating us. After we've managed to figure that one out and attract a partner worth keeping, the mate-retention subself is unwrapped from its cocoon. And of course, the kin-care subself doesn't fully mature until we've not only found and kept a mate but produced a child.

For Abraham Maslow, the top of the pyramid was the need for *self-actualization*—the desire to pursue one's own artistic and creative impulses without regard to other people's reactions. You might be surprised to find that we've knocked self-actualization off the top of our pyramid and replaced it with those mundane mammalian parenting motives. We do not deny that human beings are motivated to be creative and artistic. But a desire to self-actualize is not detached from our social goals; instead, it is directly linked to the deeper evolutionary goals of gaining status and acquiring a mate (think about how Pablo Picasso and Diego Rivera each turned his creativity into a ticket into the arms of many beautiful women).

Later in the book we take a closer look at the scientific evidence for the architectural refurbishment of Maslow's pyramid, and we also examine how different people proceed through this developmental sequence in the pyramid at different speeds (see Chapter 6, "Living Fast and Dying Young"). But for now, let's take a look at how our different subselves approach financial decisions.

THE SUBSELVES MEET MONEY

One of the authors of this book (Vlad, the former Communist bubble gum aficionado) once worked as an intern at Morgan Stanley, a giant international investment firm. His manager, who ran a multi-million-dollar fund, was a wily Vietnam War veteran who had acquired a taste for the finer things in life and liked fast cars and the sound of roaring engines. He thrived in the action-packed financial environment, blasting into work at 5 a.m. each day and taking pleasure in pulling the trigger on high-stakes decisions that could wipe him out or enshrine his hero status. It takes a certain bravado and confidence to take such large risks on a daily basis, and he was the kind of man who liked the adrenaline rush that came along with taking those calculated plunges.

But this fund manager was different from other financial traders in one important regard. Although Wall Street types are known to work around the clock (money never sleeps, after all), this particular financier adhered strictly to the opposite policy: he refused to make investment decisions at home. This practice had less to do with his desire for rest and relaxation than with his keen strategic wisdom. After years in the industry, he realized an important split in his own personality. At the office he was a maverick who approached decisions with guns blazing, but at home he was a family man with a loving wife, small children, and a cuddly puppy. The financial choices he made in the confines of his family world were much more cautious than the ones he made at the office. The same risky investment opportunity that seemed sound and calculated at work looked too precarious at home. To stay successful at his job, he had to take immense risk, but the parent in him simply couldn't take such chances.

This fund manager understood something critical about the divided nature of human nature: different subselves are activated in different social situations. This has important implications not just for investing but also for understanding the seemingly irrational biases that plague our minds.

REVERSING LOSS AVERSION

Let's take another look at the phenomenon of loss aversion—the tendency for people to weigh losses more heavily than gains. This seemingly irrational bias was discovered by behavioral economists, those fun-loving laboratory researchers who love to expose our foibles (they're the guys wearing those Rolling Stones T-shirts with the red tongue hanging out underneath their white lab coats). Loss aversion is one of those things that led to a lot of head scratching among rational economists, the sharply dressed number crunchers. From the classic rational perspective, loss aversion is mathematically irrational: $100 ought to be worth $100, regardless of whether it's coming or going. But at a psychological level, people are more moved by a loss than by a gain of an identical amount.

An evolutionary perspective provides two insights into puzzling phenomena like loss aversion. The first is that many of our cognitive and behavioral biases have deeper evolutionary functions. Recall that the seemingly irrational bias of loss aversion is not only found in humans in all corners of the globe but also shared by other primates (like those coin-wielding, apple-purchasing capuchin monkeys). Loss aversion makes sense from an evolutionary perspective, to the extent that this bias would have helped our ancestors solve some fundamental evolutionary challenges. For instance, loss aversion might be adaptive for solving the evolutionary problem of protecting ourselves from danger. When in danger our ancestors may have benefitted especially from avoiding losses so as to retain their lives or limbs.

An evolutionary perspective also provides a second important insight. By understanding the adaptive function of a given tendency, we are in a better position to predict when that tendency will be strong and when it won't. This second insight could chip away at a cornerstone assumption of classic economics—that people have stable preferences. The idea is that we're supposed to behave consistently from one situation to another. You should be loss averse at this moment, in an hour, tomorrow, and the day after. Some have even stated a precise number when it comes to the stability of loss aversion: a person should experience a loss as 2.75 times more psychologically impactful than a gain of the same magnitude.

But the idea of subselves suggests a radically different way of thinking about how people behave across situations. Rather than being one monolithically consistent decision maker, we are—led by our subselves—predictably inconsistent. If a particular bias, like loss aversion, were adaptive for solving a particular ancestral problem, we would expect this bias to ebb and flow according to the evolutionary goal currently most important to a person. We would thus expect people to be strongly loss averse in some situations but not in others.

Along with our colleagues Jessica Li and Steve Neuberg, we set out to test this possibility in a series of experiments. As other researchers had done in past studies demonstrating loss aversion, we asked people how they would feel if they gained $100 or lost $100. Before people answered these questions, though, they first read a short story designed to activate either the self-protection or the mate-acquisition subself.

If you were being primed for self-protection, you would read a story imagining yourself alone in your house at night. You hear suspicious noises outside your window. At first, you dismiss them as merely rustlings of the night winds, but as things progress, it becomes clear that someone has broken into your house. You call out, and no one replies, but then you hear footsteps right outside your bedroom. You pick up the phone to make an emergency call, but the line has been cut. Finally, the intruder lets out an evil cackle, then turns the handle to your bedroom door. The scenario ends as you see his shadow appear ominously in your doorway.

If you were instead being primed for mate acquisition, you'd have read a story about being away on vacation and meeting someone to whom you are instantly attracted. Not only is this person attractive to you, but he or she also finds you irresistible, and the two of you keep finding excuses to be around one another for hours on end. Your feelings become more and more romantic, and the scenario ends as you share a passionate kiss.

Both men and women who read the vacation story found it romantic and even sexually arousing. People who read the other story about the creepy break-in, on the other hand, experienced not the pleasure of sexual arousal but the foreboding of abject fear. What effect did priming fear versus romance have on people's loss aversion? Activating the self-protection subself made people even more loss-averse than usual. For these individuals, losses loomed much larger than gains. This finding makes sense to the extent that loss aversion was adaptive for solving ancestral challenges related to survival. When dangers lurk, it pays to worry. We would expect our inner night watchman to be particularly loss averse.

But while losses loomed large in the self-protection condition, something very different happened with those primed for mate acquisition. In fact, when this subself was running the show, loss aversion didn't just disappear, it reversed itself for men, who became oblivious to losses and amped up the importance of gains.

For men primed to attract a mate, then, gains loomed larger than losses. Why? Across the animal kingdom, failure to gain a mate puts mammalian males at critical risk of not being able to pass on their genes. Remember those young skateboarding blokes in Australia, who threw caution to the wind when a pretty young woman came to watch them perform. Potential gains in the mating domain loom large because ancestral males who were overly safe failed the most critical step in evolution.

Whereas many biases have been considered stable, it turns out that biases like loss aversion vary dramatically from situation to situation—they can be amplified, turned off, and even inverted. These variations are neither arbitrary nor irrational; instead, they reflect the operation of our deeply rational subselves. Some subselves are loss averse, like our inner night watchman seeking to protect us from danger. But others are not, like men's inner swinging-single subself seeking to find a mate. Predicting whether a person will be loss averse or not requires knowing which of the seven people in his or her head is currently at the controls.

WHO WAS THE REAL MARTIN LUTHER KING JR.?

When Martin Luther King Jr. acted very differently in different situations, was he being a hypocrite or suffering from a breakdown of his true, more rational self? And assuming that you do not always act in a perfectly consistent manner, are you a hypocrite?

The idea of subselves suggests that there is more to hypocrisy than meets the eye. If each of us is really multiple people, then we should not be surprised by hypocrisy. It might be tempting (but wrong) to think of our subselves as playing different characters at different times, like when our demeanor at a Halloween party changes to match our costume. We all realize that sometimes we pretend to be someone we really are not. But subselves are not roles. The idea of role-playing presumes that there is a single "real" you when you get off the stage or take off the mask. But if you think about yourself as encompassing several different subselves, this single you is a mirage—an illusion created by your hyperrationalizing consciousness. The notion of subselves implies that there are many real yous, not one. The you with your friends, the you on a date, the you with your family, and the you striving for a promotion are all equally the real you.

Some of your subselves have common objectives; befriending a neighbor could simultaneously serve affiliative, self-protective, and kin-care goals, for example. But some of your subselves have incompatible goals, pulling you in opposite directions. And when one subself is in charge, it doesn't much care what your other off-duty subselves might normally desire. The self-protection subself compelling you to dine at a popular, well-lit restaurant doesn't care that your idle mate-acquisition subself would rather explore the unique little out-of-the-way joint a few blocks down a dark street. When you are worried about the band of knife-wielding thugs who just walked around the corner, you are not thinking about romancing your date.

The mate-retention subself and the mate-acquisition subself are especially likely to be at odds with one another. Just because someone's mate-retention subself has chosen to wear a wedding ring and has sworn eternal faithfulness, that doesn't mean that the mate-acquisition subself has also taken a vow of chastity. King exemplified the tension between these two subselves. When a powerful, high-status man is away from home and in the presence of adoring female admirers, not only is his inner good spouse likely to be off duty, but his inner swinging single is primed to jump into the driver's seat. And when the swinging single starts pursuing its agenda, it doesn't much care what the good spouse would do if it were in charge.

This is not to say that subselves provide an excuse or a justification for immoral behavior. But they can explain why humans often behave like hypocrites: we have only one body, but our brains are inherently divided. The actions of our mate-acquisition subself often create dire consequences for our other subselves later, as when the new sexual partner feels jilted and calls a press conference. But as we saw in the study about reversing loss aversion, a man's mate-acquisition subself is not especially qualified to judge potential losses when there are immediate gains on the horizon.

NOW THAT we've properly introduced our subselves, we'll look more closely at how they do business. We must warn you, though: if you've ever taken a business class, the next chapter might inspire you to throw away your textbook. To see why, we'll first make a stop at Disneyland.

3

Home Economics Versus
Wall Street Economics

ON OCTOBER 16, 1923, Walt Disney and Roy O. Disney started a small business called the Disney Brothers Cartoon Studio. Walt was the cartoonist; Roy handled the finances. Working on a shoestring budget out of their Uncle Robert's garage, the Disney boys operated on the edge of bankruptcy for over a decade, often borrowing money from their parents and other relatives.

From the outset Walt dreamed big, sparing no expense to make the first talking animated film, then raising the bar even higher with the first cartoon in Technicolor. In 1937, they staked everything on creating the first feature-length animated film. Although immensely risky, the venture was a great success. Over seventy-five years later, we'll guess you still know the film—it was called *Snow White and the Seven Dwarfs*. The brothers followed this triumph with a string of other now-classic films, including *Pinocchio, Dumbo, Fantasia,* and *Bambi*.

Running a business together for many years, the brothers Disney had some bitter disagreements, many stemming from Walt's big-dreaming perfectionism and complete lack of attention to money. For *Snow White*, Walt hired a giant team of animators, investing an excruciating three years and $1.5 million into the film (an unheard-of sum back in the Depression-ridden 1930s). Even after the film was finished,

Walt wanted to spend another $300,000 in last-minute touch-ups—a move Roy forcefully blocked. Nevertheless, the two men stuck together through a lifetime of ups and downs, eventually expanding beyond the movie business, opening Disneyland in 1955 and Disney World in 1971, leaving behind a company that became the largest media conglomerate in the world.

Fast-forward to 1984, when Michael Eisner arrived to take his new job as Disney's chief executive. Although Walt and Roy had been gone for over a decade, the company still had the feel of a family business. Roy E. Disney, Roy O.'s son, was head of animation and vice chairman of the board of directors. Despite the company's having grown to the size of a major corporation, Disney employees faced none of the massive between-production layoffs common in the film industry. Working at Disney was more like being part of a family than a corporation. Employees even took off an afternoon every week to play softball together.

Forward again to 2003. After two decades of Eisner's leadership, the once warm and friendly family business that had given birth to Mickey Mouse, Sleepy, Sneezy, and Dopey had become a battlefield, devastated by legal and managerial feuds. Although Roy E. Disney had himself brought in Eisner, he openly criticized many of Eisner's decisions. Eisner retaliated by hatching a plot to remove Roy from the board of directors. The messy feud was covered widely in the media, leaving some dark smudges on the company's cherished warm and fuzzy family-oriented image, as well as its financial bottom line. Eisner was eventually demoted and then quit on bad terms.

Given the billions of dollars at stake, why couldn't Eisner and Roy E., who had once been friends, just follow the lead of the company's famous founders and try harder to get along?

Unless you're a hermit, most of your crowning achievements and painful failures involve other people. Sometimes people's efforts mesh beautifully, and result in something extraordinary, like *Snow White*. But negotiating the social world presents a minefield of potential conflicts, from nickel-and-dime flare-ups on the playground to billion-dollar explosions in the corporate boardroom. Why are some people successful negotiators, while others can't seem to get on the same page with their colleagues?

If we take a closer look at the rational economic rulebook for negotiation, we make a surprising discovery: rather than trying to maximize profits and minimize losses rationally, the most successful teams and CEOs operate by a very different set of rules—the ones used by our different subselves. This is useful to know because you will want to bring the right subself when you're heading to the bargaining table.

PLAYING GAMES

Brutus and Caesar, Jung and Freud, and Lennon and McCartney all had famously productive partnerships, followed by infamously nasty splits. Even the closest of relationships are occasionally staging grounds for marital spats, sibling rivalries, and parent-child conflicts. Life is a series of fragile negotiations. Does a wife clean the kitchen uncomplainingly or initiate a possible argument over the distribution of domestic labor? Does a man pick up the restaurant tab for the fifth time in a row or ask his dating partner whether she is familiar with the concept of turn taking? Does a parent yield to a toddler's screaming demands for a sugary treat at the market or say no and risk the possibility that the situation will escalate into an embarrassing full-blown public tantrum?

Rational economists, the mathematically oriented business analysts, study these kinds of negotiations using a set of ideas called *game theory*. Game theory applies cold hard mathematical logic to otherwise messy decisions. For example, should you accept an initial salary offer from Acme Corporation or drive a harder bargain and take the chance that the Acme execs will offer the slot to someone else? By applying clean numerical values to the different outcomes, economists turn confusing dilemmas into precise mathematical problems. And we humans really like logical precision—so much so that eight different game theorists have been awarded Nobel Prizes.

If you've ever taken a course in economics or social psychology, you've heard about the *prisoner's dilemma,* a prototypical example of game theory in action. Imagine you are a crook. One day you and one of your criminal associates are arrested on suspicion of a crime, and you are held in separate rooms. The district attorney comes into your cell and offers you two options: you can remain silent or confess. By remaining silent, you will be cooperating with your partner on the standard criminal pact of silence, whereas by confessing, you will be defecting on your partner.

So do you cooperate with your partner and keep mum, or do you defect and snitch? For both of you as a pair, you get the best joint outcome if both of you cooperate and say nothing. If the two of you keep your mouths shut, the worst you'll get is a short prison sentence (the DA doesn't have enough evidence to put both of you away for a long time). If both of you defect and snitch on each other, you'll both get a substantially longer sentence.

But the decision poses a dilemma: If you remain silent while your partner confesses, things will turn out really badly for you. You will be put behind bars for a long time, while your partner strikes a plea bargain and gets to walk away. On the other hand, if your partner remains loyal and stays quiet, but you choose to confess and give the DA evidence against him, you get to go free! Your outcome depends not only on what you do but also on what your fellow felon does, making this the kind of dilemma ideally suited for game theory.

Researchers often study prisoners' dilemmas in the laboratory, offering people different amounts of money for cooperating versus defecting. For example, if you and the other person in an experiment both choose to cooperate, you each get $5. But if you both defect on one another, you walk away with only $2. That might make it seem like cooperation is the best strategy, but it isn't. If you choose to defect but your partner cooperates, you win $8, while the other guy gets $0. Of course, if the reverse happens (you cooperate but your partner defects), you're the one who ends up with zilch—this is known as the "sucker's payoff."

From the rational economist's perspective, the most reasonable decision in this type of one-shot prisoner's dilemma is to defect. Defecting is rational because it gives you a relatively better payoff regardless of what your partner decides to do. If you defect, you'll be better off in the event that your partner either defects (you get $2 as opposed to $0) or cooperates (you get $8 instead of $5). According to the logical rules of game theory developed by rational economists, the rational choice is for people to defect on their partners because no one should choose to be the sucker.

Although game theory is all very logical and precise, behavioral economists and other psychologists who have studied these kinds of dilemmas point out one little problem. Real people don't play like rational economists say they should. Even in one-shot games with complete strangers who can't see or hear one another, and who will never meet, real people often spontaneously decide to cooperate.

We humans fail to behave rationally in all kinds of negotiations. In one economic game called the *ultimatum game,* you are given a sum of money (say, $100) that you need to split between yourself and another player. The other player has no say in how much you give, except that if he or she says, "No way," to your offer, neither of you gets a penny. Rational economists have argued that your most reasonable choice would be to offer very little to the other player, maybe $1 for the other person and $99 for you. Why? Because if she says yes, she gets $1; if she says no, she gets $0. So, as long as she chooses rationally, you have her over a barrel. Yet people who are offered a $1 share of $100 usually respond with what rational economists would consider irrational spite, saying, "No thanks. I'll take $0 instead!" In fact, not only do people making offers in the ultimatum game rarely act like rational economists say they should, but capitalistic Americans are surprisingly generous in their offers, often sharing equally with the other person (the one exception is that students of economics tend to play hardball, and consequently tend to leave the experiment with less money than less "rational" people).

Behavioral economists, the laboratory decision scientists who have exposed our supposed defects, have dedicated thousands of pages in scientific journals to these kinds of "anomalies," "fallacies," and "paradoxes." But do these violations of economic rationality really mean that humans are flawed? From the evolutionary psychologist's perspective, there is something deeper going on.

The rules of game theory developed by rational economists make good sense when the parties negotiating with each other are cold-blooded Econs, each seeking to maximize monetary returns. These rules work well in explaining how the Coca-Cola and Pepsi-Cola Corporations compete in the marketplace, how used automobiles are bought and sold on the open market, and how Wall Street traders exchange shares of stock or swap pork bellies on the Chicago Mercantile Exchange. But humans are not cold-blooded Econs. Corporations, market pricing, and even economics itself are all evolutionarily novel phenomena—things our ancestors would never have encountered. What our ancestors did encounter was their kith and kin. Even today, most people in the world still have most of their meaningful interactions with friends and family members. Rather than playing the rational economist's game, we play a very different game when it comes to family.

HOME ECONOMICS: THE KINSHIP GAME

What would happen if you were playing the prisoner's dilemma game, but the other prisoner was your clone? Nancy Segal has actually studied this very question. Segal is a behavioral geneticist at California State University, Fullerton, just up the road from Disneyland. Segal studies twins. She looks at the similarities and differences in twins' preferences and behaviors, like whether twins separated at birth have similar personality traits when they are reunited thirty years later. Segal believes that studying the relationships between twins offers an unusual opportunity to study one of evolutionary biology's most powerful principles: *inclusive fitness*. The idea is simple: because evolution favors behaviors that help an organism pass on its DNA, natural selection favors greater cooperation between organisms who share common genes. Since we share some of our genes with relatives, this means that helping a relative is, from a genetic perspective, almost as good as helping ourselves.

The principle of inclusive fitness provides the scientific explanation for why blood is thicker than water. But the principle doesn't just say that people will help family members more than strangers. It is much more precise: people will tend to give more help to those family members who share more genes with them. For example, if you're going to run into a burning building to save another, the principle of inclusive fitness suggests that risking your own life will be genetically worthwhile if you can save two siblings (each sharing about half, or

0.5, of their genes with you), four nephews or nieces (each sharing one-quarter, or 0.25, of their genes with you), or eight cousins (each sharing one-eighth, or 0.125, of their genes with you).

Hundreds of findings across the animal kingdom support this principle. Ground squirrels are more likely to risk their lives by giving a loud alarm signal to warn of a predator if doing so will save their brothers and sisters, as compared to their second cousins. White-fronted bee-eaters are more likely to share food with full siblings than with half siblings. And aid within human families tends to run along genetic lines as well. Of the inheritance money left in people's wills, 92.3 percent goes to family and only 7.7 percent to nonfamily. And of the money left to genetic relatives, 84 percent goes to those sharing 50 percent of the benefactor's genes, 14 percent to those sharing 25 percent, and less than 2 percent to those sharing 12.5 percent or fewer genes.

The power of shared genes shows up in bold relief if you compare the way parents treat children who are related to them by blood as compared to by marriage. In the classic fairytale, Cinderella's nasty stepmother treats her like a lowly servant, all the while showering rewards and affection on her two evil daughters. Sadly, the real world resembles the cruel fairytale. Parents are 5.5 times less likely to help pay college costs for stepchildren versus biological children. And while they are shut out of many rewards, stepchildren are often dealt more than their share of punishments. Children living with a stepparent are forty times more likely to suffer physical abuse than those living with two genetic parents, with much of the abuse coming from the stepparent. Even more shocking are the data on homicides. Although murders of small children are rare, children living with a stepparent are forty to one hundred times more likely to be killed! Is this because stepchildren live in poorer families, or because of some other confounding variable? No. Even for parents who have both biological children and stepchildren living with them in the same house (for whom all the possible confounding variables are equated), stepchildren are nine times more likely to be abused than biological children living under the same roof.

Nancy Segal, the twins researcher, wondered whether the principle of inclusive fitness would apply to the extreme case in which siblings share more than the usual number of common genes. To explore this question, she compared identical (or monozygotic) twins with fraternal (or dizygotic) twins. While both types of twins tend to be born into the same family at the same time, they differ in the proportion of genes they share. Fraternal twins share the usual brotherly 50 percent, while identical twins share 100 percent of their genes. Identical twins are in fact clones.

In her research, Segal repeatedly finds that identical twins have closer and more cooperative relationships than fraternal twins. Identical twins feel closer to one another's children than fraternal twins. And when a member of a pair of identical twins dies, the surviving twin feels a more intense and longer sense of mourning than that felt by the surviving member of a pair of fraternal twins.

In one study, Segal and her colleague Scott Hershberger had twins play a prisoner's dilemma game. To be consistent with the economic rules of the game, the researchers gave the twins instructions designed to encourage self-interested play, explaining that each person's goal should be to win as much money for him- or herself as possible and not worry about what happens to the other player. Yet even when spurred to think about maximizing their own self-interest—rational economist style—the twins had a hard time defecting on one another. Instead, they spontaneously chose to cooperate much of the time.

The most interesting finding was the difference in cooperation between twins who shared half versus all of their genes. Compared to fraternal twins, identical twins were 27 percent more likely to cooperate. We're not suggesting that twins were making relatedness calculations in their head before they decided to cooperate. Identical twins simply feel more cooperative toward one another than fraternal twins, in the same way that most of us feel more willing to lend money to a sibling (who shares 50 percent of our genes) than to Cousin Myrtle (who shares only 12.5 percent).

The twin study shows not only that blood is thicker than water but that the blood of genetically closer kin is thicker than that of less closely related kin. Our preference for those who share our genes is not simply due to the fact that we have spent more time with our closer relatives. Even after being raised separately and then reunited, identical twins regularly become closer to one another than do reunited fraternal twins.

HOME ECONOMICS VERSUS CORPORATE ECONOMICS

Let's go back to the Disney example and consider the two different pairs of men who ran the company. The founding brothers, Walt and Roy O., had many disagreements and fierce negotiations, but they found a way to cooperate and stuck together through a lifetime of ups and downs. Roy E. and Michael Eisner, however, were unwilling to see eye to eye; instead, they aired their dirty laundry in public and let the company and its image flounder.

Each of these conflicts can be analyzed using game theory. Let's say that Eisner and Roy E. are playing the prisoner's dilemma in the laboratory and can win up to $100. The situation is a zero-sum game: If Eisner receives $100, that's $100 that Roy won't get. If Roy gets a larger payout, on the other hand, Eisner will have to take less money. The rules of rational economics predict that when interests conflict, the best strategy for each player is to defect—to avoid being the sucker. Roy E. and Eisner followed the rules of the game perfectly, playing with pure self-interest and generating a relatively dismal outcome.

But now consider the case of two brothers, like Walt and Roy O., playing the same game. Unlike Eisner and Roy E., the two brothers share 50 percent of their genes. This is important because, from an evolutionary perspective, if your brother benefits, so do you. Anything that contributes to your brother's survival and reproduction gets tallied in your own evolutionary success ledger. This makes the dilemma a positive-sum game: a $100 benefit for your brother is a $50 benefit for you. Indeed, sometimes a family member can still win by losing.

When one of the authors of this book, Doug, and colleagues Federico Sanabria, Jill Sundie, and Peter Killeen joined to recalculate the prisoner's dilemma in these terms, they found that the dilemma often disappeared if two brothers were playing. Under most conditions, the deeply rational strategy was no longer to defect but to cooperate. Thinking about this makes it easier to understand why Roy O. was able to tolerate his brother Walt's financial eccentricities in a way that Roy E. could not for Michael Eisner, who was connected to the Disney clan only through dollar signs and not genes.

The fact that siblings are genetically related doesn't mean they will always get along. Brothers and sisters often fight bitterly, and even lifelong business partners Walt and Roy spent a long period avoiding one another and communicating through intermediaries. Eminent evolutionary biologist Robert Trivers has noted that some degree of sibling rivalry is to be expected from an evolutionary perspective. Except in the rare case of identical twins, siblings share only half their genes. From your genes' selfish perspective, every dollar mom and dad invest in you is perfectly well spent, but the same buck invested in your brother wastes fifty cents (on those unshared genes).

Despite the fact that siblings are not completely cooperative with one another, however, they cooperate more with one another than with nonrelatives. Conflict between family members is hardly impossible; it's just less vicious than conflict between nonrelatives. All else being equal, Roy Disney prefers a dollar spent on Roy Disney. A dollar spent on a member of the Eisner clan, on the other hand, is worth nothing. The same dollar spent on brother Walt is at least worth fifty cents.

THE RULES OF THE GAME
(THEORY) FOR DIFFERENT SUBSELVES

When it comes to game theory, then, there are at least two different games in town—one based on Wall Street market pricing and another based on kinship bonds. But are there more? As it turns out, each of the different subselves we met earlier has its own set of rules for how to play the game. Because our evolutionary interests align differently when it comes to corporations, blood relatives, friends, bosses, dating partners, and spouses, each subself negotiates according to its own set of rules. And whether a particular subself comes out to play depends on who else is on the playground.

TEAM PAYOFFS: THE AFFILIATION GAME

Friendships can be quite rewarding. Your buddies can provide a shoulder when you need one to cry on and an extra pair of arms and legs when you need to move a large piece of furniture. And if you read the cast of characters in any individual's financial success story, you will usually find a few friends playing key supporting roles. Take the case of the person listed in the *Guinness Book of World Records* as "the most successful musician and composer in popular music history." This individual has had sixty separate records go gold (selling more than a half million copies), and a single one of this person's songs has been covered by over two thousand other artists. That song, "Yesterday," helped make its author (a fellow named Paul McCartney) one of Britain's wealthiest men, with a net worth of approximately $741 million in 2010.

But none of this would have happened if not for a powerful friendship McCartney formed as a mere lad of fifteen years, when he went to hear a local skiffle band called The Quarrymen. The lead singer of The Quarrymen, a cocky seventeen-year-old named John Lennon, invited McCartney to join the band, and the two later formed a songwriting partnership in which they agreed to take equal credit for any of the tunes they wrote. They cowrote approximately 180 songs during their decades-long friendship, most of them recorded by their band, whose name they later changed from The Quarrymen to The Beatles.

Lennon and McCartney's share-and-share-alike arrangement is common among friends. A couple of decades later, when Steve Wozniak and his young buddy Steve Jobs started Apple Computer, Inc., they had a precisely equal share in the company's stocks. The two friends agreed on a fifty-fifty split, even though Wozniak's father thought it grossly unfair since his son had designed the Apple I computer with little or no technical help from Jobs.

Alan Fiske, an anthropologist at the University of California, Los Angeles (UCLA), believes that the human mind has separate systems for calculating exchanges between different types of people. Fiske's theory grew out of his anthropological fieldwork in West Africa. Living among the Mossi people of Burkina Faso, he observed that the villagers switched between very different modes of exchange, depending on whom they were dealing with. Fiske was struck by the fact that he had observed the same patterns of exchange growing up in the United States and later uncovered them in other cultures he visited in his roles as a Peace Corps volunteer and field anthropologist.

We have already met two of Fiske's models. The first, *market pricing*, is the cold-blooded monetary system that rational economists presume people use for most of their decisions. But Fiske detailed several other systems that he observed humans regularly using across the globe. Fiske's second model, *communal sharing*, is that used between close relatives, like Walt and Roy O. Disney or the twins in the prisoner's dilemma. This set of kinship rules involves giving what you can, taking what you need, and not keeping track of individual contributions. Communal sharing is the model used by the kin-care subself we met earlier.

Fiske's third model, *equality matching*, describes exchanges between peers or friends, such as Lennon and McCartney or Jobs and Wozniak. The affiliation subself typically uses this set of rules. When the mind is running this program, it feels fair when everyone gets the same amount and has an equal turn. Friendly kids on the playground use this system, as do teenagers on athletic teams, adults in carpools, and members of babysitting cooperatives. Between friends, strict mathematical calculation isn't necessary. If I invite you over to dinner or pay for lunch, next time you'll take your turn. As turn-taking friends, we don't worry about the fact that you're a studied chef who lays out a five-star presentation to highlight your special steak tartare, whereas I have to stretch my capacities to fry up a humble repast of breaded chicken and home fries.

Fiske contrasts this buddy system with the rational economist's market-pricing system, in which people pay for commodities in proportion to what they receive, carefully calculating market value, with everyone bargaining to get the best deal for themselves and allowing those with more capital to get a larger share of the goodies. To appreciate the contrast between the rational economic model and the model used between friends, imagine finishing a dinner at a friend's house and receiving a bill that calculated the difference between the value of the fine wine, steak, and selected mushrooms they'd served against the estimated value of the beer, chicken, and potatoes you'd served the week before, with an extra 50 percent surcharge added in for the additional preparation time and culinary skills your friend had brought to bear. This is more or less exactly what gets calculated into the bill when you go to a fine restaurant. The rational economic model applies to how goods are exchanged on the open market, but it would be highly inappropriate, indeed positively insulting, between friends. Friends take their turns, and both are satisfied with the deal.

One study found that people cluster the rewards other folks provide into several distinct categories. Sometimes other people provide you with love; other times they give you status; and still other times they give you money or goods. The researchers asked participants to imagine that they had given one of those rewards to another person, for example, love ("You convey to a person that you feel affection for him and enjoy being with him"), status ("You convey to a person your respect and esteem for his talents"), or goods ("You give a person certain objects that you possess"). They then asked what participants would prefer to get back in each case. If you gave someone love, for example, would you prefer that the other person give back affection, merchandise, money, or a willingness to run an errand for you?

In contrast to what one might expect from the rational economist's perspective, the researchers found that money was the last thing their subjects wanted back from other people, unless they had given them money in the first place. Money and love were even viewed as negatively linked to one another. Not only can't money buy me love, as The Beatles put it, but an offer of cash in exchange for your girlfriend saying she loves you may buy you a ticket to ride—one-way, back to your bachelor pad.

The focus on balance in friendly relationships has a negative side. When friends start to feel a gross imbalance, they may feel resentful and respond with spiteful tit-for-tat exchanges of negativity. This happened when Lennon and McCartney split up The Beatles, and the former moptops starting singing a much less harmonious tune. They began wailing about exactly which one of them should get credit for which lyrics and melodies in which particular songs, and insulting one another in public (Lennon wrote a nasty tune called "How Do You Sleep?" with lines like "the only thing you done was 'Yesterday'").

The originators of Apple avoided such an acrimonious split, but Wozniak was bothered for years after learning that Steve Jobs had deceptively neglected to share a few dollars of bonus money Jobs had earned when Wozniak helped him with a programming project at Atari during their younger years. "I wish he had just been honest. If he had told me he needed the money, he should have known I would have just given it to him. He was a friend. You help your friends."

The equality-matching rulebook, used by our affiliation subself, is very different from the one used by our kin-care subself. Next we turn to our status subself, which has its own specialized instructions for navigating social hierarchies.

PYRAMID PLAY: THE STATUS GAME

It's good to be king, right? Kings, presidents, and CEOs of major corporations have access to palatial dwellings, personal airplanes, and servants to prepare their food, clean up after them, and deliver their purple robes to the dry cleaners. As CEO of the Disney corporation, Michael Eisner earned a cool $40 million in 1987 alone. But Eisner was a mere peasant compared to Bhupinder Singh, Seventh Maharajah of the state of Patiala in India, who lorded over immense areas of land, collected Rolls-Royces, and had hordes of wives and concubines waiting in line to please him. Even down in the humbler towns and villages where most of us mortals live, our fellow townies with higher status get larger paychecks, better parking spaces, offices with views, personal secretaries, and houses on the right side of the tracks.

And yet, not everyone wants to be a leader. Steve Wozniak insisted on remaining an engineer and refused to take a managerial position when he and Steve Jobs started Apple. In many universities, most faculty eligible to chair a department run from the opportunity for a big raise, a secretary, and a corner office. When an opening for a new chair arises, many faculty take the same position as famous Civil War general William Tecumseh Sherman did when he was being considered as a candidate for president: "I will not run for the office, and if elected, I will not serve." People's ambivalence about climbing the ladder stems from the fact that the higher rungs bring not only boosted benefits but also elevated expectations.

Alan Fiske, the UCLA anthropologist, points out that leaders and followers use rules of exchange that are very different from those that guide brothers and sisters, friends, or consumers and shopkeepers. Fiske calls this hierarchical system *authority ranking*. In this mode of exchange—the one used by our status subself—people receive different benefits and pay different costs depending on their position in a status hierarchy, and nobody gets by for free. The underlings bestow loyalty and special privileges on the higher-ups, but in turn they expect leaders to provide resources, money, protection, and direction. For example, the US president gets to live in the White House, fly on Air Force One, and speak on television whenever he feels the impulse, but his constituents expect him to reduce unemployment, increase everyone's paychecks, provide a first-rate education for their kids, stand up to military threats all around the world, and reduce taxes along the way.

Leadership is found in a wide range of species, including our close relatives chimpanzees and gorillas, as well as capuchin monkeys, zebras, antelopes, wolves, and homing pigeons. Even some sheep are leaders. Most members of all those species, however, like most members of the human race, are followers. From the perspective of game theory, it is often better to be a member of the herd than a lone wolf who goes it alone, even if it means allowing the leader to have first shot at benefits, like the best drinking position at the watering hole. Without a leader willing to decide whether to head south to the river, north to the pasture, or east to the berry patch, the herd members would disperse randomly and thereby lose the benefits of traveling in a big group when a hungry predator came along.

Human followers, of course, often become very disappointed if their leaders do not provide direction and inspiration. Only a few years after starting Apple, Steve Jobs, who was frequently rude to his team members, was fired by his own board of directors. Michael Eisner, who also developed a reputation for being ruthless and autocratic, was booted out as head of Disney. The office of the US president may be the highest-status position in the world, yet every president in recent history has had to endure a continual barrage of angry and insulting media attention during his term. Bill Clinton was almost removed from office for behaving a bit too much like the amorous Maharajah Bhupinder Singh, and Richard Nixon was in fact forced out of office for his role in the Watergate cover-up. Being humiliated before the eyes of the world seems a high price to pay, but it went even worse for John F. Kennedy, James Garfield, William McKinley, and Abraham Lincoln, who were all killed by unhappy constituents before they could finish their presidential terms.

An important insight is that leaders and followers play the status game differently. Followers offer loyalty, obedience, and special privileges for the leader, but this offer is contingent on the leader's reciprocating by protecting their interests and having the vision to move the group in the right direction. In a sense, a leader and a follower are playing a real-life version of the "ultimatum game" described earlier, in which the follower expects the leader to show a sense of *noblesse oblige* and not keep all the goodies for himself.

So far we have talked about the different rulebooks used by our status, kin-care, and affiliation subselves. But which of our subselves actually uses the rules of market pricing as developed by rational economists? You might be afraid to find out.

FOXHOLE ECONOMICS: THE SELF-PROTECTION GAME

In 1221, the residents of the Persian city of Nishapur confronted the ultimate game theory dilemma. Their city was surrounded by one hundred thousand Mongolian warriors on horseback, led by Genghis Khan, who sent a messenger with the following ultimatum: "Commanders, elders, and commoners, know that God has given me the empire of the earth from the east to the west. Whoever submits shall be spared, but those who resist, they shall be destroyed with their wives, children, and dependents."

Surrendering to an alien army rarely results in a happy outcome. Throughout history, conquering tribes have tended to regard the conquered as somewhat less than human and have rarely felt compelled to be fair as they exploited the vanquished people's resources, stole their women, demanded tribute, and often forced the vanquished young men into military service. Genghis Khan would compel the men in the last town he conquered to march before his troops into their next battle, then use his horses to push them into the moats of the next city on their warpath, allowing the Mongol horsemen to ride over their bodies. But for the residents of Nishapur, even these possibilities were better than having Genghis Khan's army slaughter every-one on the spot. The negotiation with Genghis went quickly: Nisha-pur surrendered.

But sometimes intergroup negotiations are less nasty: outsiders have things we want, and it can be useful to form alliances with them. Despite his sometimes brutal acts of conquest, Genghis Khan set up the world's most important trade routes, connecting Asia, the Middle East, and Europe. Of course, human beings become especially wary about possible unfairness when they're exchanging goods or services with members of other tribes, Mongolian or otherwise. Unlike your kin, the members of the other tribes do not share your genes, and un-like your friends and associates, strangers share no history of reciproc-ity and trust with you.

This is where market economics come in, providing a system to regulate the careful accounting of costs and benefits. Monetary sys-tems provide an elegant means to directly compare the value of Hon-eycrisp apples, Apple iPads, Kotex minipads, text-messaging services, and erotic massages. But in market exchanges, sellers count every penny, and buyers are wary of shoddy merchandise, with each side quick to anger at any hint of unfairness. The rules of rational econom-ics are deeply rational when the top priority is protecting yourself from getting burned. And this is why our wary self-protection subself operates using the rules of market pricing.

While market pricing is relevant to understanding how people deal with wary strangers, it does not represent how the mind calcu-lates exchanges between relatives, friends, or people higher or lower in the status hierarchy. Yet if you peruse the expansive literature on decision making, you will discover that the majority of theorists and researchers have presumed that some variant of market pricing drives all human decisions. This makes sense to the extent that economists are trying to understand how investors deal with competitors on Wall Street. These rules might also help psychologists understand how people interact with perfect strangers, like most of the people they meet in laboratory experiments. If someone is a perfect stranger, it makes sense that he or she might defect in a prisoner's dilemma.

But a central point in this book is that economically rational market principles apply to only a fraction of human decisions. Most of the time, we're dealing with relatives, friends, neighbors, coworkers, and long-term business partners. We even come to have relationships with the people who sell us groceries or automobiles. Only rarely do we deal with total strangers. And most of the time, rather than trying to skulk away with the biggest bag of money, we stick around and try to get those other people to like and respect us and care about our welfare. If you use the rules of free market rationality with the people around you, you are likely to find yourself without too many intimate associates to worry about. Indeed, a tendency to treat others in a coldly calculating manner and to try to get them to serve your interests, while giving as little as possible in return, is an indicator of sociopathy, which psychiatrists consider a mental disorder.

Speaking of intimate associates, we haven't yet discussed two more exchange systems, those used to calculate costs and benefits between romantic partners and between spouses. Unless all of your intimate relations resemble those between a prostitute and a john, you are unlikely to be using the rules of free market rationality in your amorous relationships. The rules of the mating game are so interesting that we dedicate an entire chapter to sexual economics (see Chapter 8). For now, let's reconsider the rules of market economics in the business world in light of what we've learned about how our different subselves reckon self-interest.

IS MARKET ECONOMICS ANY WAY TO RUN A BUSINESS?

Although market economics doesn't apply to relationships with friends and relatives, at least we can assume it makes sense in the business world, right? It's only business, after all.

Actually, no. Unless you're involved in a onetime negotiation with a total stranger about how many pesos to pay for a pound of pomegranates, market economics typically makes for bad business. Cold, hard rational self-interest might make sense in dealing with potentially hostile strangers you'll never see or hear from again, but it doesn't work too well when you're dealing with people with whom you'll be doing business for any length of time, be they coworkers, clients, or simply repeat customers.

Frederick Winslow Taylor, the father of "scientific management," was the ultimate capitalist philosopher. Working in the steel industry around the turn of the twentieth century, he observed, "The fundamental principle upon which industry seems now to be run in this century is that the employer shall pay just as low wages as he can and that the workman shall retaliate by doing just as little work as he can." His ultrarational solution to this problem was to calculate the precise amount of financial incentive that would motivate workers to boost production rates and allow his company (Bethlehem Steel) to fire the majority of its less efficient coworkers. One biographer notes that Taylor was "so deeply hated by the men that he had to walk home under armed guard for fear of an attack on his life." The same biographer suggests that Taylor's rational scientific-management approach inadvertently "contributed more to labor unrest than AFL founder Samuel Gompers and Socialist party founder Eugene V. Debs combined."

So, things don't go so well if you treat your colleagues like strangers negotiating over the price of a mango in a crowded marketplace. And as we've seen, the rules of the marketplace get completely thrown out when we're dealing with family members. But if you're not running a family business, is there anything you can do to foster a more cooperative and trusting environment?

BRINGING HOME ECONOMICS TO WALL STREET

One key difference between the hard-negotiating market-pricing model and the easygoing family model is trust. Remember that even according to the economic rules of game theory, the best outcome in a prisoner's dilemma comes when both people trust each other enough to cooperate. The problem arises when you can't trust the other person. Will your fellow crook really honor that pact of silence? Because the other person has large incentives to defect on you, many economists presume that he or she will. If that's the case, the most rational decision for you is to defect as well, unless you want to end up with the sucker's payoff.

But unlike in the Wall Street game, there is less incentive to defect in the kinship game. If your brother cheats you out of some benefit, he is also, from an evolutionary perspective, cheating himself out of half that benefit. Because the two of you are aligned genetically, you trust that he is, compared to a stranger in the marketplace, less likely to defect on you, making you more likely to cooperate.

An important implication of all this is that people can negotiate or run a business using a mistrusting psychology of market economics or a trusting psychology of family relations. The key is to switch people from one to the other, even if they aren't your relatives.

In one interesting study, evolutionary psychologist Lisa DeBruine came up with a clever way to convert wary strangers into kin. She had people play a version of the prisoner's dilemma called the *trust game*. In the game, you are given some money (say, $10) and presented with two options. One option is that you can completely dictate how to divide the money between yourself and another person (you can take $9 for yourself and give that other person $1 if you want, because the other person has no say at all). Alternatively, you can let the other person dictate the terms, giving the other person complete control over how to split the money. If you choose to let the other player dictate the terms, the amount of money to be divided will be substantially larger (say, $30). This means that if you let the other person divide the money, you could get a larger payout than if you choose to divide the money yourself. Your choice in the game depends on whether you trust the other person. Do you think the other person will be a malevolent or benevolent dictator?

DeBruine suspected that people's choices would differ depending on whether they played the game according to the mistrusting psychology of market economics or the trusting psychology of family relations. So at the beginning of the study, DeBruine took everyone's photo. This means that as you made your decision, you saw a photograph of the other player you were paired with, who was always a complete stranger. DeBruine found that people were not especially trusting of the other person. Even if they could make more money by letting the other person choose, people were generally unwilling to take that risk. When gazing at the face of a stranger, people behaved like employees at Bethlehem Steel, wary that this person might take their money and run.

But in another condition in the study, DeBruine morphed your photo with the photo of the other person. As a result the other player looked like your long-lost relative. Playing the game with someone who looked like a potential family member activated the kin-care subself. Now, all of a sudden, people trusted the other person and gave him or her the opportunity to dictate the terms of the game. In return, they got larger payoffs themselves. Even though none of the participants realized that their own faces had been morphed into the other person's, giving money to the other person was like giving money to a family member, because they were, literally, a part of that other person.

A FAMILY COMPANY

Even if it's not very practical for you to start morphing photos of your employees and customers, the trust game study provides an important lesson: people will trust and cooperate more with others if they feel like they are part of a family. This is exactly what happened at Southwest Airlines under longtime CEO Herb Kelleher. As one former Southwest employee observed, "Rather than being a megacorporation with thousands of employees, Southwest is a large family with many members."

Unlike CEOs in the rest of the cutthroat airline industry, Kelleher dealt his employees in on the corporation's profits. To further the familial atmosphere, Kelleher also installed rocking chairs throughout the corporate offices and encouraged employees to wear pajamas to work for a day. After September 11, 2001, when the airline industry suffered a massive crash in business and most of the airlines resorted to massive layoffs, Kelleher appealed to the workers' team spirit, asking them all to share a general pay cut to prevent the company's having to start selectively firing other members of the family. As a consequence, Southwest Airlines employees have never gone on strike, and *Fortune* magazine has frequently listed Southwest as one of the best places to work, as well as one of the most admired corporations in America.

Customers noticed the happier family feeling projected by Southwest employees and have been extremely loyal to the airline. Ironically, by avoiding the cutthroat, profit über alles Wall Street approach, Southwest has been a financial success story, thriving during years when its competitors watched their profits disappear.

Southwest's secret of success was, in essence, to activate the kin-care subself at work, inspiring unrelated people to treat each other like family. This is a variant of the same principle used in the photograph-morphing study. Southwest managed to psychologically morph all its employees into members of the same family.

Southwest Airlines is, of course, not a family; it's a large corporation. But its story indicates something important about your different subselves: they are flexible; they can be turned on and off to fit your current social context. Although your trusting kin-care subself usually comes out when you are around relatives, it can be primed by appropriate circumstances. And when it is running the show, your economic decisions will be more familial. By encouraging employees to think of themselves as members of a big family, companies like Southwest are able to shift the rules of the game psychologically.

And the same thing can happen at an even broader societal level. Martin Luther King Jr.'s "I Have a Dream" speech is full of images that encourage people of different races to think of one another as members of a common tribe—as fellow citizens living in the land of Abraham Lincoln, the US Constitution, and the Declaration of Independence—and even as members of a common family, making repeated reference to brotherhood and to children. That speech has been repeated to generations of children in the years since Dr. King gave it, and its familial imagery may have done more to improve race relations than all the laws passed to punish civil rights violations.

Let's think about the Walt Disney Company in light of what we know about how people's different subselves do business. Disney not only started out as an actual family company but continued to operate on familial principles even after Walt and his brother left the scene. But then Michael Eisner arrived. Eisner brought to the company a hard-nosed Wall Street emphasis on the bottom line, and the result was a harsher, more cutthroat atmosphere. Whereas Walt and Roy O. kept the Disney family together despite occasional downturns in the bottom line, when Eisner started losing money, he was treated like a foreign invader from a strange land, and Roy E. arranged to have him thrown out on the street.

EACH OF OUR SUBSELVES negotiates according to a different rulebook. Rather than treating everyone according to the same set of cold, objective, self-serving rules in every situation, we have a different set of biases depending on whom we're playing with. Those biases often lead us to put shallow self-interest aside. But putting self-interest aside, and doing so in different ways for friends, relatives, and business associates, was good business practice for our ancestors. Those biases led to more beneficial exchanges between our progenitors and their family members, friends, and trading partners.

But some of the biases that served our ancestors so well can sometimes produce costly errors and mistakes. We next take a closer look at our biases and mistakes in an attempt to understand seemingly senseless phenomena from everyday overconfidence to egregious miscalculation. Next stop—Africa, where one particularly potent ancestral bias led the people of one country to choose to starve rather than accept help.

4

Smoke Detectors in the Mind

ON MAY 30, 2002, the African nation of Zambia declared a food crisis. Even before this catastrophe, the country had been in bad shape. The nation was mired in chronic poverty, with a typical family earning $395 per year, and one in ten infants dying soon after birth. In 2002, though, things went from bad to worse. The rainy season that usually begins in November and runs into April came to a sudden halt in mid-January. Thousands of acres of crops planted the previous fall withered and died. By mid-spring, with the country's food reserves running out, Zambians had to resort to boiling poisonous wild roots for eight hours to make them edible and killing protected elephants for meat. Despite these desperate measures, 3 million Zambians were on the verge of starvation, when President Levy Mwanawasa declared a national food emergency.

With the emergency declared, things began to look more hopeful, as the world swiftly came to Zambia's aid. Within weeks the United States had sent thirty-five thousand tons of food to the distressed nation, enough to sustain the population until the next harvest. Much of the food consisted of donations from American farmers, some of whom had surpluses from a bountiful harvest.

But few could have anticipated what happened next. To the shock of the world, President Mwanawasa rejected the aid!

Some observers speculated that this startling episode might be a ploy by an evil dictator hoping to bring his people to their knees. As a wealthy leader, after all, he wasn't the one who was going to starve. But in reality President Mwanawasa had support for the food boycott from the government and from much of the population. Other observers conjectured that perhaps the food aid was so low in quality as to be barely edible. But the supplies sent to Zambia were identical to the food many Americans consumed on a daily basis. Instead, at the heart of the matter were two words that appeared in small print on the food crates: "genetically modified." Many outraged Zambians refused to even touch the crates, leading President Mwanawasa to categorically assert, "We would rather starve than get genetically modified foods." To the Zambians the thirty-five thousand tons of crops from the United States were not food but poison.

Although observers decried Zambia's decision as an error of astounding proportions, we suspect that many people in President Mwanawasa's shoes would have reacted just as he did. The president's decision may have been an error, but it stemmed from a deeply rational bias designed to avoid a much costlier mistake. Here we take a closer look at the ancestral biases guiding people's decisions. While biases are often viewed as deficiencies and equated with poor decision making, an evolutionary perspective stresses that many biases stem from adaptive tendencies that helped our ancestors solve evolutionary problems. We humans are born to be biased—and for good reason. Although these innate biases can sometimes lead to errors, the very nature of these errors often reveals a deeply intelligent brain.

DEFECTIVE BRAINS

We have already looked at a few of the human biases discovered by behavioral economists, the scientists wearing Rolling Stones T-shirts under their white lab coats, who enjoy having a good chuckle at human behavior. And why not? It's sometimes hard not to chuckle at our long list of gross errors in judgment. Our perceptions of reality are grossly warped by phenomena such as the *false consensus bias,* our tendency to overestimate the degree to which other folks agree with us, which results in half of us being shocked after every election. And reality is further warped by the *overconfidence bias,* the tendency for most of us to believe we are better than average on most traits, even though this is mathematically impossible (half of the population is, by definition, below average on any given trait, but of course we don't mean you or me). Overconfidence sometimes reaches absurd levels, as in the case of people hospitalized after auto accidents, who persist in believing they are better-than-average drivers.

Scrolling down the long list of documented errors and biases, it's easy to see humans as being like Keanu Reeves's character Neo in *The Matrix*. Our perception of the world is so skewed by our brains that we seem to be out of touch with the true nature of reality.

But from the evolutionary psychologist's perspective, it would be surprising if the human mind were really so woefully muddled. If our ancestors were so out of touch with reality, how in the world would they have managed to survive, let alone reproduce and then raise offspring who themselves survived, thrived, and reproduced? Brains are expensive mechanisms, requiring more energy than most other bodily organs (our brains make up only 2 percent of our bodily mass yet gobble up as much as 20 to 30 percent of the calories we consume). These calories are not wasted, though. Human brains, like those of other animals, are designed with incredible efficiency, allowing us to thrive in an incredible range of environments.

We are not saying that the brain is free of biases or that people don't sometimes make moronic choices. But we are saying that it's time to reconsider what it means for judgments and decisions to be considered smart.

DOES ADAPTIVE = ACCURATE?

A critical distinction between a traditional and an evolutionary perspective involves the question of whether it's always smart to be accurate. According to most social scientists, people should strive to uncover and know the pure and undistorted truth, which would therefore enable us to make more accurate and correct judgments. But will natural selection necessarily build organisms designed to seek truth? Maybe not. Indeed, in some instances evolution might even disfavor truth and accuracy. What matters instead is that people's judgments enhance fitness. And if it so happens that being biased and inaccurate helps achieve that end in some cases, then in those cases we should expect to see a mind that consistently produces biased and inaccurate judgments. "The principal function of nervous systems," according to cognitive scientist Patricia Churchland, is "to get the body parts where they should be in order that the organism may survive. . . . Truth, whatever that is, definitely takes the hindmost."

We are not saying that someone who is hopelessly delusional and incapable of ever seeing the truth is going to be evolutionarily successful. For most problems, it usually pays a higher dividend to be accurate rather than inaccurate. But the mind is not designed to strive for accuracy and truth 100 percent of the time. As we'll see, there's a good reason why it sometimes makes evolutionary sense to warp reality.

Consider the following example: if an object is moving toward you at 20 feet per second, and is currently 120 feet away, how long will it take for the object to hit you? The accurate answer is 6 seconds (6.001 seconds if you're a physicist concerned about air friction). A guess of four seconds would certainly be inaccurate; indeed, it would be a clear error in judgment. Yet the mind is wired to intentionally make this exact error. When our eyes see an approaching object, our brains tell us that this object will hit us sooner than it actually will. In fact, merely hearing the sound of an approaching object (the swoosh of a bird diving through the air, the rustling of someone in the bushes) will result in the same error. The bias to sense that approaching sounds are going to arrive sooner than they really will is known as *auditory looming*. One study found that this "error" was made by 100 percent of people.

Like many errors and biases that seem irrational on the surface, auditory looming turns out, on closer examination, to be pretty smart. Other animals, like rhesus monkeys, have evolved the same bias. This intentional error functions as an advance warning system, manned by the self-protection subself, providing individuals with a margin of safety when confronted with potentially dangerous approaching objects. If you spot a rhinoceros or hear an avalanche speeding toward you, auditory looming will motivate you to jump out of the way now rather than wait until the last second. The evolutionary benefits of immediately getting out of the way of approaching dangers were so strong that natural selection endowed us—and other mammals—with brains that intentionally see and hear the world inaccurately. Although this kind of bias might inhibit economically rational judgment in laboratory tasks, it leads us to behave in a deeply rational manner in the real world. Being accurate is not always smart.

NOT ALL ERRORS ARE CREATED EQUAL

Although many of our decision errors and biases might look like random design flaws at the surface level, a deeper look often reveals that they aren't random flaws at all. The mind evolved not simply to be biased but to make specific kinds of errors and not others. Consider one of our friends, who recently purchased a house with his family. During the first night in their new home, the family endured a frightening ordeal. As everyone was sleeping, a ceiling-mounted smoke detector sounded a piercing alarm. Our friend woke up to an acrid smell and quickly remembered in horror that he had left several boxes of packing materials next to the stove. His wife hustled frantically to get the kids out of the house, while he managed to call 911.

Thankfully, it was a false alarm. There was no fire after all—the neighbors were just burning wood in their grungy, resin-coated fireplace. A few weeks later the smoke alarm shrieked again, waking everyone in the wee hours of morning. Once again, there was no fire. A few weeks later, there was another false alarm, and then another. Annoyed that the smoke detector was making so many errors, our friend decided to adjust the device to reduce its sensitivity. As he was about to make the smoke detector less responsive, though, his young daughter became visibly distraught. "But daddy," she cried, "what if there is a fire and the alarm doesn't sound?"

This is the smoke detector dilemma. Do you want to set your smoke detector to be less sensitive or more sensitive? This depends on how much you value not being annoyed versus not being trapped in a burning home. Most people would rather have an oversensitive smoke detector, because by tolerating the occasional irritating error they ensure that their families remain alive. We intentionally bias the judgments of our smoke detectors because this helps ensure our survival.

The smoke detector dilemma is the same conundrum natural selection had to resolve in designing many of our own built-in decision-making systems. For many decisions, our brains are wired like ancestral smoke detectors. A smoke detector is designed to make judgment calls despite having incomplete information. When it senses trace amounts of airborne particles that might resemble smoke, the device needs either to start screaming, "Fire! Fire! Fire!" or to remain silent. Our brains have similarly evolved to make judgment calls without having all the pertinent information.

Imagine you're about to run an errand and need to decide whether to take an umbrella. You must choose whether to lug this clunky bumbershoot around town all day or take a chance and leave it at home. Your decision will depend on whether you think it's going to rain. The forecast says there is a 50 percent chance of rain, and you see some clouds in the sky. But you also know there can be clouds without rain, and weather forecasts are notoriously inaccurate. Like a smoke detector, you need to make a decision based on imperfect information.

The decision-making process will inevitably produce some errors. We simply can't be right all the time in a world with imperfect and incomplete information. But not all errors are created equally. There are two fundamentally different types of errors, one of which is much costlier than the other. In the umbrella case, one type of error is that you bring the umbrella, and it doesn't rain. Known as a *false alarm,* this error is like that of a smoke detector sounding without a fire. It's annoying but not a huge deal. Alternatively, a second type of error is that it rains, and you fail to bring your umbrella; this is known as a *miss.* Misses are often much costlier than false alarms in detecting threats. In the umbrella case, a miss means you may be drenched to the bone and ruin your new dress jacket. In the smoke detector case, a miss has even more dire consequences: you could die.

Natural selection creates systems, like the brain, that are biased to minimize the costlier error. This built-in bias to avoid evolutionarily expensive errors is known as the *smoke detector principle*. Evolutionary psychologists Martie Haselton and Randy Nesse believe that natural selection engineered human judgment and decision making to be biased according to the same principle. Like a good smoke detector, our brain is rigged to sound the alarm even when there is no fire, forcing us to tolerate the inconvenience of false alarms to avoid potentially lethal misses. Because our evolutionary tendencies steer us toward avoiding costly errors, our decisions will result in more small errors. But we are disposed to produce little errors so that we avoid big mistakes.

MONEY UP IN SMOKE

The smoke detector principle underlies a plethora of decision errors, such as when you expend the extra effort to put on your seat belt, then don't get in an accident. The decision to wear a seat belt produces an error 999 times out of 1,000. In the overwhelming majority of situations, we drive around strapped into an irritating harness that provides no benefit (it's akin to lugging around an unwieldy umbrella on a sunny day). Yet after a few decades of griping, most sensible people now happily choose to commit the seat belt error, and the result has been a dramatic drop in auto fatalities compared to our belt-resisting grandparents' day. The smoke detector principle leads people to make this small error to avoid the much costlier mistake of getting into an accident without wearing a seat belt.

The smoke detector perspective on decision errors is radically different from how such errors are normally viewed. Many economists, for example, argue that people are especially prone to making errors when it comes to money. Books such as *Why Smart People Make Big Money Mistakes* and *Mean Markets and Lizard Brains* allege that people are foolish financial investors. They claim that one of the most common money mistakes is that people take too little risk with their financial investments—humans are notoriously risk averse. Because US stocks have historically outperformed all other types of investments over the long run, many rational types are befuddled that more people are not investing in stocks. If you have saved up $5,000 and have many years left before retirement, the smart and rational Econ would put this money in a mix of investments that include a fair share of risky stocks. Instead, many people choose to tuck the $5,000 away in a bank—where it is likely to earn a piddling interest rate that barely covers the loss due to inflation. From a traditional economic perspective, this seems irrational.

But think about the same financial decision in light of the smoke detector principle. The decision about what to do with your $5,000 life-savings account could produce two types of errors. One possibility is that you put the money in the bank and the stock market booms. Instead of having a nice return on your investment, you have only your $5,000 plus a measly 1.8 percent interest. This is the supposedly egregious error that makes risk aversion appear so irrational.

We agree that this is an error, but making this error won't cost you your shirt and tie (and your life savings). Consider the other possibility: you invest all your money in stocks, and the market plummets. Now your life savings are gone. Indeed, one of us moved a good portion of his retirement funds from low-interest bond accounts into stocks in 2001. Within a few months of that decision, the stock market took a historically unprecedented dive in value and then another nosedive a short time after that. As we mentioned in the book's opening pages, he is now in a position to retire sometime around age seventy-nine or eighty and, even then, may have to live out his golden years in a modest hut somewhere in Ecuador.

The smoke detector principle has preset our brains to be wary of situations in which we could lose our resources, because this is the much costlier error. The human tendency toward risk aversion may lead to errors, but it is a calculated bias—engineered by natural selection to avoid a much bigger mistake.

DIFFERENT BIASES FOR DIFFERENT SUBSELVES

When are we inclined to be overly conservative in our judgments, and when are we inclined to be more carefree? It depends on which of our subselves is currently in charge of making judgments and decisions. Different subselves have different evolutionary goals, and the criteria for what makes a smart decision differ quite drastically depending on whether you're currently worried about disease as opposed to seeking a mate or caring for your children. Let's go inside the mind of our different subselves to see how this works.

THE BEHAVIORAL IMMUNE SYSTEM:
IN THE MIND OF YOUR DISEASE-AVOIDANCE SUBSELF

Think about the last time you sneezed. Was your body in real danger? Probably not. When we sneeze, our body has frequently made an error, because there is no real threat. Instead, some dander particle or a whiff of chili powder sets off a false alarm. But we are physiologically wired to sneeze at the slightest of respiratory irritations because our body's defenses evolved to be safe rather than sorry.

Our immune system is rigged the same way. An army of white blood cells is ready to go to war if it senses any germ-like substance swimming in our bloodstream. But sending the entire body to war can be expensive, using up precious bodily resources. So natural selection endowed us with a crude first line of defense against pathogens—what evolutionary psychologist Mark Schaller calls the *behavioral immune system*. This psychological system is a set of disease-avoidant thoughts and behaviors operated by our disease-avoidance subself.

The behavioral immune system is a pathogen detector. Just as smoke detectors are sensitive to anything that could resemble smoke, the behavioral immune system is hypersensitive to anything associated with disease. The system is triggered by the sight, smell, or sound of people, places, or odors that could signal dangerous pathogens in the vicinity. Its alarm goes off anytime we're exposed to unsightly sores on someone's arm, the scent of decaying meat, or a man coughing on the bus. When our senses detect something or someone that smells, looks, or sounds strange or different, our disease-avoidance subself makes sure that our behavior changes accordingly.

One study by Josh Tybur and Angela Bryan found that when people were exposed to an unpleasant odor, they were more willing to use condoms. In this case the pathogen cue was superficial and harmless (a squirt from a gag aerosol with a sulfur dioxide scent reminiscent of flatulence and descriptively named "Liquid Ass"). Nevertheless, the harmless stench triggered people's behavioral inclination to protect themselves from sexually transmitted disease.

The realm of psychology (the behavioral immune system) and the realm of biology (the physical immune system) are often thought of as independent spheres. But evolution has harnessed both psychology and biology in a brilliantly coordinated, deeply rational system. As it turns out, activating the behavioral immune system in turn triggers a red alert in the body's physical immune system, the standing army of T cells and other germ-killing lymphocytes. Mark Schaller conducted a clever experiment to test just how closely the two systems work together. He and his team asked people to watch a slide show containing pictures of people who looked sick. The photos depicted folks with rashes and pox, as well as images of people coughing and sneezing as mucus spewed out of their noses. Study participants gave blood samples both before and after watching the images. The researchers then exposed these samples to a bacterial infection to measure the presence of interleukin-6 (IL-6), a pro-inflammatory cytokine that white blood cells make when they detect microbial intruders. A higher level of IL-6 indicates that the body has begun to mount a more aggressive immune response to infection—it's the equivalent of the immune system's troops preparing to go to battle.

By measuring inflammation before and after the slide show, the researchers were able to determine whether seeing pictures of disease-y people actually stimulated the immune system to fight infection—and it did! Merely seeing images of people who might be sick triggered white blood cells to mount a vigorous response to bacterial infection. The researchers even found that the immune system was deeply rational about the types of images that set off a biological response. A different group of participants viewed photos of people who looked dangerous. Some of the people in these photos brandished guns pointed right at the camera, thus aimed directly at the participants themselves (these kinds of images trigger the self-protection subself). Although the dangerous pictures were rated as even more distressing than the disease-y pictures, exposure to images of physical danger had no effect on immune system reaction. Only exposure to disease cues prompted the immune system to kick into higher gear.

REVISITING ZAMBIAN AID AND MUTANT FRENCH FRIES

The behavioral immune system produces an array of responses designed to help prevent infection. Some of these responses may initially appear irrational and completely unrelated to disease. For instance, priming the disease-avoidance subself leads people to be more prejudiced against foreigners from exotic places like Sri Lanka and Ethiopia. While this seems a little strange at first blush, it makes much more sense when one considers that strange outsiders have historically been likely to carry diseases foreign to our immune system, making us especially vulnerable. Most of the post-Columbus decline in the Native American population was due merely to coming into contact with diseases carried by the Europeans. The massacre at Wounded Knee was nothing compared to smallpox. Our psychological disease-avoidance system facilitates deeply rational responses by spurring us to avoid contact with anything or anyone that might require a physiologically costly mobilization of our real immune system.

Given what we know about our behavioral immune system, let's revisit the Zambian food-aid predicament, in which even hungry people refused to eat genetically modified food. When people think about eating genetically modified substances, they often imagine ingesting something physically unnatural, strange, and unknown into their bodies. We want our fruits and vegetables to be "natural." Labeling them as "genetically modified" conjures up unnatural science fiction images—a disfigured blue potato or a red banana with lumpy outgrowths.

Aid workers were outraged at the Zambian president for rejecting genetically modified food aid, especially because many Americans were already eating genetically modified foods on a daily basis. In 2000, around the time of the Zambian aid fiasco, all french fries served in American McDonald's restaurants came from genetically modified potatoes. But it turns out that while consumers loved the taste of these super McSpuds, the vast majority were unaware they were eating genetically modified potatoes.

When Americans learned about the true origin of their fries, it sparked a national outrage in the United States not too different from the indignation in Zambia. American citizens insisted that they would only eat "normal" potatoes. It didn't matter that agricultural inspectors had deemed the genetically modified potatoes perfectly safe. Nor did it make any difference that the World Health Organization has never found ill effects on human health from eating genetically modified foods. Cognitive reasoning has little effect on people when the disease-avoidance subself takes charge. As a result of the protests, McDonald's had no choice but to switch back to the old "natural" potatoes. In the same way that Zambians refused to ingest genetically modified food, Americans refused to touch mutant french fries.

SEX DETECTORS: IN THE MIND OF MEN'S MATE-ACQUISITION SUBSELVES

Thus far we have focused on ancestral biases geared for successful defense, such as those used by our disease-avoidance subself that protect us from disease. But in the game of natural selection, a good defense is only part of the story. Evolutionary success involves both solving the challenges of danger and disease (having a good defense) and taking advantage of opportunities to make friends, gain status, and reproduce (having a good offense). In fact, a good offense can be even more critical from an evolutionary perspective. If a successfully defensive person lives to be one hundred years old, his genes will die with him unless he can send some of them out on a mating mission. By contrast, the genes of a mediocre defender who only manages to live to age thirty still have a chance as long as he sends some of his genes out on a few successful quests.

Just as animals have detection systems to spot danger and disease, they have other sets of mechanisms to detect opportunities. Take the silkworm moth, known to fluent Latin entomologists as *Bombyx mori* and to the ancient Chinese as a flying cash crop. When female silkworm moths are interested in mating, they release a chemical called bombykol. The evolutionary success of male moths depends on whether they can detect the presence of an interested female. But there's a problem: females produce only the tiniest amounts of this sex pheromone. So males have evolved extremely sensitive bombykol detectors, enabling them to detect this chemical in concentrations as low as 1 molecule in 1,000,000,000,000,000,000 air molecules (that's a quintillion, in case your cash supplies don't typically require you to count that many zeroes). With that level of sensitivity, a guy moth can detect the scent of a lady moth over ten kilometers away. When it comes to mating, male silkworm moths are like sharks, which can detect a drop of blood in a bay full of water and dart toward their target.

In the same way that evolution has endowed humans with intentionally biased smoke detectors for superb defense, natural selection has also produced intentionally biased sex detectors for conducting a mating offense. Unlike the shrill wail of a smoke detector, which leads us to avoid deadly mistakes, the sound of a sex detector alarm is a pleasant melody, propelling us toward reproductive opportunities. Men, for example, are notorious for making judgment errors when it comes to gauging women's romantic interest. As many women can attest, men are often delusional—a guy may think a woman is romantically interested in him when nothing could be further from the truth. If an attractive woman does so much as look a man's way, many men think: She wants me.

In one of our studies, we asked men to look at photos of attractive women. Although the women all had perfectly neutral facial expressions, the men in the study were told that the models were suppressing a specific emotion. The men were told that the point of the study was to see if they could pick up on "microexpressions" in other people's faces, which might, in this case, leak the true emotions the women were feeling. Before being asked to determine what emotion the women in the photographs might be suppressing, some of the men watched a film clip that elicited romantic feelings—it depicted a highly attractive woman falling for a handsome man. After having his mate-acquisition subself awakened, a typical man believed that he could detect subtle signs of suppressed sexual interest in the attractive women's expressions. It didn't matter that these were photos of women that had been preselected for their perfectly neutral, stoic expressions. In a sense, the men were convinced that the beautiful female models were flirting with them.

The mate-acquisition subself has preset men's sex detectors to be overly sensitive. While this setting leads men to make errors in judgment, it's an evolutionarily calculated error. This bias is the flip side of the smoke detector principle, which biases judgment to avoid costly errors. Recall that there are two types of errors: misses and false alarms. In the case of men trying to infer female interest, a false alarm means that a man perceives sexual interest when there is none. But a miss means that a man fails to perceive sexual interest when a woman is in fact interested. From an evolutionary perspective, the cost to a man of overlooking a sexual opportunity (a miss) is greater than the cost of occasionally wasting time pursuing a disinterested woman (a false alarm). Because a typical man doesn't get all that many mating opportunities, it is especially important not to let one slip by.

Natural selection has rigged men's mate-acquisition subself to overestimate the extent to which women are interested in them. This might frequently lead men to appear like delusional fools, but evolutionary success in the mating domain is a numbers game—the more you're willing to ask, the more mates you're likely to get. In fact, if an average-looking male college student walks up to a female student who is single and asks her out on a date, studies show that he will be successful in scoring a date about 50 percent of the time. Obviously, a guy who thinks a woman is interested in him is more likely to ask her on a date, whereas a guy who guesses she's uninterested will shy away, even though there is a good chance that she would have said yes. If you're a guy, you might never get a date unless you're occasionally willing to make a fool of yourself.

Women, on the other hand, do not show the sexual overperception bias. Instead, they are generally wisely skeptical when it comes to men—though, as we'll see, not always.

SEXY BAD BOY DELUSIONS:
IN THE MIND OF WOMEN'S MATE-ACQUISITION SUBSELVES

Many women believe that a good romantic partner is someone who is reliable, dependable, and will make a good father. Yet many of these same women have their hearts broken after pursuing a man who is charismatic, sexy, adventurous, and hopelessly unreliable—think of the dapper Don Draper on *Mad Men* or Christian Grey in *Fifty Shades of Grey*. Whereas dating guides for men teach bachelors how to be the dangerous bad boy women can't resist, dating guides for women implore them to steer clear of commitment-phobic sexy cads and instead choose the reliable "Mr. Good Enough." How is it, then, that, despite continuous warnings and recurring heartbreak, some women keep going after the wrong guy?

Recall that women's shopping behavior and exotic dancing prowess is subconsciously influenced by their ovulatory cycles, which cause women to seek sexier clothing and act in more enticing ways. Ovulation is a hormonal trigger for women's mate-acquisition subself. And during the few days around ovulation when they are most fertile, women subconsciously become more attracted to the George Clooneys and James Bonds of the world—men who are charming, physically attractive, masculine, and adventurous.

Even though such men are obvious playboys, some women convince themselves that these handsome Don Juans are just the kind of men they can tame and turn into good husbands. Some evolutionary psychologists have argued that natural selection engineered ovulating women to be drawn to these handsome specimens because symmetry, masculinity, and social dominance are biological markers of male genetic fitness. George Clooney's handsome, masculine appearance might be a signal that he is bearing genes that will make for healthier, stronger, and sexier offspring (kids who will grow up to play both good defense and good offense). But because other women are also likely to throw themselves at these strapping specimens, such men often have a problem with commitment, making them less-than-ideal relationship partners.

Because most women are more interested in long-term commitments than one-night stands, why would they ever think it wise to pursue a relationship with precisely the men who are most likely to cheat, lie, and then leave them for the next woman who comes along?

It turns out that ovulation warps women's perceptions of sexy bad boys. In one study, ovulating and nonovulating college-age women were introduced to two different men. The women got to know the guys over a videoconferencing system. One of the men (actually an actor) played a convincing role as a reliable "good dad" type: nice, caring, reasonably good-looking, and wanting nothing more than a committed relationship and a family. But despite these desirable characteristics, this nice fellow was also shy, boring, and unsure of himself. A second guy (also a trained actor) was more intriguing: he was a sexy bad boy, a gorgeous hunk with an athletic body and a magnetic charisma. This fellow knew how to take charge and show a woman a good time, but he also sent up all the clear red flags that he was unreliable and undependable.

After they interacted with both guys, the ovulating and nonovulating women rated each of the two bachelors. When they were evaluating the "good dad," ovulation had no effect. Women thought he seemed pretty sweet but was nothing special, regardless of where they were in their cycle. But when evaluating the sexy bad boy, ovulating women became delusional. Women under the influence of their own natural fertility hormones came to believe that the sexy cad would become a committed and stable relationship partner and that he would magically transform into a dream husband and father—the kind of magical transformation that happens at the climax of almost every women's romance novel. When their ovulatory hormones were flowing, women deluded themselves into believing that the James Bond type would not only change diapers, cook, and happily give the baby baths but even take on *more than half* of the parental care! When looking at the sexy bad boy through ovulation goggles, Mr. Wrong looked exactly like Mr. Right.

The research suggests that fertility hormones trigger women's sex detectors. Rather than being skeptical of a sexy bad boy's intentions, ovulating women are ready to go on the offensive—by unwittingly allowing themselves to believe that they can transform sexy cads into good husbands and dads. Because natural selection engineered women's minds to find ways to extract high-quality male genes, this ovulatory delusion may be the extra push some women need to participate in sexual encounters with men high in genetic quality. Occasionally, the right woman does successfully inspire one of these playboy types to settle down—even Brad Pitt was finally persuaded to become a devoted husband and father. Ovulation seems to delude women into thinking that they could be "the one."

REASON FOR OPTIMISM: IN THE MIND OF YOUR STATUS SUBSELF

We talked earlier about how Steve Jobs partnered up with his buddy Steve Wozniak to start Apple. Jobs is considered by many as one of the most brilliant visionaries of the modern age. Yet few would describe him as having had an accurate grasp of reality. Jobs was notorious for being supremely confident in his own ideas—so confident that those closest to him believed his perception of the objective world was permanently warped by a "reality distortion field." And this wasn't just because Jobs had the inflated ego that sometimes comes with great success. As a twenty-three-year-old college dropout in the late 1970s, Jobs already had the gall to show up to corporate meetings barefoot and reeking of body odor. It didn't matter that he was trying to convince investors to give him millions of dollars; Jobs showered once a week and refused to wear deodorant, certain that his diet of apples rendered it unnecessary. Despite heading a fledgling company without a proven product, Jobs was so convinced of the brilliance of his ideas that he felt corporate investors shouldn't care at all if he looked and smelled like a vagrant.

A surprising number of people share Jobs's inclination toward overconfidence. When men are asked to rank themselves on athletic ability, 100 percent of men rate themselves in the top 50 percent. Every first-year MBA student at the University of Chicago expects to receive an above-average grade in his or her first class, even though fully half of them will fail to do so. Psychologists call this the *overconfidence bias*, and there is no arguing that it is mathematically irrational. It's simply not possible for everyone to be better than average. But although this bias can lead us to appear foolish and irrational, it may actually be smart when it comes to taking advantage of opportunities to gain status.

Political scientist Dominic Johnson finds evidence that confidence, especially overconfidence, can be an evolutionarily adaptive bias. Confidence is an essential ingredient of success in job performance, sports, and business. While some people presume that confidence makes people lazy and careless, the exact opposite is actually true. Confidence serves to increase ambition, resolve, and persistence. Confident individuals are more likely to remain optimistic and keep on trying in the face of uncertainty. For example, overconfident life insurance agents who view setbacks as mere flukes, rather than accurately viewing them as signs of incompetence, are more likely to persist and eventually sell more policies.

Using sophisticated mathematical models, Johnson and his colleague James Fowler found that overconfidence is actually likely to enhance an individual's evolutionary fitness when competing for resources. This is the domain of our status subself, which is especially prone to the overconfidence bias. Confidence is adaptive because it leads people to approach opportunities and persist in the face of failure rather than sit on their butts and miss out on what could have been. Too much overconfidence can certainly produce arrogance and occasionally lead to very disastrous choices (overconfidence has been blamed for World War I, the Vietnam War, the war in Iraq, and the lack of preparation for many deadly environmental disasters). But being optimistic about our chances of winning is what inspires us to swing the bat and actually hit a home run rather than stand there hoping that something good will happen if we hang around on the bench. Confidence also has a lot to do with getting promotions at work. People who are seen as confident are also seen as more competent. And when it's time to select a leader, studies find that the top jobs go to people who are seen as competent, regardless of the reality.

The most successful titans of industry share the overconfidence bias. People like James Cameron, the mastermind filmmaker behind *Titanic* and *Avatar*, are extremely confident—overconfident, by the account of many who have worked with them. Cameron's production of *Titanic* went so far over budget that the studio executives stopped paying bills and demanded that he accede to their desires. Rather than heed their demands, though, Cameron refused to negotiate. Instead, he used his own money to pay for the movie, which cost a whopping $270 million—more than any previous movie had ever cost. In the end, Cameron's confidence was vindicated. The movie went on to rake in $2.1 billion worldwide, making it the highest-grossing film at the time, since topped only by Cameron's own *Avatar*, which grossed $2.7 billion.

And despite his hobo appearance and pungent scent, Steve Jobs didn't do too shabbily either. Jobs was so convinced of his own ideas that he didn't see any reason not to follow his gut. But not everyone shared his confidence. Jobs initially convinced Ron Wayne, an engineer at Atari, to become the third partner with him and Steve Wozniak in the proposed Apple company. After watching the overconfident Jobs borrow start-up money, however, Wayne got cold feet and sold his 10 percent share in the new company back to Jobs and Wozniak for $800. Jobs's persistent self-confidence paid off, and Apple became the single most valuable company in world history. If Ron Wayne had shared Jobs's confidence, his $800 investment would have been worth $2.6 billion in 2010.

BORN TO BE BIASED

"Bias" is often seen as a dirty little word. We are taught that we should avoid bias and instead strive to be accurate, rational, and smart. Yet the reality is that our minds evolved to be biased—to predictably make specific types of errors and decisions that appear irrational. As we've been discovering, what seems foolish and even delusional from a traditional perspective can be smart from an evolutionary vantage point.

Whether we are conscious of it or not, our brains have been designed to do whatever it takes to solve perennial evolutionary challenges. When it comes to danger and disease, our minds are set to be overly sensitive to strange outsiders and to the smell and sight of sickness. This produces occasional paranoia or hypochondria, but it beats the alternative—being naively inattentive to people who might beat us up or sneeze a lungful of deadly viruses all over us. Similarly, when a man's mate-acquisition subself is at the helm, his mind is biased to be hypersensitive to any remote signs of interest from desirable women. And when a woman's ovulatory phase triggers her mate-acquisition subself, her mind is biased to think that a big handsome Lothario will finally settle down with her. Both sexes occasionally make fools of themselves, but if we always played the statistics, we'd remain celibate. By occasionally warping our perception of reality, our brains are better able to accomplish their job—to keep us alive, reproducing, and solving perennial evolutionary challenges.

Consider what might be the grandest of all delusions. If you are a typical American, you are perfectly aware that about 50 percent of marriages end in divorce; yet 86 percent of people believed that their marriage will last forever (of 1,000 newlyweds, then, at least 360 of the 500 that break up will have made an overconfident prediction). These individuals might be foolish and irrational, but without this grand delusion veiled as love, they might never get married. And here is where our evolutionary tendencies can be seen pulling our emotional strings from behind the curtain of consciousness. Marriage is of course a powerful predictor of having children. People who get married tend to have kids soon after, often producing several offspring within only a few years of saying "I do." This means that any delusion that motivates people to get married is a bias that enhances the likelihood that their genes will replicate. So yes, love does make people irrational when it comes to the accuracy of their judgments, but the underlying system is based on a deeply rational foundation.

EACH OF OUR subselves is biased to make occasional errors (like ignoring the base rates on divorce when we exchange wedding bands), but those same biases often lead us to avoid big evolutionary mistakes (like failing to replicate our genes). Does this mean that our deep-seated biases always incline us to make smart decisions? No. In fact, sometimes they produce serious problems, because those biases, though well fitted to an ancestral village, are mismatched with the modern world full of strangers, skyscrapers, and SAT college admissions examinations. We next examine how a better understanding of this mismatch can dramatically improve our decisions, starting with investigation of a curious question: Why do uneducated tribespeople from deep in the Amazonian jungle easily solve logical problems that stump sophisticated students at Harvard?

5

Modern Cavemen

DEEP IN THE AMAZON RAIN FOREST, on the shores of treacherous rivers between Ecuador and Peru, live the Shiwiar. Tucked away in the middle of nowhere, the Shiwiar people have had almost no contact with outsiders, and their way of life mirrors many aspects of our evolutionary past. They gather nuts and fruits, spear fish, and hunt a range of animals from armadillos to toucans, often taking down their prey with a blowgun. The Shiwiar are wary of outsiders and interact mostly with close relatives. Daily life entails a smidge of gossip, a dab of witchcraft, and the ever-present threat of disease and death. Venomous snakebites and insect stings pose ubiquitous dangers, as do malaria and other infections. And if the parasites don't get you, your skull might be impaled by a jaguar—a local carnivore who likes to bite prey through the head to deliver a fatal blow directly to the brain.

Larry Sugiyama, an anthropologist who studies the Shiwiar, is interested in human reasoning and cognition. He's the kind of guy who enjoys giving tricky logic tests to see who's smart enough to get the correct answer. Sugiyama had just finished giving a test to students at Harvard when he began to wonder how the Shiwiar would do on the same mental challenge.

"It is difficult to imagine two populations that differ more than Shiwiar villagers and Harvard students," Sugiyama explains. The Harvard students, selected for possessing the brightest minds in the world, have been exposed to over twelve years of Western schooling and have consequently absorbed an immense amount of humanity's accumulated wisdom. The Shiwiar, by contrast, are illiterate, with no formal schooling at all. While the Harvard kids grew up with Baby Einstein brain puzzles to exercise their minds, Shiwiar children were given machetes and sent into the jungle to bring home dinner. Given the educational gap, it hardly seems fair to compare the Shiwiar and Harvard students' performance on logic tests.

But just how big is the intellectual gap between inhabitants of an ancestral-style society and those living in the ultrasophisticated modern world anyway? Well, when Sugiyama conducted his reasoning test in the Amazon, he discovered something astonishing. The Shiwiar aced the tough problems. They not only matched the performance of the budding brainiacs who make the pages of the *Harvard Crimson*, they actually did a little bit better. How is it that illiterate jungle dwellers could outmatch the reasoning abilities of students at one of the most prestigious academic institutions in the world?

To understand this puzzle, we first need to know more about the ancestral nature of the human mind. In this leg of our tour, we'll rummage through our evolutionary past, exploring the surprising implications of the idea that our modern skulls house Stone Age brains. Indeed, there is an emerging body of evidence to suggest that we are all modern cavemen, approaching the problems of our complex contemporary world using brains that evolved to confront ancestral problems.

By better understanding how the ancestral mind works, though, researchers like Sugiyama have discovered that many of our highly touted deficiencies in decision making are less the fault of the test takers and more the fault of the tests and the test makers. And by applying insights from our evolutionary past, Sugiyama and his colleagues have found that small alterations to complex questions can instantly transform test takers from seemingly dim-witted dodos into deeply rational savants.

LOGICALLY DEFICIENT MINDS

Unless you decided to skip the first half of this book to read about why illiterate jungle dwellers outperform Harvard students, you have by now picked up a central theme of our argument: that many of our seemingly irrational biases in judgment and decision making turn out to be pretty smart on closer examination. Seemingly irrational biases like loss aversion, overconfidence, and men's overperception of female sexual interest seem a bit more rational when viewed through an evolutionary lens. On average, those biases ultimately produced wise choices for our ancestors.

But not all errors mask an underlying wisdom. Sometimes an error is just an error—and many human errors are quite tragic. In the United States, about sixty thousand people die each year from mistakes in medical decision making. Medical errors are in fact the sixth-most-common cause of death in the United States, more likely to cause death than Alzheimer's disease, breast cancer, suicide, or homicide. These are not small errors that help us avoid big mistakes—these errors are the big mistakes, and they cost thousands of lives each month.

Studies find that people are particularly error-prone when it comes to problems that require a little bit of math and logical reasoning. Consider the classic "Linda problem" below, developed by pioneering behavioral economists Daniel Kahneman and Amos Tversky:

> Linda is thirty-one years old, single, outspoken, and very bright. She majored in philosophy. As a student, she was deeply concerned with issues of discrimination and social justice and also participated in antinuclear demonstrations.
> Which is more probable?
>   A. Linda is a bank teller.
>   B. Linda is a bank teller and is active in the feminist movement.

The correct answer is A. It's a better bet to guess that Linda is simply a bank teller. Yet Kahneman and Tversky found that almost 90 percent of people incorrectly answer B. Most people believe that it's more probable that Linda is not just a bank teller but also an active feminist. This answer is a bad bet because the probability of two events

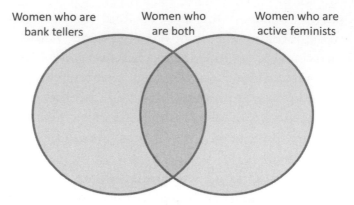

Figure 5.1. A visual depiction of the Linda problem

occurring together is less than the probability of either one occurring alone. To see why, look at Figure 5.1. Even if there is only a small chance that someone like Linda is a bank teller and a large chance that she's an active feminist, we already know she is a bank teller— both option A and option B state that she works at a bank. Given that both options include the presumption that she is a bank teller, the probability that Linda resides somewhere in the circle on the left (all bank tellers) has to be larger than the probability that she is both a bank teller and a feminist and thus resides somewhere in the tiny overlap of the two circles. Mathematically, there are simply fewer women who are bank tellers and feminists than there are women who are just bank tellers, so the odds are strongly stacked against you if you choose option B.

Behavioral economists and psychologists find that people get stumped by all sorts of questions that aren't really all that difficult (you don't need any knowledge of trigonometry, calculus, linear algebra, or differential equations to solve the Linda problem). Yet hundreds of studies have exposed the limitations of the human mind. The common explanation for such poor performance is that people are generally inept when it comes to math, logic, and reasoning. In that view, the way to fix this deficiency is to provide more formal training in these areas. If only people had more education and practice, the argument goes, they would surely come to the correct conclusion.

But there is a problem with this explanation for people's poor performance. It turns out that very smart people, including those with college degrees from Harvard, Yale, and Princeton, make the same errors at almost the same high rates. Despite many years of formal education, including classes in math, logic, and reasoning, most people nevertheless have difficulty solving basic problems like the Linda problem. And what about those sixty thousand deaths each year that stem from medical errors? These are errors made by university-educated experts, with years of training in life-and-death decision making. Yet they too have problems with making good decisions.

On closer inspection, there is something strikingly peculiar about the kinds of questions that give people so much trouble. As in the Linda problem, once people have the logic explained to them (once they see the picture with the two circles), the answer makes perfect sense—the question is not that difficult. Yet it was almost impossible to see this simple answer when the question was asked in its original form. Although the answer is obvious, this obviousness was obscured. This pattern provides an important clue about what could be producing so many errors in decision making. Our errors might have less to do with our lack of mental ability and more to do with the way the questions are being asked.

TALKING VERSUS WRITING

Some things in life are easy. Consider learning how to talk. Most children start talking by age two. By age three the average kid knows hundreds of words and can often use a new word after hearing it only once. And by the ripe old age of four, kids from Cambridge to Cambodia are already master communicators, expounding on which toys they want, which foods they hate, and which parent they love bossing around more. The ability to talk seems to bloom independently of how much it is nurtured by the kid's parents. Some parents begin a continual stream of chitchat with their tots from day one. Others find it a waste of time to have extended monologues with nonverbal newborns. It doesn't much matter. As long as they overhear an occasional conversation, children learn to talk. You need only turn on *Sesame*

Street and let kids listen to Elmo, Big Bird, Kermit, Miss Piggy, and Oscar the Grouch, or let them crawl around the kitchen listening to their parents and grandparents gossiping, and they will eventually start talking spontaneously. If only everything in life were as easy as learning to talk.

Other things in life are difficult—like mastering the written as opposed to the spoken word. Reading and writing (whether with a pen, a typewriter, or a cell phone) are hard. You can give your baby girl as many crayons and *Sesame Street* books as you like, but she is not going to spontaneously start expressing her thoughts in comprehensible prose. Without a parent or a teacher providing years of incentives and instruction—connecting sounds to letters, letters to words, and punctuation to spoken pauses and emphases—the likelihood that a child would ever write a coherent sentence is approximately zero. Reading and writing are so difficult that modern schooling devotes year after year of formal instruction to developing these skills. We practice and memorize, and then practice and memorize some more.

Yet, despite all that practice, the same kids who are eloquent speakers (perhaps even poetic rappers) suddenly become deficient communicators if asked to express their ideas in writing. Many people in the world never learn to write at all, including the Shiwiar tribespeople in the jungles of the Amazon. And even among the educated urbanites who are drilled in writing for years, most will never feel completely comfortable communicating through this channel. As university professors, we hear nonstop complaints about how poorly college students write—and they have been explicitly taught how to write in school for over twelve years!

Why is learning to talk easy while learning to write is difficult? The answer lies in our evolutionary history. Our ancestors have been talking for hundreds of thousands of years. The ability to talk gave such an advantage that humans across the world have been naturally selected for being good talkers. Talking is like walking. We don't need to sign up for a walking class—we just do it. But writing is very different. The written word is the new evolutionary kid on the block. From the perspective of our 2-million-year hominid lifespan, we have been writing for only a brief time. And most of the writing in the last few thousand years has been done by a tiny number of select individuals. Even in the modern world, the majority of people are still illiterate—they speak but don't read or write. Whereas talking is like walking, writing is like doing ballet. If you buy your child a pair of ballet slippers, it's highly unlikely she will spontaneously start doing triple pirouettes. You'd be fortunate if the kid merely starts hopping clumsily up in the air without hitting her head on the floor. If you want anything even vaguely resembling *Swan Lake,* better sign her up for a few years of ballet classes.

Many things in life are like talking—evolutionarily old and easy. We don't have to try hard to learn how to see, breathe, eat, or run. But many other things in the modern world are like writing—evolutionarily novel and difficult. This includes most of the skills we need to read, write, play the violin, perform brain surgery, and do rocket science. And when it comes to making decision errors, many of them stem from something we've all spent over a dozen years and thousands of hours desperately trying to learn: math.

WHY CAN'T JOHNNY DO THE MATH?

Imagine you are a woman at your gynecologist's office. Your doctor suggests a mammogram to screen for breast cancer, and your worst fear comes true: it comes back positive. But you've heard that these kinds of tests aren't always right, so you ask your doctor, "Does this really mean I have breast cancer? What's the likelihood?"

It would certainly make a huge difference if your chances of having cancer are 1 percent or 90 percent. And many people assume that every physician knows the precise answer. But we shouldn't be so sure. In a recent study, 160 respected doctors were provided with the relevant statistical information needed to calculate the chances that a woman with a positive test actually has the disease. Here is everything you need to know:

- The probability that a woman has breast cancer is 1 percent.

- If a woman has breast cancer, the probability that she will test positive is 90 percent.

- If a woman does not have breast cancer, the probability that she will nevertheless test positive is 9 percent.

If a woman tests positive, what are the chances that she has breast cancer?

The correct answer is roughly 10 percent. Given the odds above, if a woman tests positive, there is about a 10 percent chance that she actually has breast cancer. (If you do the math, you'll see that nine out of one hundred women who don't have breast cancer will be false positives, and a little less than one in one hundred will be a true positive. So just about one in ten who test positive, or 10 percent, actually has breast cancer.)

But of the doctors who were asked this question, only 21 percent got it right. This should already be pretty disturbing, but the situation is much more disconcerting than that. For starters, these doctors were all gynecologists. These are the people who actually do mammography screening! The doctors could have simply recalled what they should already know about false positives, but that didn't happen. Even more troubling is the range of responses. Almost half of the doctors said the likelihood of having breast cancer was 90 percent! And one in five doctors said the likelihood was only 1 percent! But here is the final kicker. The question was multiple choice—there were only four options (90 percent, 81 percent, 10 percent, and 1 percent). This means that monkeys would have likely done better in answering this question correctly, since randomly guessing the answer will lead monkeys to be right 25 percent of the time, while only 21 percent of doctors got it right.

The literature on judgment and decision making is overflowing with these kinds of shocking studies. It is tempting to present such findings as prime evidence of the stupidity and inability of humankind. Errors are in fact being made—gross errors by the people who should know best. But before condemning humanity as hopelessly deficient, let's take a step back and think about the situation. The people making these errors are doctors. They've been full-time students receiving formal education from the age of five to thirty. And it's not just the schooling. You have to be pretty smart and motivated to get into medical school in the first place, not to mention finish it and pass all your exams. It hardly makes sense to relegate this group to the category of stupid people.

From the evolutionary psychologist's perspective, it's unlikely that the brain evolved to be dumb. Instead, the problem might be not with the test takers but with the test makers. The breast cancer problem is asking us a question on a frequency our brains don't receive. And it's pretty important that we adjust the antenna.

COMMUNICATING ON OUR NATURAL FREQUENCY

In the modern world, we are awash in numerically expressed statistical information. You may have spent enough years in math classes to cognitively understand that a 0.07 probability and a 7 percent likelihood are the same thing, but many of us will still furrow our brows and squint our eyes when digesting a statement about a 0.07 probability. Probabilities and likelihood estimates are a common way to present statistical information, but they are also an evolutionarily recent invention. Mathematical probabilities were invented in Europe in the mid-1600s. And thanks to this statistical renaissance, we now have a really smart way to present numbers—so smart that probabilities often outsmart even us.

Gerd Gigerenzer, a decision scientist at the Max Plank Institute, is not a fan of mathematical probabilities or likelihood estimates. He has long realized that trying to understand probabilities and likelihoods is the evolutionary equivalent of writing as compared to talking—an unnatural and difficult variant of something that's easy in another format. Hence, statistics presented in probability format can lead to a lot of problems. Just as even well-educated writers have problems spelling words like "dumbbell," "embarrass," and "misspell," smart doctors can have problems figuring out the likelihood that you have breast cancer if your mammogram comes back positive.

Instead of presenting information as conditional probabilities or likelihood estimates, Gigerenzer has demonstrated that people are much better at computing statistical information if it's presented in terms of *natural frequencies.* "Natural frequencies represent the way ancestral humans encoded information," Gigerenzer explains. Whereas probabilities are like writing, natural frequencies are like talking.

Let's take a boat upriver to the Shiwiar village. Imagine that the village chief wants to catch dinner today, and he's trying to decide whether it would be worthwhile to go hunting in the nearby red canyon. For the Shiwiar, as for most of our ancestors, the only database available to make any kind of calculation consists of their own observations and those communicated by a handful of close others. When the chief is trying to determine whether it's wise to go hunting in the red canyon, he can consider what happened the last twenty times people went hunting there. The chief observes natural frequencies—five out of the last twenty hunts in the red canyon were successful. He doesn't think in terms of probabilities, though. Neither did our ancestors, who did not observe probabilities in their natural environment. As a consequence, our brains do not process probabilities ("0.25 probability of success") in the same way as they do natural frequencies ("5 out of 20 were successful"). Years of formal math training have taught most of us that these two statistical statements mean the same thing, but decades of writing training still hasn't outmoded spell-checkers.

Gigerenzer has found dramatic improvements in both novices and experts when hard questions are asked in terms of natural frequencies rather than probabilities. Take the probability-laced breast cancer question asked earlier—the one that dumbfounded our panel of doctors. Here is the same exact information translated into natural frequencies:

- Ten out of every one thousand women have breast cancer.

- Of these ten women with breast cancer, nine test positive.

- Of the 990 women without breast cancer, about 89 also test positive.

If a woman tests positive, what are the chances that she has breast cancer?

When Gigerenzer asked doctors this question, the difference was remarkable. Whereas only 21 percent of doctors answered correctly when the question was presented in terms of probabilities, 87 percent answered correctly when it was presented in terms of natural frequencies. One question is hard; the other is easy—even though, to a mathematician, both are asking the same exact thing.

And remember the Linda problem mentioned earlier? It suffers from the same problem: it asks people a simple question in terms of complex probabilities. Below is the Linda problem translated into natural frequencies:

> Researchers polled one hundred women with the following features. They are on average thirty-one years old, single, outspoken, and very bright. They majored in philosophy. As students, they were deeply concerned with issues of discrimination and social justice, and also participated in antinuclear demonstrations.
>
> Which is larger?
>   A. The number of women out of that one hundred that might be bank tellers.
>   B. The number of women out of that one hundred that might be bank tellers and active in the feminist movement.

Whereas only about 10 percent of people answer the Linda problem correctly when it is asked in probability format as presented earlier, almost 100 percent get the right answer when it's presented in natural frequency format. Mathematically, both versions ask the exact same question. But the first version is confusing and leads to errors, whereas the second one is surprisingly easy.

TAPPING THE ANCESTRAL WISDOM OF OUR DIFFERENT SUBSELVES

To tap into the innate intelligence of the human brain, we need to understand how the mind expects to take in information. Because our brains are designed to receive information in the way our ancestors would have received it, people will be much better problem solvers when problems are presented in ancestral formats—such as presenting math problems by using natural frequencies (five out of one hundred) rather than probabilities (0.05).

We should also expect that people will be superb problem solvers when it comes to ancestral challenges—solving the types of evolutionary problems faced by our subselves. And because each of our subselves specializes in different types of problems, we should be able to improve our reasoning abilities by making complex problems relevant to our different subselves. In the remainder of the chapter, we look at two cases that unlock the wisdom of our inner team player—the affiliation subself.

DETECTING CHEATERS

Cognitive psychologists have developed some particularly difficult problems to test people's abilities in deciphering what's known as *conditional logic*. A classic problem of this sort is known as the *Wason Task:*

> Figure 5.2 shows four cards. Each card has a number on one side and a letter on the other. Which card(s) should you turn over in order to test whether the following rule is true: If a card has an even number on one side, then it must have a consonant on the other side?

Figure 5.2. The Wason Task

The correct answer is that you need to turn over two cards: The card with the "8" and the card with the "A." You don't need to turn over any other card. If you turn over the card labeled "3" and find that the second side has a consonant, this does not invalidate the rule (which says nothing about odd numbers). Likewise, if you turn over the "B" card and find an odd number, this also does not break the rule.

Don't feel too bad if you didn't get the right answer. People are not very good at these kinds of problems. Only about 10 percent of college students get the right answer. The Shiwiar of the Amazon got it right 0 percent of the time. We can take comfort in knowing that the payoff from many years of formal education is a boost in those test scores—to 10 percent. And in case you're wondering, paying over $40,000 per year for a Harvard education may improve scores even further—all the way up to 12 percent.

The Wason card problem is difficult for most people, in the same way that learning to write is difficult. Unless you took advanced conditional reasoning in college, it's not that easy to derive the right answer—it's like asking an illiterate person to write an essay. Even philosophy professors and mathematicians tend to get the answer wrong (in fact, we wrote the wrong answer when writing this book and had to go back and correct it two separate times).

But what if there were a way to make this problem less like doing ballet and more like walking? Leda Cosmides, an evolutionary psychologist at the University of California, Santa Barbara, has figured out how to do just that. Although solving abstract logic problems is evolutionarily novel and therefore difficult, Cosmides suspected that humans have been solving all sorts of complex logical problems for hundreds of thousands of years. As it turns out, solving one of those ancestral problems requires the same exact complex logic as solving the Wason card problem.

This ancestral problem is a specialty of our affiliation subself, which is a master manager of life in social groups. Here's why: Living in social groups brings many advantages. With ten heads working on a problem, the odds of discovering a solution rise dramatically. But anyone who has ever worked on a group project knows that there's also a downside to working in groups—some people end up taking the credit without doing their part. When our ancestors were living in small groups and facing frequent dangers of starvation, it was critical to figure out which people were taking more than they were giving.

Having a couple of group members who ate their share of the food but didn't do their share of the hunting and gathering could mean the difference between starvation and survival. Our ancestors needed to be good at detecting social parasites—the cheaters in our midst.

Leda Cosmides realized that the logical reasoning people use to detect cheaters involves the exact same logical reasoning needed to solve the Wason card problem. Let's revisit the card problem, except this time we'll state the problem in a way that allows the affiliation subself to process this information in the way our ancestors did:

> Figure 5.3 shows four cards. Each card has a person's age on one side and the beverage he or she is drinking on the other. Which card(s) do you need to turn over in order to test whether the following rule is true: If a person is drinking alcohol, he or she must be over eighteen?

Figure 5.3. The Cheater Detection version of the Wason Task

When presented with this translated version of the problem, most people instantly get the right answer: turn over the card with "16" and the card with "beer," while leaving the other two cards unturned. It's pointless to turn over the card with "21" because we know that this person isn't a cheater. It's similarly useless to turn over the card of the person who's drinking a Coke because that person did not receive the benefit that could come from cheating.

The complex logic required to solve the cheater problem is mathematically identical to the complex logic needed to solve the Wason card problem we gave you earlier. Cosmides tried dozens of versions of the problem, always finding the same results. Regardless of whether the question was about familiar things like the drinking age or unfamiliar things like the right to eat cassava roots, if the problem involved detecting a cheater, most people became brilliant logicians.

Larry Sugiyama, the anthropologist we met at the beginning of the chapter, had the Shiwiar try to solve this problem. Whereas the Shiwiar solved the original Wason card task 0 percent of the time, they solved the evolutionarily translated version 83 percent of the time. This was in fact one point better than Harvard students, so in an intellectual Olympics, the unschooled Shiwiar would have beat out the well-educated Cambridge team on the natural version of this problem.

Cosmides and Sugiyama demonstrated something extremely important. It's not the case that people are incapable of doing complex logic. Instead, most academic problems are written in such a way that they never engage the sophisticated talents of our subselves. It's like asking a car mechanic to solve the problem of lifting a car not by using a jack but by demonstrating the answer in terms of mathematical vectors and energy exchange.

One of us just tried the cheater detection problem on our seven-year-old son, who has yet to be educated in multiplication, much less conditional probability. He had a difficult time understanding the Wason card task, wanting to turn over every card. But when the problem was framed in terms of people who either had or had not paid the fee to play a special Lego Universe computer game, he nailed the answer easily. Whereas the original card task is tough, like writing an essay about family relations in the modern world, the evolutionarily translated version is like chatting with a neighbor about how your kids are doing. Writing is hard, and talking is easy, even when you are attempting to communicate the same exact thing.

THE LARGE NUMBERS PARADOX

Imagine you learn that there was a plane crash, and all two hundred people aboard perished. You wouldn't be human if you didn't feel some sadness and grief in response to this news. Now imagine instead that it was a larger plane, and the crash resulted in six hundred fatalities. How would you feel?

Most people would again feel grief and sadness, but they wouldn't feel three times as much grief and sadness. In fact, people experience about the same level of emotion in both situations—and sometimes they experience less emotion when more people perish.

This is known as the *large numbers paradox*. You can find it all around you. Many Americans, for example, are outraged when they learn that the US military presence in Iraq and Afghanistan in the first decade of the twenty-first century cost taxpayers over $1 billion. But those people wouldn't feel much more outrage if they were told that the endeavor cost over $1 trillion—even though the latter amount is over a thousand times greater and, in fact, closer to the actual cost. It's mathematically equivalent to the difference between the clerk at the corner store charging you $4 versus $4,000 for the same sandwich. Yet when government expenses are multiplied a thousand times, people don't get any angrier!

To understand this paradox we need to navigate through the jungle back to the world of the Shiwiar. The Shiwiar live in small villages of about fifty to one hundred people. Each villager knows most of these people, many of whom are relatives or close friends. The range of fifty to one hundred is important because it appears again and again around the globe and across time. Modern hunter-gatherers, from Africa to South America to Oceania, live in bands of about fifty to one hundred people. If you were the first explorer to contact a tribe of people who had never seen an outsider, smart money says you'd find about fifty to one hundred people in that tribe. Archaeological evidence suggests that if you traveled back in time one hundred thousand years to visit your great, great, great . . . great-grandmother, you'd likely find her living in a nomadic band of fifty to one hundred people. Today many of us live in cities of millions. Yet our social networks—the people we interact with—still include about fifty to one hundred people.

If you went up to a Shiwiar chief and told him that six hundred people might perish, he'd probably scratch his head and say, "Hunh?

What does this mean?" Hunter-gatherer societies tend to have very few words for numbers and amounts. You might find "one," "two," "a few," "tribe size." Were we to start discoursing about 200, 600, 1 million, 1 billion, the Shiwiar's eyes would likely glaze over (just as ours do at the distinction between a billion and a trillion).

Making reasoned decisions involving calculations with large numbers is an evolutionarily novel concept—it's like writing, not talking. While it's perhaps amusing to think about how the Shiwiar might respond to large numbers, keep in mind that your brain is pretty much evolutionarily identical to a Shiwiar's brain, which is in turn similar to the brains of the common ancestors of all human beings, who migrated out of Africa approximately fifty thousand years ago. We are all modern cavemen. Many of us have spent long years in math classes, and we cognitively comprehend that we need to add three zeros to turn a thousand into a million. Yet, as the paradoxical plane crash and taxpayer examples illustrate, our brains get a bit numb when numbers get big. What's a light-year again, or what's 10^{12} nanometers? To our brains, the very big number is a fuzzy concept devoid of evolutionary relevance. This really matters if we want to understand people's erroneous and irrational decisions. Asking the average person to reason out logical questions laced with large numbers is a bit like asking him or her to perform *Swan Lake* at the Metropolitan Opera House.

ERASING ERRORS BY ENGAGING THE AFFILIATION SUBSELF

Daniel Kahneman and Amos Tversky make up the dynamic duo whose groundbreaking research in judgment and decision making garnered a Nobel Prize. Among their many contributions to behavioral economics, they are known for devising a number of particularly clever questions to expose the fallibility of human reasoning. One such question goes like this:

> Imagine that the United States is preparing for the outbreak of an unusual Asian disease, which is expected to kill six hundred people. Two alternative programs to combat the disease have been proposed.

Program A: If Program A is adopted, two hundred people will be saved.

Program B: If Program B is adopted, there is a one-third probability that six hundred people will be saved and a two-thirds probability that no people will be saved.

Which of the two programs would you favor?

The first thing to notice is that both options have the exact same "expected value" for the average number of people who are expected to remain alive—two hundred out of six hundred. The difference between the two options is this: whereas Program A provides a precise number for how many people are going to be saved for certain, Program B is fraught with uncertainty. Tversky and Kahneman found that the majority of people (72 percent) chose the more certain Program A.

But discovering that people like the more certain option didn't win them the Nobel Prize. The important twist is what happened next. A second group of people were given the same Asian disease problem and provided with the same options. But the options were framed just a little bit differently:

Program A: If Program A is adopted, four hundred people will die.

Program B: If Program B is adopted, there is a one-third probability that nobody will die, and a two-thirds probability that six hundred people will die.

Which of the two programs would you favor?

It's critical to note that this second problem is logically and mathematically the exact same problem as the first one. Again, both options have the same expected value for the average number of people who are expected to remain alive—two hundred out of six hundred. The only difference is that the options are never framed as losses instead of gains. However, when presented with the latter two options, the majority of people (78 percent) now chose the less certain option B. This preference reversal seems to reveal a blatant miscalibration in decision making.

People's fickle preference reversal in the Asian disease problem is often presented as a hallmark of human irrationality and a crushing blow to the central assumptions of the classical economic model of rational man. It's not that people are bad at math (the numbers in the problem are intentionally round so that all college students can easily calculate the expected values in their head). Instead, people just seem irrationally inconsistent in dealing with mathematically identical decisions.

But before we close the case and conclude that educated individuals are mostly moronic decision makers, let's do a little detective work with our evolutionary magnifying lens. We know that our ancestors lived in bands of one hundred people or fewer. And we know that our brains are not designed to comprehend large numbers. Remember, our ancestors would not have encountered such quantities.

Decision scientist X. T. Wang suspected that the classic Asian disease problem might be an evolutionarily novel contraption that fails to tap our deeper ancestral logic. Wang thought that the problem is like asking an illiterate person to write, or like asking Doug and Vlad to perform a few ballet movements from *Swan Lake* (take our word for it, you don't want to see either of us in tights).

Because the size of hunter-gatherer groups rarely exceeded one hundred people, Wang reasoned that people might respond to the problem very differently if it involved numbers that would have made sense to our ancestors. What if, rather than six hundred people, the problem involved sixty people—a number within the range that our ancestors' affiliation subselves had to deal with?

Wang performed an experiment in which he presented people with the exact same problem that Kahneman and Tversky used. The only difference was that the number of people in Wang's question now approximated the size of an ancestral band. Subjects in the study had to decide between one program that would save twenty people versus another program with a one-third probability that sixty people would be saved (with a two-thirds probability that no people would be saved). Others needed to choose between having forty people die versus taking a chance on a program with a one-third probability that nobody would die (and a two-thirds probability that sixty people would die).

Wang made a surprising discovery. When the size of the group was sixty (rather than six hundred), the framing made no difference in people's choices. Whether the problem was framed as a loss or a gain, people consistently made the same choices. Wang's findings throw a monkey wrench into the model of humans as irrationally fallible by showing that people are perfectly capable of avoiding errors. The trick is to ask questions in an ancestrally relevant way.

HOW TO HELP SUICIDAL TURTLES (AND IRRATIONAL HUMANS)

Sea turtles lay their eggs on dry, shallow beaches. The eggs hatch in the wee hours of the night, with hundreds of hatchlings crawling down the beach toward their ocean home. It's a glorious sight. As Crush, the turtle in *Finding Nemo*, explains in his charming surfer accent, "Oh, it's awesome, Jellyman. The little dudes are just eggs, we leave 'em on a beach to hatch, and then, coo-coo-cachoo, they find their way back to the big ol' blue."

But recent generations of sea turtles have been making some awesome errors in their decision making. When presented with the option of crawling either toward the ocean or away from the water onto asphalt full of oncoming eighteen-wheelers, thousands of turtles have been choosing the latter, fatally irrational option.

A Florida man was recently inspired to find a cure for this new wave of chelonian self-destructiveness. A news article titled "Fort Lauderdale Saves Turtles from Suicide" explains his radical solution for reducing turtle decision errors: turning off the distracting lights.

Turtle hatchlings have, it seems, evolved to crawl toward the light. For millions of years this was a highly rational and effective strategy because the light on a dark beach represented the reflection of the moon and stars on the water's surface. Following the lights led baby turtles back home to the sea. The problems started when humans began building beachfront homes and sparkling hotels on the other side of the beach. Now after hatching, Fort Lauderdale's turtles heading for the brightest nearby lights were being guided straight into traffic.

Are self-destructive sea turtles naturally irrational? Yes, in the modern world. But there's a deeper truth. Turtles are basing their decisions on simple cues that were perfectly rational for their ancestors; these days, however, their evolved decision-making mechanisms are being blinded by modern lights.

Modern humans have something in common with suicidal turtles. We too have deeply rational decision-making mechanisms, and our machinery is also sometimes blinded by features of the modern world.

Behavioral economists and psychologists studying judgment and decision making have constructed a hilarious house of errors, often showing with great fanfare that humans are like suicidal turtles. Step right up, folks, and see the amazing Stupidman! Just pay your $20 and look in the mirror! And for a mere $50, you can look twice!

But lost in this carnival of human idiocy is a deeper truth about humanity: not only is *Homo sapiens* one of the most successful species on the planet (suggesting that we're doing something right), but we hominids have mastered extraordinarily complex problems such as speech perception, grammar induction, and facial and object recognition, outperforming the most powerful computers.

When blinded by modern lights, though, we too can fail at many simpler tasks. But many of our errors and irrationalities are less the fault of our abilities and more the fault of the disabling ways our abilities are tested. By making small alterations to present information in ancestrally relevant ways—by turning off the blinding lights—even we seemingly dim-witted dodos can be instantly transformed into deeply rational savants.

ALTERING DIFFICULT QUESTIONS to tap into our wise ancestral psychologies can drastically decrease errors and improve our decisions. But it turns out that the same decision can be deeply rational for one person and irrational for another. We next take a closer look at a fundamental biological difference between two types of people. To see why this matters, we start by asking a simple question: Why do people who go from rags to riches often later end up in bankruptcy court?

6

Living Fast and Dying Young

CHANCES ARE YOU have heard of Stanley Burrell, though you might not recognize him by that name or know all the details of his fascinating life story. Raised by a single mother, Burrell grew up with eight siblings crammed into a small apartment in the East Oakland housing projects. To earn money, the young Burrell sold stray baseballs and danced with a beat box in the Oakland Coliseum parking lot. His energy and flair were so infectious that after seeing him rouse fans while doing splits, Charles O. Finley, owner of the Oakland A's major-league baseball team, hired eleven-year-old Stanley as a batboy. One of the players thought the new batboy bore a resemblance to baseball legend Hammerin' Hank Aaron, so they started calling him "Hammer."

By age twenty-seven, Stanley had channeled his performing energies into a career as a superstar musician, known to the public as MC Hammer. The masses went wild over his flamboyant dance moves, trademark parachute pants, and hits such as "U Can't Touch This." In 1990, *Forbes* magazine estimated that the once-poverty-ridden Burrell, having sold over 50 million records, was worth $33 million.

Yet only a few years later, in 1996, Burrell was forced to file for bankruptcy. He had not only lost all that fortune but was now $13 million in debt. While Hammer was an adept master of ceremonies (earning him his "MC" moniker), he could not master the concept of saving. His expenses included a Xanadu-like twenty-acre California compound complete with tennis courts, two pools, a built-in movie theater, a seventeen-car garage, and a sound system that required twenty-two miles of wiring. He also felt compelled to purchase several racehorses, a helicopter, and solid gold chains for his four Rottweilers. But he didn't limit his lavish spending to himself: maintaining the Hammer hype required an entourage of two hundred people at a yearly cost of $6.8 million.

MC Hammer is not unique in his journey from rags to riches to bankruptcy. According to an article in *Sports Illustrated*, 78 percent of professional football players will go bankrupt in their lifetimes, and 60 percent of pro basketball players are broke within five years of retirement. This is despite the fact that the minimum yearly salary in the National Football League is $375,000. And for players in the National Basketball Association, the average salary is a whopping $5.15 million a year.

Where does all the money go? New York Knicks center Patrick Ewing once explained it this way: "We make a lot of money, but we spend a lot of money too." Boxer Mike Tyson epitomized the big-spending athlete, dropping $188,000 for two white Bengal tigers (to wrestle for fun), shelling out a cool $2 million for a single bathtub for one of the thirty-eight bathrooms in his mansion, and buying a house with seven kitchens and its own nightclub—only to stay there one night. Although Tyson earned over $300 million during his fighting career, he was over $24 million in debt when he filed for bankruptcy in 2003.

The compulsion to splurge is not limited to athletes or entertainers. The book *The Millionaire Next Door* reveals that many well-respected professionals, including doctors, spend more than they earn, often ending up broke later in life. Even longtime CNN interviewer Larry King was forced to declare bankruptcy when he couldn't pay his debts, although it didn't prevent this former poor boy from Brooklyn from racking up still more debt—and more wives (King is currently on his eighth bride).

Why do so many people who strike it rich not only fail to save for the future, but spend so outlandishly beyond their means? Although many of these impulsive choices might appear foolish and irrational, let's consider how living for the moment and spending like there is no tomorrow may reflect a deeper rationality. Here we examine the evidence that different people are disposed to follow very different strategies in life. Some, like MC Hammer, aspire to race up from rags to riches, following a "fast" trajectory associated with risk raking, impulsivity, and a dangerous lifestyle that can often lead to early death. Others are on the "slow" path, which involves delaying gratification and playing it safe. Neither strategy is intrinsically better; rather, each one makes the best of the circumstances into which people were born. Understanding these two strategies—and the circumstances that produce them—is important because they explain why the same decision can be irrational and maladaptive for one person, yet completely rational and adaptive for another.

LIFE HISTORY THEORY

Although more money doesn't always lead to more problems, the question of how to spend money can present a dilemma. If you have $100, for example, you can spend it on many different things: you can stock up on food, buy a few dozen long-stem roses for your loved one, invest in a couple of violin lessons for your child, buy a new outfit that might include a pair of parachute pants, or even download MC Hammer's complete music catalog, including his 1992 hit "2 Legit 2 Quit" and its accompanying ten-minute music video, which cost $2.5 million to make (an unheard-of price tag back in 1992). The dilemma arises because money is a limited resource. If you have only $100 to spend, you can't fill your entire refrigerator with food and buy a new outfit and pay for violin lessons for your kid. When it comes to allocating limited resources, you have to prioritize some things over others.

Limited resources are not limited to money. Time is a limited resource, as is the caloric energy contained in food. Decisions about how to use each resource require us to make trade-offs. If you have one hour of time, for example, you can spend it playing with your kids or responding to a batch of e-mails or taking a nap. The time spent on one activity cannot be spent on another. Similarly, if you consume one hundred calories' worth of energy, your body can use it to do maintenance work on your immune system, or it can move your muscles (you can dance in your parachute pants), or it can store the energy in your own personal fatty savings account for later use.

Our friends the rational economists have devoted an entire field of study—microeconomics—to understanding how individuals and firms allocate limited resources. Microeconomics is generally concerned with the decisions of people, but the need to allocate limited resources is not limited to human beings. Be it a single-cell bacterium, a Rottweiler, a Bengal tiger, or a long-stem rose, every living organism must make trade-offs. And it turns out that the underlying trade-offs faced by humans are the same as those confronted by all species.

To understand how organisms of all sorts allocate their limited resources, biologists have developed a powerful set of ideas called *life history theory*. Life history theory is like microeconomics, except that it's about biological trade-offs. The theory addresses questions like these: How long should an individual animal grow and develop before it starts to make babies? Should that animal allocate resources to caring for those offspring after they are born? If so, how much care should the animal invest in the offspring before leaving them to fend for themselves?

According to life history theory, the fundamental tasks of life for all organisms are divided into two broad categories: *somatic effort* and *reproductive effort*. Somatic effort is the energy an animal expends to grow and maintain a healthy body (the "soma"). Reproductive effort is the energy spent to replicate the organism's genes. You can think of somatic effort as like depositing money into a growing bank account. Reproductive effort, on the other hand, is like withdrawing money from that bank account to spend in ways that will help replicate one's genes. Just as people don't save money merely for the sake of generating a large bank account, animals don't invest in somatic effort merely to have a large body. Instead, investment in somatic effort is investment in future reproduction. By building a larger bank account now, an animal can create more successful offspring in the future.

Life history theory highlights how all animals make the same underlying trade-offs. At any one point, you, your pet cat, or the sparrow nesting outside your window can spend limited resources on either somatic or reproductive effort.

Different animals resolve this trade-off in different ways, leading to what are known as different *life history strategies*. Some animals follow a "slow" life history strategy, investing a great deal of time and effort in somatic development before turning to reproduction. Other animals follow a "fast" strategy, skimping on somatic investment to reproduce faster. For example, tenrecs (hedgehoglike mammals found in Madagascar) are on the fast path, reaching sexual maturity only forty days after birth. As soon as they are physically capable, tenrecs become prolific replicators, generating litters of young as large as thirty-two at a time. Elephants, on the other hand, are on the slow path, taking a hundred times longer to reach sexual maturity. Even after they are physically ready, elephants might wait years more to produce young. And when they do finally get around to it, they have one offspring at a time and then wait many more years before making a sibling for little Dumbo.

We humans are closer to elephants than to tenrecs in our life histories. We invest a great deal in somatic development, biding our time before we reach sexual maturity. Even after our bodies mature, we may wait anywhere from a few years to many decades before having children. And like elephants, we typically dedicate a great deal of energy to parenting, caring for our slowly maturing, large-brained babies— helpless little things that historically have not thrived without resources provided by both mothers and fathers.

In fact, for elephants, humans, and any animal that gives birth to relatively helpless babies, reproductive effort is about much more than just copulation. Successful reproduction is subdivided into two very different tasks: *mating effort* (energy resources spent on things like competing for status, attracting a mate, and copulating) and *parenting effort* (energy resources spent to ensure that their offspring are capable of surviving and reproducing on their own). Human life histories, like those of elephants, involve a lot of growing, a bit of mating, and then a lot of parenting.

THE THREE STAGES

By looking at ourselves through the lens of life history theory, we can see that, like other animals, we follow a predictable developmental sequence across the lifespan. Like other critters, our life histories can be divided into three stages, each characterized predominately by one type of effort: somatic effort, mating effort, and parenting effort. These stages help explain how our priorities and psychologies change across the lifespan. In fact, each of our specific subselves is more likely than others to direct our choices during some life stages. Recall the developmental pyramid from Chapter 2 (see Figure 2.1 for a reminder). That pyramid depicts how, as we mature, each of our subselves builds upon the ones that came before.

All animals must first survive and grow before they can reproduce. The first life stage of somatic effort provides a necessary developmental foundation before mating effort can unfold. During this initial stage children develop physically, build up their immune systems, and start learning social skills that enable them to form a network of friends. During the somatic stage, the self-protection and disease-avoidance subselves come online. Toddlers are particularly wary of outsiders (stranger danger peaks between ages two and three), and they are averse to ingesting novel foods, often preferring to eat the same food day after day after day (the thousandth peanut butter sandwich is welcomed with a smile, but those walnuts and avocados—positively yucky!). Children become concerned with making friends only much later, which is when the affiliation subself comes online to usher in the second life history stage.

If you have raised a teenage son or daughter, or if you just recall your own high school years, you might remember that during the second stage, involving mating effort, things get testy. For both men and women, mating effort peaks in young adulthood, the period from our mid-teens through the late twenties. After those innocent and asexual elementary school years, mating effort suddenly starts to monopolize an inordinate amount of a high schooler's time and effort. Am I popular or good-looking enough? Are other kids impressed with my status or are they looking down on me? Do I fit in with the in crowd? Do I stand out enough to draw attention? And the ultimate question: Can I land a date with that charming and attractive kid who sits next to me in history class?

Across the animal kingdom, mating effort is associated with rampant aggression and conspicuous showing off. The same is true across human societies. People at this age get the largest rush of adrenaline from doing things like jumping off bridges and spelunking into bottomless holes. Young adults are most likely to experiment with drugs, intoxicants, and risky sexual behavior. It's no coincidence that car crashes are the leading cause of death for American teenagers. Not only are teens less likely to be wearing their seat belts, but they are also more likely to be overconfident about their driving abilities, to be intoxicated, and to be driving around with more passengers—the ones they might want to impress with their recklessness.

The vigor of our mating effort is directly related to the amount of testosterone flowing through our bodies, which rises substantially in the mid-teens and peaks in our twenties. Testosterone stokes the flames of competition, rebellion, and lust. When men and women are injected with testosterone, they become more aggressive and more interested in sex. In one study of 4,462 military veterans, those with high testosterone levels had been in more trouble with the law, been more violent, and racked up an unusually large number of sexual partners.

The pubertal surge of testosterone marks the emergence of the mate-acquisition and status subselves, which dominate our behavior throughout most of the second life stage. The testosterone rushing through our veins also suppresses the self-protection and disease-avoidance subselves that were highly active when we were younger. After all, it's difficult to take wild risks and impress others when you are worried about your health and physical safety.

The decreased concern for safety can make the mating stage especially dangerous. Examining homicide patterns from Canada to Kenya and from medieval Europeans to the !Kung San of the Kalahari Desert, evolutionary psychologists Martin Daly and Margo Wilson found that killers everywhere are disproportionately young adults. Compared to a more mature fellow in his early forties, a young man in his early twenties is 400 percent more likely to kill another man.

And what's the main motive for all this violence? The single most common cause of murder, accounting for up to 37 percent of all homicides, is what's officially termed a *trivial altercation*. Police call such altercations trivial because they begin over relatively petty issues, such as a few words of insult, a curse, or one person bumping into another. As one Dallas homicide detective put it, "Murders result from little ol' arguments about nothing at all. Tempers flare. A fight starts, and somebody gets stabbed or shot. I've worked on cases where the principals had been arguing over a 10 cent record on a jukebox, or over a one dollar gambling debt from a dice game." Daly and Wilson pointed out that most violence has to do with status and mates—especially the lack thereof. In one study of Detroit homicides, 41 percent of the perpetrators were unemployed, and 73 percent were unmarried.

If a person survives the mating-effort stage (and for some young men, the homicide statistics tell us that this is a real if), he or she is likely to reach the third life stage, involving parenting effort. This final stage is associated with forming a long-term bond with another person, usually a marriage partner. This relationship creates a foundation for producing and successfully raising offspring. Although there is no official timetable for the beginning of the parenting stage, the average age for becoming a first-time parent in the United States is twenty-five for mothers and twenty-seven for fathers, although people in some other countries start families later (average age of first-time mothers is 29.2 in Japan and 29.5 in England, for example). Most people are in the parenting stage by the time they hit forty. And this third phase lasts longer than just the years spent raising your own kids—parenting effort for human beings also includes grandparenting.

The parenting stage brings about decreases in aggression and competitiveness. In one study, researchers observed amateur hockey players in Canada, comparing the games played by younger, unmarried men in their twenties with those played by older, married men in their thirties. The older players were fully three times less aggressive than the younger players. And when the older guys bumped or yelled at one another, most of the incidents were humorous—just minor teasing and joking around. For the younger men, there was nothing funny about the competition. The younger players not only got angry more easily but were four times more likely to display what the researchers called "cold hostility"—intentionally pushing, shoving, or hitting another player with no hint of a smile or an apology.

As men and women hit their thirties, testosterone levels start to decline. This hormonal decrease doesn't just follow a preset biological timer; it depends on whether you've entered the parenting-effort stage. Testosterone levels go down when a person gets married, and they decrease even further after the birth of a child. Philippine women who have had a child, for instance, have 30 percent less testosterone than women of the same age and socioeconomic status who don't have children. Likewise, North American men's testosterone levels drop when they get married, and then drop again when they have a child.

The parenting stage is when our mate-retention and kin-care subselves take center stage. Interacting with a long-term partner and a new baby continually activates the subselves devoted to being a good spouse and parent. Meanwhile, the neglected self-protection and disease-avoidance subselves experience a bit of a resurgence, since we now need to stay alive and healthy to raise our offspring and to protect them from various threats. By the time people are married with children, it's just not as fun to go jumping off bridges or running red lights, and they feel less need to explode violently over an insult or get hostile during an athletic game.

THE AGE OF ENTREPRENEURISM

Our shifting priorities through the different life stages have important consequences for how we approach financial decisions at different points. Thanks to high testosterone levels in young adulthood, the mating stage leads people to have the greatest appetite for risk, adventure, and gambling.

Consider the ages of the players in the World Series of Poker—a giant tournament that takes place in Las Vegas each year. Of the roughly eight thousand entrants, who each fork over a $10,000 entry fee, the average age is about twenty-five. Each year, savvy older poker veterans such as Phil "The Poker Brat" Hellmuth notoriously complain that today's young upstarts are playing the game with reckless abandon, bluffing and going "all in" when it's completely irrational to do so. But this kind of brazen play appears to have some payoffs. The last five people to win the grand prize (worth around $9 million) have been twenty-two, twenty-one, twenty-three, twenty-two, and twenty-four. Hellmuth, who is now nearing his fifties and is married with two kids, hasn't won the tournament himself since the ripe old age of twenty-four.

Age and testosterone don't affect just bets in Vegas. We can witness their effects in the daily activities of the whole financial sector. One British study followed futures traders at the London stock exchange (who were on average 27.6 years old), measuring their testosterone levels every morning for several weeks. On the days when the traders' testosterone levels were higher than average, they made eight times more profit than on the days when their testosterone count was hovering at the average level. The researchers attribute this enhanced success to the fact that testosterone increases persistence and fearlessness in the face of novelty.

After this study came out, clinics in New York City reported a rise in treatment for testosterone deficiency. Upper West Side doctor Lionel Bissoon, who performs hormone-replacement therapy, believes that testosterone is becoming the drug of choice for Wall Street traders seeking an edge over their professional rivals—90 percent of his patients are men in the finance industry in their thirties and forties who hope that testosterone boosters will help them perform better at work and enable them to put in longer hours. "If you're going to be trading on Wall Street or dealing with large sums of money, you had better be confident," Dr. Bissoon explains. "The man who is wishy-washy is not going to be successful."

Given that testosterone peaks in the early twenties, age might be a particularly important factor in entering careers that require immense risk taking, such as entrepreneurial ones. MC Hammer was twenty-two when he took a big risk by borrowing $40,000 from former Oakland A's players Mike Davis and Dwayne Murphy to start a record label called Bust It Productions. Selling records from the trunk of his car and marketing himself relentlessly, CEO Hammer soon recorded his own album, *Feel My Power*, on which he began aggressively waging war against rival rappers such as Doug E. Fresh and LL Cool J by calling them out in his songs and declaring himself "second to none."

And when it comes to the world of Internet tycoons, at least one venture capitalist thinks that "Internet entrepreneurs are like pro basketball players. They peak at 25. By 30 they're usually done." Larry Page and Sergey Brin were both twenty-five when they founded Google in 1998. Bill Gates was twenty-one when he founded Microsoft, Mark Zuckerberg was twenty-one when he started Facebook, and Steve Jobs was twenty-one when he started Apple with his twenty-five-year-old buddy Steve Wozniak. Apple was initially supposed to be a three-man operation with Jobs, Wozniak, and Ronald Wayne each owning a significant chunk of the company. We met Wayne earlier in Chapter 4 on smoke detectors in the mind; he's the guy who would have had $2.6 billion today if he hadn't decided to pull out of the deal after two weeks, explaining that he didn't have the stomach for such a risky entrepreneurial venture. Might age have had something to do with his cold feet? Unlike the youthful Jobs and Wozniak, Wayne was forty-two at the time.

The testosterone-juiced young are not just willing to stomach more risks; they are also more aggressive in their dealings with other businesspeople. One study, examining 357 mergers and acquisitions deals, found that young CEOs were more combative, more likely to try to acquire other companies, and more likely to resist being acquired themselves. Young moguls seek to protect their turf fiercely, while aggressively expanding their empire. This has some powerful implications for negotiation.

Imagine that a man must share $40 with you, so he makes you an offer. If you accept the offer, each of you gets to take home the agreed-on amount. But if you reject the offer, neither of you gets anything. If the man offered you only $5 out of $40, would you take it?

When researchers examined this exact question, they found that men's responses depended on their testosterone level. For men with below-average testosterone, 93 percent accepted the offer, happily taking $5 for themselves while letting the other man have $35. But of the men with above-average testosterone, almost half—45 percent—rejected the offer, choosing to take $0 rather than lose face by accepting a raw deal. And of the men in the study with the highest level of testosterone, fully 71 percent outright rejected the low offer.

Because the young are more restless and prone to risk taking, they are more willing to test their luck in risky professions such as fishing in the unforgiving, icy waters of Alaska, logging giant trees with chainsaws, or starting their own business. But while younger individuals are more likely to test their luck, does this always make them better entrepreneurs? The answer appears to be no. Because young adults are more likely to be blinded by myopic optimism and naïve enough to bet everything on one hand, a few will succeed. But many more will fail. A study of 549 successful entrepreneurs found that those who succeeded in their ventures were, on average, older and more experienced when they started the company that ultimately went on to be successful. Of course, successes are often preceded by many failures from risky ventures undertaken when people were younger. While older individuals might be wiser when they do take risks, they are less likely to enter into risky ventures in the first place.

FAST VERSUS SLOW STRATEGIES

Imagine you're one of the five-year-old children who showed up for a now classic study at Stanford University. As you wait by yourself in a room free of distractions, you are offered a tasty marshmallow, planted temptingly on the table right in front of you. You are told it's alright to munch the tasty treat if you really want to, but if you can wait for a little while without giving in to temptation, you will be rewarded with two marshmallows. What would you do?

After the researcher left the room in the study, each child was observed through a one-way mirror. Whereas some of the kids gobbled the marshmallow right away, others tried to resist. The scientists observed that some of the latter kids would "cover their eyes with their hands or turn around so that they [couldn't] see the tray." A few began kicking the desk or tugging on their pigtails. And one even started to "stroke the marshmallow as if it were a tiny stuffed animal."

The marshmallow study tested people's ability to delay gratification. A decade later, when the children from the study had grown into adolescents, those who had resisted eating the marshmallow as five-year-olds were more competent teenagers as judged by their parents and teachers. And a few years later, those same individuals scored higher on their SAT exams. The message is simple: impulsiveness bad; delayed gratification good.

But is delaying gratification always a good thing? And might acting impulsively sometimes be smarter? Life history theory suggests that there is more to the marshmallow test than meets the eye. So far we have talked about how people's general priorities change across the lifespan. But life history theory emphasizes that there are important differences among people who are pursuing different strategies. Although just about everyone goes through the mating stage, for example, some people in this phase have an eye on tomorrow, while others seek to live for today. And as we'll discover, it turns out that impulsivity is sometimes the best strategy.

HIGH RISK, NO REWARD

Ray Otero works as a building superintendent at 106 East Eighty-fifth Street in New York City. A former car mechanic with a happy-go-lucky disposition, Otero has an unusual investment strategy. He "invests" $500 to $700 every week in the lottery. He plays the game in shifts, placing one bet in the morning at eleven o'clock and another in the midafternoon. His bets range from $10 to $20 on a scratch-off game or on the daily numbers, and he picks his digits from the license plates of parked or passing cars.

Otero is fully committed to his investment strategy—so much so that he spends a whopping $30,000 a year on the lottery! In 2008, Otero's buddy Richie Randazzo, the doorman for the building across the street, won $5 million in the Set for Life scratch-off game. The forty-four-year-old Randazzo, now set for life, immediately started dating a leggy, twenty-three-year-old Swedish model (who was later charged with promoting prostitution at Big Daddy Lou's Hot Lap Dance Club). But Otero himself has thus far failed to recoup his staggering investment. He has won only three times, earning $1,000 on a scratch-and-win and pulling in $2,000 on the Pick Five twice. But all of it was reinvested. "No matter how much I get," he says, "I always spend it back."

Why doesn't Otero just save his money instead of essentially gambling it away? It turns out that Otero is not alone in his enthusiasm for the lottery. John Charlson, a spokesman for the New York State Lottery, points out that 75 percent of all New Yorkers have, at one time or another, put money on the games, with an average New York lottery player spending about $350 a year. But even more intriguing is that the lottery has attracted more "investors" in the last decade. While consumer spending generally decreased right after the 2001 tragedy of September 11, spending on the New York State Lottery has increased every year after 2001. Are millions of people foolish and irrational, or might Otero's behavior reflect some kind of deeper logic?

At the heart of this puzzle is the question of the best strategy for investing money. While the specifics of financial investing entail limitless small print and shady complexity, there are really just two types of broad investment strategies. One option is the high-risk, high-reward route. You can, for instance, buy shares in a new start-up company, play amateur venture capitalist by funding your college buddy's zany business idea, or perhaps invest your money in excavating a new diamond mine in a faraway country. If just one of these ventures succeeds, you're going to be rich—possibly rich enough to put gold hubcaps on your Cadillac and maybe even to buy a luxury yacht and retire.

Ray Otero clearly favors the high-reward strategy. This is because spending money on the lottery is not all that different from buying risky stocks. If you pick a winner, like the $5 million doorman Richie Randazzo did, you'll be set for life. A key part of the high-reward strategy is that it promises the possibility of not only large but also immediate payoffs. You don't have to wait to enjoy that twenty-three-foot sailboat with your AARP buddies—you might be able to cruise around in your own luxury yacht right now!

But there's a reason the "go for it" strategy is called high risk. There's a good chance you won't make any money—and you'll likely lose everything. The new start-up you invested in may well go belly-up when the next bubble pops, your college buddy's scheme may well turn out to be as harebrained as you'd suspected, and the guaranteed largest-ever diamond mine in a faraway country is more likely to yield a record-size pile of rocks and dirt. Ray Otero's desire for big and fast rewards has not yielded much on his $30,000 yearly investment, most of which has been an unintended gift to the New York State Department of Taxation and Finance.

If you're not too comfortable with the possibility of losing your savings, there is an alternative investment strategy: the safe and boring route. This strategy entails doing things like putting money in a savings account or buying some bonds. While this isn't too exciting, you will earn some interest each year. Let's say that you earned 4 percent a year. While 4 percent isn't a huge return, it's far more than the 80 percent loss you can expect every time you buy a lottery ticket. The safe route will also enable you to take advantage of the extraordinary power of compound interest. If Ray Otero put $30,000 a year into a savings account with 4 percent interest, in ten years he'd have $419,000—and in twenty years this would grow to a cool million. Of course, Otero would have to wait two decades to get his hands on that kind of cash.

So which strategy is better: takings large risks in hopes of winning big now or playing it slow and steady to reap rewards later?

To all you college-educated types who read books about rational animals, it may certainly seem like it's smarter to resist the temptation of an easy but highly unlikely big score, and instead control your impulses and delay gratification. After all, slow and steady wins the race, doesn't it? This is why our parents want us to get an education in a practical field like accountancy and find secure employment rather than dropping out of school to start a risky new business or become a rock musician.

But the answer to the question of which investment strategy is better is neither that simple nor that obvious. In fact, it relates directly to the life history strategies we discussed earlier. Asking about how best to invest your money is very much like asking whether it's better to follow a fast or a slow life history strategy. As we discuss below, the answer is, "It depends." And when it comes to people, an evolutionary perspective suggests that some may be better off running at full speed rather than trudging along slowly and steadily.

FAST AND SLOW PEOPLE

Recall that some animals, like tenrecs, follow a fast life history strategy (investing very little in somatic effort and instead focusing on mating), while other animals, like elephants, follow a slow strategy (investing heavily in somatic effort and delaying reproduction). Life history theory emphasizes that neither strategy is inherently better. Instead, each is evolutionarily suited to different environments.

Fast strategies are adaptive in environments that are dangerous and unpredictable, like that of tenrecs, whose life is treacherous and uncertain. Not only must tenrecs endlessly scour for dinner in a desiccated Madagascar desert, but predators lurk behind every bush, on the lookout for a delicious tenrec dinner themselves. For critters living in a dangerous and unpredictable world, following a fast strategy is a necessity. If they delay investing in reproductive effort, they risk not reproducing at all. Tenrecs simply can't afford to build a larger bank account, because they might not be around later to spend their savings.

Slow strategies, on the other hand, are adaptive in safer and more predictable environments. Unlike tenrecs, elephants feed on a predictable diet of regional vegetation, and their massive size and power protects them from most predators. The adaptive strategy for elephants is to take their time, grow, and learn more about their world. With the luxury of being able to pad their somatic bank account, elephants invest more in somatic effort, thereby making themselves more competitive as mates in the future and, ultimately, better parents.

But here is where things get even more interesting. Differences in life history strategies don't just apply across different species. Individual animals within a given species also differ in their life history strategies. Some elephants and tenrecs reproduce earlier, while other elephants and tenrecs reproduce later. The same is true for humans. Although humans are relatively slow compared to other species, some people start families earlier, and others start them later. In the United States, for example, although the average age of first-time mothers is twenty-five, more than one in five first births occur to women under age twenty, while one in ten occur to women over the age of thirty-five. Some people are faster than average; others are slower. And on closer examination, these differences are not just random variations in whether or not a woman happens to become pregnant. Instead, fast and slow strategies are associated with vastly different psychologies and vastly different orientations toward everything from family to sex to money.

Slow strategists tend to be late bloomers. They actually grow up less rapidly, start puberty at later ages, and age biologically at a slower rate. They start having sex later in life and have fewer sexual partners, preferring monogamous relationships. People on the slow path also tend to have fewer children, to have them later in life, and to be married when they do so.

In sharp contrast, people on the fast track grow up more rapidly, start puberty at earlier ages, and age biologically at a faster rate (if you've ever been to a high school reunion, take a look at how some people look a lot older than others, even though everyone is the same age). Fast strategists are sexually precocious, having their first sex at an earlier age and having more sexual partners both earlier and later in life. Lots of sex often results in their having children earlier in life and in having more of them. People on the fast path are also more likely to be single parents, either because they never settled down or because they have divorced—an outcome made more likely by the fact that fast strategists are attracted to other fast strategists, who are quicker to move on to new mating opportunities.

Fast and slow people also have different personality traits. Whereas slow strategists are long-term planners, delaying immediate gratification to increase future payoffs, fast strategists are short-term opportunists, taking immediate benefits with little regard for long-term consequences. The cautious and calculated trudge along in the slow lane, while the reckless, the horny, and the shortsighted zoom by in the fast lane. As the noted lyrical philosopher MC Hammer said during his rapid rise to fame and fortune, "U Can't Touch This"!

RAISED TO RUN

Why do some people follow a fast strategy while others follow a slow one? Part of it has to do with the genes inherited from our parents.

But another part has to do with our environments. In particular, our life history strategies hinge on the environment we encountered early in childhood.

Developmental psychologists Bruce Ellis and Jay Belsky have found that two aspects of our childhood environment are critical in determining our life history strategy. First, strategies speed up if people grow up in dangerous environments—places rife with violence or disease. A study of 170 different countries found that local mortality levels (the likelihood of death) were strongly related to the age at which mothers had children, with higher mortality leading to much earlier age at first birth. In Niger, for example, which has the fourteenth-highest death rate in the world, over 50 percent of women have had their first child by age eighteen. In Vietnam, which has a low death rate, 165th in the world, only 3 percent of women give birth by age eighteen. Similarly, in a study of Chicago neighborhoods, the median age of mothers giving birth was 27.3 for the ten neighborhoods with the highest life expectancy but only 22.6 in the ten neighborhoods with the lowest life expectancy. Life history strategies are not merely related to general crime. When we examined records for 373 counties in the United States, we found that earlier age of first birth is specifically related to higher rates of physically dangerous violent crimes (homicide, assault, rape) but not property crime (theft, car theft, burglary). And the patterns persisted even when controlling for income.

The second factor that speeds up life history strategies is being raised in a fluctuating environment. Environmental fluctuations include frequently moving from place to place, having an unpredictable income, or seeing different people move in and out of the house. For example, girls living in a household without a consistently present father figure start puberty earlier—they begin menstruating, on average, nine months before girls who have a consistently present father figure. Earlier onset of menarche is a clear marker of a fast strategy. Similarly, having an insecure and more unpredictable relationship with one's mother in infancy is also linked to earlier onset of puberty. And just like those of dangerous environments, the effects of fluctuating and unpredictable environments remain strong even when researchers control for socioeconomic status or genetic factors, such as the mother's own age of menarche.

Just as we saw for tenrecs, it has been evolutionarily adaptive for people in dangerous and unpredictable environments to follow a fast strategy. Such environments are associated not only with a shorter lifespan but also with uncertainty about where resources are going to come from—or if there will be any resources at all. A fast strategy emphasizes getting the rewards and cashing them in immediately. In a dangerous and unpredictable environment, this can be adaptive, since you don't know whether you'll be around later to enjoy the benefits of compound interest on long-term investments. For the same reason, investing time and energy in acquiring skills and knowledge (such as getting a college education) makes evolutionary sense only if a person expects to be around for a while. If not, evolutionary success may be better served by foregoing the time, effort, and cost associated with education and instead expending those resources on tasks with more immediate evolutionary payoffs—like reproduction.

Our childhood environments serve as blueprints for what we can expect as adults. When Jeff Simpson, Vlad, and their colleagues examined what kinds of childhood experiences were most associated with a fast strategy in adulthood, they found that the experience of living in a fluctuating environment during the preschool years was the strongest predictor of having more sexual partners, being more aggressive and delinquent, and having a criminal record as an adult. The importance of the first five years suggests that even if our young minds are not consciously ready to analyze what's happening around us, our brains are nevertheless encoding what's going on. If you're being raised in a world where there is little you can do to avoid violence, and it's impossible to know what tomorrow might bring, you need to make the most of today. And if access to resources is unpredictable, a "get while the getting's good" attitude may be evolutionarily adaptive.

It's no coincidence that many people who live fast come from difficult childhoods. MC Hammer, Mike Tyson, and Larry King have all lived fast. They also all grew up in poor and dangerous neighborhoods (in the East Oakland projects and the tough Bedford-Stuyvesant and Bensonhurst neighborhoods of Brooklyn, respectively). Each was raised by a single mother after his father either abandoned the family or died, and each had to find ways to get what he needed (Tyson had already been arrested thirty-eight times by age thirteen).

These kinds of harsh and fluctuating early-life environments calibrate the brain to enact a fast strategy—the kind adaptive for evolutionary success when life is expected to be nasty, brutish, and short. Looking through an evolutionary lens, it becomes clear why these three men started spending their monetary windfalls as soon as the money hit their bank accounts: their brains were calibrated to live fast because they did not know what tomorrow would bring. Not only do the majority of people who win the lottery come from poor and unstable backgrounds, but many lottery winners go on to lose their fortunes within a few years. By contrast, growing up in a safe, stable, and predictable environment calibrates the brain to enact a slow strategy. It pays to go slow and steady when you know what's coming next and you're expecting to be around to reap the fruits of your labor.

Let's reconsider the marshmallow test from earlier, in which kids were given the choice between having one marshmallow now or two marshmallows later. Which choice is smarter? From a life history perspective, the wisdom of waiting depends on the nature of your environment—on whether you live in a predictable or unpredictable world.

Scientists at the University of Rochester recently performed the marshmallow test once again, except they made the child's environment either predictable or unpredictable. Before giving the kids the test, a researcher first showed them a few crayons and promised that if they waited, they would get to play with a large box of fun art supplies. In one condition, the researcher came back with the art supplies as promised. But in another condition, the researcher came back with nothing, telling the children that he had made a mistake and there were no art supplies. In both conditions, the kids were then offered the standard marshmallow deal. As each child sat alone in the room looking at the treat, the researchers recorded how long each boy or girl waited before eating the marshmallow.

When the kids had experienced a predictable environment with the reliable person, they waited an average of twelve minutes before grabbing the marshmallow. But when they had instead experienced an unpredictable environment with the unreliable person, the children grabbed the marshmallow after just three minutes. Children's ability to delay gratification is not carved in stone. Their brains adjust their impulsivity depending on their situation, in the same way that our adult life history strategies are adjusted depending on our childhood environments.

WIN, CRASH, OR BURN

So is it always wise to delay gratification and play it slow and steady? Or might it be wiser instead to take large risks in hopes of winning big now? From an evolutionary perspective, the answer depends on whether one is following a slow or a fast life history strategy.

If life were an athletic event, slow and fast strategists would be participating in completely different races. Slow strategists are on a long march. A defining feature of slow strategies is their low variance. This means that few slow strategists will end up as millionaires, but few will end up bankrupt either. Instead, there is relatively little variability in the slow game—the vast majority of such strategists find themselves somewhere in the middle, with decent, stable jobs, perhaps a white picket fence, and a small nest egg. Slow strategists are the backbone of every community. They include many of our teachers, administrators, nurses, middle managers, and accountants. These are not freewheeling types throwing around money or swimming in massive amounts of debt. They live within their means and expect to be alive to enjoy the fruits of their labor in retirement, when they finally get to cross the finish line of life's long march.

Fast strategists, on the other hand, are racing in a sprint hurdle. They have to dash rapidly and jump high in hopes of clearing the many impediments that are likely to trip them up. A defining feature of fast strategies is their high variance. Compared to those on the slow path, more fast strategists will come up from the streets to become millionaire movers and shakers. These are the visionary artists, entertainers, and entrepreneurs—of both the legitimate and illegitimate varieties. Through fearless enterprising, maniacal hard work, and a lot of luck, some fast strategists like MC Hammer, Larry King, and Mike Tyson rise to the top. But while a few fast strategists will taste success, even if for a short while, many more will crash and burn. The same riskiness and shortsightedness that lead some to rise to the top lead many more into debt, debilitating addiction, or prison (Mike Tyson, for example, was prosecuted for rape, and Larry King was arrested for grand larceny).

Some fast strategists won't even live long enough to spend their "easy-come" fortunes or go to prison. That's because living the fast life is inherently dangerous. The same traits that produce ambitious entrepreneurs, visionary artists, and attention-grabbing entertainers can lead to massive health problems and tragic accidents.

At least fifty-three successful rock stars belong to the infamous "twenty-seven club" of rockers who lived fast, partied hard, and died at the age of twenty-seven. These include raspy-voiced singer-songwriter Janis Joplin (heroin overdose), psychedelic guitar icon Jimi Hendrix (mixing alcohol with barbiturates), generational poet and Doors front man Jim Morrison (heart failure from a drug overdose), original Grateful Dead keyboardist Ron "Pigpen" McKernan (stomach hemorrhage from heavy drinking), eclectic singer Amy Winehouse (alcohol poisoning), and the original Rolling Stones guitarist Brian Jones (found at the bottom of a swimming pool, with the coroner's report ruling that the cause was "death by misadventure").

Whereas the average age of death in America is 75.8 years, one informal study of 321 rock stars found that their average age of death is 36.9 years. Certainly not all rock stars die. When Motley Crüe front man and "Dr. Feelgood" singer Vince Neil crashed his exotic De Tomaso Pantera sports car while driving drunk in 1984, he lived—but he did kill his twenty-five-year-old passenger, Nicholas "Razzle" Dingley. Neil managed to stay alive long enough to file for bankruptcy in 2005, despite selling over 80 million albums in his career.

Even if you're not a rock star and don't always live on the edge, your own fast or slow tendencies are likely etched deep into your psychology. Animal research has found that tendencies imprinted in childhood are most likely to surface in times of stress and uncertainty. In studies with Bonnet macaques, for example, adult monkeys respond to stress very differently depending on their childhood environment. After the monkeys were born, researchers had placed them in different environments. Some were raised in stable and predictable environments (their mothers could obtain food every day in the same place in a predictable manner). Other monkeys were placed in fluctuating environments (the researchers kept switching the locations of their food supply, so that the mothers didn't know how, where, or when they were going to find food each day). When the monkeys grew up and were exposed to stress as adults, those reared in a consistent and predictable environment coped well and explored multiple ways to deal with the situation; those reared in fluctuating and unpredictable environments panicked.

Research in Vlad's laboratory has found a similar pattern in humans. In these studies, some people first read stress-inducing news articles—daunting descriptions of recent economic recessions or increases in homicide. Other people read calming news articles that didn't induce any stress. Then everyone was asked to make several choices that tapped into desires for risk and willingness to delay gratification. For example, they could choose between receiving some real money for sure versus gambling for a larger amount (would they rather get $25 for sure or have a 50 percent chance of getting $40, for example). Other questions gave them a choice between receiving some money tomorrow versus receiving a much larger amount in the future (would you rather get $25 tomorrow or get $60 in one year, for example).

When people read the calming news story, their choices were similar regardless of their childhood environment. But reading the stressful news article produced markedly different responses, depending on the person's childhood environment. People raised in more predictable environments (as measured by having grown up in relatively wealthier homes) responded by adopting a slow strategy, avoiding gambles, and delaying gratification. When stressed out, people who grew up relatively well-off wanted to go slow and steady. By contrast, people raised in less predictable environments (as measured by having grown up in lower-income homes) responded to stress by adopting a faster strategy, preferring the gambles and becoming more impulsive.

When stressed out, people who grew up with fewer resources became more risk seeking and impatient.

Both the studies with monkeys and with humans show that childhood environments influence life history strategies. Although tendencies associated with fast versus slow strategies might be dormant during good times, they emerge in times of stress.

OFF TO THE RACES

At the surface level, behaviors associated with fast strategies can seem wildly irrational and foolish. Frittering away $30,000 a year on lottery tickets or buying a $2 million bathtub makes little sense when considered from the rational economist's perspective. Yet, like many of the other puzzling phenomena discussed in this book, impulsive behavior might reveal a deeper logic when you consider it from the evolutionary psychologist's perspective.

Let's revisit the example of lottery investor Ray Otero. As with MC Hammer, Otero's behavior is likely rooted in his childhood. Otero grew up poor in Puerto Rico, moving from place to place, and he eventually immigrated to the Bronx. By the time he moved to New York, Otero's psychology had already been calibrated to follow a fast strategy, but his true colors might not have completely manifested themselves until a particularly stressful local event. Otero was in New York City to witness the horrific tragedy of September 11, 2001—a salient reminder of the fragile nature of life in a dangerous and unpredictable world. It was around this time that he became especially impatient and disenchanted with his long-term prospects and began investing his resources in the lottery—along with the millions of other people who contributed to increasing post-9/11 lottery sales.

Are Otero and others like him foolish and irrational? It might appear that way to many of his slow strategy neighbors, one of whom described Otero's behavior as "crazy"—"He's got a ton of worthless tickets!" But Otero doesn't see it that way. As he explained to the *New York Times*, "Working for poor uneducated men is a sucker's game, where one must run increasingly fast to keep one's place in line." From the perspective of someone who has grown up expecting to live in an uncertain and dangerous world, the fruits of a slow, long-term strategy might never be realized. As Otero describes it, "If all you're doing is working, you're never going to win." And for a fast strategist, taking chances for a big win now is better than never even having a shot.

LIFE HISTORY THEORY highlights that humans proceed through a particular developmental sequence, with different subselves emerging during different life stages. Some people go through this sequence slowly, but others, like Ray Otero, go faster. What do you think Ray Otero would do if he won the lottery? Would he buy a luxury yacht with a gold toilet? As we'll describe next, he might instead invest in a green Toyota Prius, but not because of its fuel efficiency.

7

Gold Porsches
and Green Peacocks

WHEN THE EDITORS OF *Consumer Reports* prepare their annual list of "Best Buys," they are unlikely even to consider the Porsche Carrera GT. The vehicle has very little cargo capacity and only two seats, gets terrible gas mileage, and is frightfully expensive to repair. Whereas $15,900 could buy you the top-rated consumer-pleasing Honda Civic, which has more cargo capacity, better mileage, and room for three more passengers, the Porsche will run you over $480,000, not counting the $14,800 dealer prep charge and the $5,000 delivery fee. And if you think that sounds like a lot of dough, the standard price wasn't high enough for one fellow—a Russian man had his Porsche meticulously plated with over forty pounds of gold. Why would anyone shell out so much money for a speedy sports car and then spend even more to weigh it down with a layer of heavy metal?

In his 1899 classic *The Theory of the Leisure Class*, Thorstein Veblen coined the term "conspicuous consumption" to refer to people's tendency to buy and show off expensive goods—with the goal of impressing other people with their wealth or status. The gold-plated Porsche may seem like an extreme example of this phenomenon, but it pales in comparison to other acts of extravagance. Greek shipping magnate Aristotle Onassis's opulent yacht was larger than a football field and featured a mosaic-tiled dance floor that could be retracted to reveal a swimming pool. The barstools on the boat were covered in garishly expensive soft leather, custom made from the foreskins of whale penises. And the excess even extended into the bathroom—the toilet fixtures were made of solid gold!

Conspicuous consumption is not some rare phenomenon found only among the superrich. Thousands of young people scraping by in poverty-ridden housing projects expend their scarce dollars on gaudy jewelry and $200 sneakers. In one popular hip-hop song, the rappers proudly show off their diamond-encrusted gold and platinum "grillz," devoting a good portion of the lyrics to bragging about how much cash they dropped for these custom-made retainer-like decorations on their front teeth. While a Porsche Carrera can at least transport you to your destination, a set of diamond-encrusted grillz is worse than useless. Not only are they a handicap when eating and closing your mouth, but as one of the rappers observes, wearing them is like "chewin' on aluminum foil."

Why do people spend money they don't really have on things they don't really need to impress people they don't really like or know? Here we examine the deeper reasons behind conspicuous consumption. By looking under the surface, we will discover something very important: we often don't really know why we do the things we do. Although we're aware of some of the surface motives for our actions, the deep-seated evolutionary motives often remain inaccessible, buried behind the scenes in the subconscious workings of our brains' ancient mechanisms. This is important because it means that asking people why they throw money around the way they do will rarely yield the underlying evolutionary reason. But by knowing where to look, we can see our subselves pulling the purse strings.

WHY DO WE THROW MONEY AWAY?

An abundant literature on excessive consumerism paints the following picture: conspicuous consumption is rampant in American culture, and it is linked to materialism, which is promoted by the American media. American television, movies, and magazines depict attractive and fast-living people sporting a hyperabundance of expensive material possessions. Bedecked in designer clothes and shiny jewels, these showy characters drive top-end luxury cars from their well-appointed beachside homes to chic urban bistros, where they bask in the company of crowds of other glamorous high rollers. One need merely turn on the television or drop in at a nearby movie house to find abundant evidence consistent with this cultural media explanation of materialism and conspicuous consumption.

Social scientists point out that this kind of Western materialism is not only rampant but harmful, leading people to de-emphasize personal relationships, feel decreased satisfaction with their incomes, and reduce their charitable giving, as they greedily pursue more wealth, bigger houses, and more expensive cars. Even worse, poor people are seduced by these glamorized images into foregoing life's necessities so that they can scrape together enough money to make a credit card payment on frivolous luxuries.

American culture is no doubt materialistic to a fault, but is that the primary cause of conspicuous consumption? On closer examination, there's a very big problem with the cultural explanation. These same excessively showy phenomena, although abundantly visible in American society, can also be found in other societies. From Argentina to Zanzibar and everywhere in between, people flaunt their wealth. In fact, in developing his classic work on conspicuous consumption over a century ago, Thorstein Veblen had already observed that people around the world have paraded their luxury possessions throughout human history.

The pharaohs of ancient Egypt, who, as far as we know, had never seen a single episode of *MTV Cribs*, nevertheless conspicuously displayed their wealth with golden thrones, elaborate artworks, and giant pyramids. And long before the advent of *Better Homes and Gardens*, Incan potentates dwelled in immense palaces surrounded by gold, and Indian maharajahs built extravagant and ostentatious palaces on expansive estates, where they kept collections of rare and exotic animals. Conspicuous displays of wealth were also abundant in feudal Europe, imperial China, and ancient Japan, where wealthy nobles constructed lavish castles filled with gold, jewels, and beautiful works of art. And these extravagances were not limited to the grand societies of history. Even among traditional people living in the remote regions of Melanesia, Iceland, and Amazonia, those who had wealth flaunted it. Rather than pointing to modern Western culture as the main reason for conspicuous consumption, anthropologists and historians have discovered that ostentatious displays of wealth have occurred in every corner of the globe for millennia.

So if we can't blame American culture, what's responsible for conspicuous consumption? Another explanation comes from our friends the economists. University of Leicester economist Gianni De Fraja notes, "Conspicuous consumption for its own sake enhances utility." But as De Fraja points out, the insight that conspicuous consumption stems from a desire to enhance "utility" is woefully unsatisfying and incomplete. Sure, we will pay good money for things that we expect to be satisfying in some way and not for others that we don't. But we need to explain why people believe some conspicuous things, and not others, will bring them satisfaction. Why exactly is it that people are willing to trade food, shelter, and health care to possess a luxury good, which may have no survival value at all?

Economists have never been much concerned with the roots of our preferences, generally ignoring the question of why we desire one thing as opposed to another. But without a better account of what people find satisfying and why, the argument that our choices stem from a desire to maximize utility is circular. How do we know something enhances utility? Because people are willing to pay for it. Why are people willing to pay more for some things? Because those things enhance utility. Much like explanations that point to culture, explanations that point to utility are not very useful for understanding the deeper reasons for behavior.

ARE WE OUT OF TOUCH WITH THE CAUSES OF OUR OWN BEHAVIOR?

One reasonable method for determining what motivates people's choices is simply to ask them. After some introspection, perhaps they will be able to reveal their real reasons for tricking out their Porsches or dropping cash on diamond-encrusted grillz.

Asking people about their needs and wants is common practice, with many businesses running focus groups, conducting interviews, and gathering surveys to better understand their clients' desires. But there is a key presumption behind asking people to explain the reasons for their behavior: that people know why they do things. This presumption might seem utterly reasonable, except that a mountain of carefully controlled scientific studies show that people are often completely clueless when it comes to explaining the reasons for their behavior. In study after study, people are superb at providing elaborate explanations for why they made a certain choice, but after reviewing the evidence, psychologists Richard Nisbett and Tim Wilson observe that we are a bit too adept at "telling more than we can know." Humans are simply not wired to be conscious of all the reasons they do things. This hidden wiring poses a real problem in uncovering the deeper motives underlying behavior.

Consider the reason why over 1 million Americans have bought a Toyota Prius, a popular hybrid gas-electric car. One of the most vocal Prius owners has been Hollywood leading man Leonardo DiCaprio, who proudly proclaimed early on, "I own a Toyota Prius. It's a step in the right direction." Because the Prius has lower emissions, it produces a smaller carbon footprint than conventional combustion engine cars. This is important to DiCaprio and to many of his Prius-owning celebrity pals, such as Cameron Diaz, Julia Roberts, Woody Harrelson, Bill Maher, and *Seinfeld* creator Larry David, all of whom are staunch environmentalists. DiCaprio even has his own foundation for environmental awareness, spending his free time lobbying to ban the sale of shark fins in California and bringing portable solar panels to power his movie sets, such as during filming of the blockbuster film *Inception*. In 2007, DiCaprio and former US vice president Al Gore even drove Priuses to the Academy Awards.

But to find out why normal people want the Prius, we need to get off Hollywood Boulevard and ask regular folk why they really buy hybrids. It just so happens that a 2007 study by the Topline Strategy Group called "Why People Really Buy Hybrids" asked Prius owners just such a question: "What was your primary motivation for buying the Prius?" The responses couldn't have been clearer. The overwhelming majority, 66 percent, said they bought a Prius because they wanted to be environmentally friendly. Like Leonardo DiCaprio, most people say they drive a Prius because they want to do their part for the environment.

But while many people say they buy the Prius to do good for the environment, is this really their reason? Vlad and his colleagues Josh Tybur and Bram Van den Bergh suspected that there might be a different motive at play, one involving the status subself. Rather than seeking to help Mother Nature, is it possible that people are instead seeking to help themselves—by going green to be seen?

To test this idea, the researchers had people choose between two cars: a luxurious nongreen model and an equivalently priced but less luxurious green hybrid. For example, people could choose between two versions of the Honda Accord, each costing $30,000. The nongreen version was a top-of-the-line EX-L model with a sporty V6 engine, leather seats, and all the desirable trimmings offered by the manufacturer. The alternative option was a Honda Accord hybrid. This option did not have the same level of luxury or performance, but it sported an enticing "H" (for "hybrid") on the back of the car, publicly proclaiming the owner's environmental concern and awareness.

Before people made their choices, however, the researchers activated the status subself in half of the study participants. These subjects read a short story in which they imagined arriving for their first day at a high-powered job. Impressed by the upscale lobby and well-appointed decor, they learned that they would be competing with several others for an opportunity to move into a prestigious corner office. Much like reading a biography of a highly successful individual, envisioning this scenario lights a flame in the mind, putting the status subself squarely in charge and producing a subconscious desire to move up in the status hierarchy. After having read the story, people make choices that will get them status.

The study revealed that people's car choices changed dramatically when the status subself was driving. Without a desire for status, most people chose the top-of-the-line combustion car model over the dinkier hybrid. But when the inner go-getter was in charge, people's choices reversed. More than half of the status-minded people chose the hybrid. In fact, these go-getters also preferred other green products such as ecologically friendly dishwashers and recycled backpacks over their conventional counterparts.

Why did a desire for status lead people to sacrifice luxury and go green? Were these budding go-getters somehow inspired to be altruistic and self-sacrificing for the environment? Not exactly. Instead, a second study found that a status motive led people to go green only if they could show off their green wares to others. If neighbors couldn't easily see the sacrifices they were making to help the planet, such as forgoing the Corinthian leather seats and the powerful V6 HEMI for a sluggish one-hundred-horsepower hybrid, then it wasn't worth it.

The "going green to be seen" research suggests that the Prius phenomenon can sometimes be just a different version of conspicuous consumption. Driving a Prius is a very public form of conspicuous conservation. Michael Marsden, dean of St. Norbert College and an expert on automobile history, explains that the Prius represents classic car-buying behavior: "Automobile culture has always been about status. The whole industry is based on symbols. With the Prius, you're bringing attention to yourself." A Prius is essentially a mobile billboard conspicuously advertising the owners' environmental concerns.

Like putting up any advertisement, having your own portable billboard will cost you. The Prius costs about $5,000 to $7,000 more than a conventional, yet still highly fuel-efficient, car such as the Honda Civic—the one *Consumer Reports* calls a "Best Buy." Does it make sense for people to fork up an extra seven grand merely to advertise their environmentalism? The answer appears to be yes, but only if the status subself is behind the wheel. Economists Steve and Alison Sexton have found that owning green products like the Prius increases people's networking opportunities and produces more business connections. They estimate that in some especially green places, like Boulder, Colorado, this step up the social ladder is worth just about $7,000—justifying the price premium of a Toyota Prius over a Honda Civic.

Recent reports indicate that Leonardo DiCaprio no longer drives a Prius. But don't worry—he still really cares about the environment. We can tell because he has recently been seen in a new hybrid. DiCaprio was the first person on the planet to take delivery of the exclusive Fisker Karma, a $116,000 high-performance hybrid sports car that is sure to attract even more attention than the Prius. Spending over a hundred grand on a car must be really beneficial to the environment, because the second person on the list to receive the Fisker Karma is DiCaprio's Academy Award companion Al Gore. Unfortunately, we suspect that both Al and Leo will soon need to find new cars. The Fisker Karma doesn't seem bound for the *Consumer Reports* "Best Buy" list. When the consumer group bought a brand-new one and took it for a test drive, it broke down and could not be restarted. "We buy about 80 cars a year," the bewildered folks at *Consumer Reports* explained, "and this is the first time in memory that we have had a car that is undriveable before it has finished our check-in process."

MULTIPLE EXPLANATIONS FOR THE SAME BEHAVIOR

How would you guess Prius owners responded to the study suggesting a scientific link between a desire for status and green behavior? After the "going green to be seen" research was publicized in the press, Vlad was bombarded with scores of angry letters, phone calls, and e-mails from hybrid owners. Entire blogs and chat rooms were dedicated to arguing against the idea that green behavior is related to status seeking. These individuals had not purchased their hybrids to show off, they protested, but to help the environment. And darn it, they wanted to be sure that everyone knew about their purely unselfish motives!

Were the hybrid owners lying to themselves about their motives for buying their energy-saving automobiles? Not completely. These people almost certainly spent a lot more time thinking about how their hybrids would help the environment than they did about showing off to their neighbors. But this brings us back to the central question: What motivates conspicuous consumption? Are Prius owners altruistically helping the environment, as they sincerely believe? Or are less conscious, selfish motives driving them to show off? It turns out that both explanations may be correct.

At the heart of the debate is a critical issue we met earlier in the book: the distinction between proximate and ultimate motives for behavior. Recall that proximate explanations refer to the surface reasons for why we do things, whereas ultimate explanations refer to the deeper evolutionary reasons behind our behavior. This distinction is important, because if you ask people why they have behaved a certain way, they are likely to be in touch with the immediate proximate triggers (events in the environment and their thoughts and feelings about those events) but completely unaware of their deeper ultimate function.

But to understand any behavior, we have to understand both its proximate and its ultimate causes. Think about what motivates people to buy Priuses. Do people buy them out of an altruistic motivation to help the environment, as most owners say? Or do they buy them to show off, as the "going green to be seen" research suggests? The answer depends on whether we're talking about proximate or ultimate causes. The decision to buy a Prius can certainly be driven by altruistic motives at the conscious proximate level ("I want to be nice and help the environment") and at the same time by subconscious selfish motives at the ultimate level (being nice and pro-environment enhances a person's status). As demonstrated by the many Prius owners outraged by Vlad's research, people needn't have any awareness that their well-intentioned and environmentally friendly acts are actually selfish at a deeper level. Natural selection has already ensured that the desire to be helpful is associated with ultimate benefits.

THE ULTIMATE DRIVING MACHINE

Let's park our hybrid cars for a while and return to the more general question of why people engage in conspicuous consumption. What ultimately inclines humans everywhere to fritter their resources on lavish commodities with no survival value, such as gold-plated Porsches or giant pyramids? As Thorstein Veblen himself observed over a century ago, conspicuous consumption is linked to status. But why? And why does showing off our status matter so much to us?

The answer to these questions might be found by considering the role of conspicuous displays in other animal species. Let's travel to the Australian Outback, to take a peek at the antics of the male satin bowerbird, which engages in a behavior that shares a striking resemblance to conspicuous consumption in humans. As we'll see, the bowerbird's antics may shed some light on the ultimate roots of the human inclination toward flashy spending.

BOWER POWER

The male satin bowerbird is a natural architect. He carefully constructs an elaborate grass structure called a bower. It takes him weeks and weeks of effort to build his towering grass castle, which can end up being several times taller than he is. The bowerbird pays special attention to aesthetics, making sure that his elaborate abode is precisely symmetrical and arranged just so. After he finishes construction, he embarks on a second phase of his architectural adventure: exquisitely decorating his mansion and its expansive front yard. He flies around searching for blue flower petals, blue berries, or even blue candy wrappers or clothespins, lugging them back to the bower and meticulously placing them in prominent positions (the color blue is scarce in his natural Outback environment, making shiny blue trinkets the bowerbird equivalent of rare jewels). Once his estate is ornately furbished, he begins standing guard, on the lookout for rivals, some of whom may be seeking to fleece his prized possessions.

You might guess that bowerbirds build bowers because these nests will eventually function as their homes. But that's not the case—the bowers aren't nests at all. Instead, the bower's only function is to attract mates. After spending months erecting and adorning his showpiece, the male patiently waits for females, who periodically drop by for an inspection. As females scrutinize the size, symmetry, and décor of his mini-mansion, the male performs an elaborate dance in the front yard, rhythmically flashing his lovely array of satin-sheened feathers, in hopes of persuading the female to stick around a little longer. If the female is impressed, the couple will copulate for a few seconds, after which the female flies back home to raise any future offspring. And when the mating season is over, the male also returns to his old bachelor pad, completely deserting the bower that took months of work to build, only to start construction on another one from scratch the following year.

The satin bowerbird is one of countless examples of conspicuous display in the animal kingdom. Looking across a wide array of species, we can make two generalizations about conspicuous displays. First, if you see a critter showing off its colorful plumage, dancing up a rhythmic spectacle, or belting out a melodious song, it's a good bet that mating season is in full swing. These kinds of conspicuous displays increase specifically during the mating season. Sometimes the displays stop completely when the mating season is over, as when colorful birds trade their brilliant plumage for a duller, camouflage-friendly outfit and quiet their singing to the point where they become difficult to find in the trees. This seasonality tells us that the display is linked to mating.

The second generalization we can make about those conspicuous displays is that if you see an animal showing off, it's a good bet you're looking at a male. Across a wide range of species, males do most of the boastful swaggering. The reason is that for most species, including humans, females enjoy a buyer's market, and males have to sell themselves. As we will discuss more fully in Chapter 8 on sexual economics, this is because females produce the offspring, which requires a much more costly investment—whether it's laying a large egg and sitting on it, avian style, or carrying a fetus inside her body and nursing it, mammalian style. Males in the animal kingdom often provide little more than a donation of sperm. Because one male can fertilize many females in the same season, but one female cannot carry offspring for multiple males at the same time, this makes individual males more expendable when it comes to reproduction.

As a consequence, females across most species tend to be very choosy about which males will suffice as mates, especially if the fellows' only contribution will be a droplet of DNA. And to be selected by a choosy female, males have to compete vigorously. Blokes need to pull out all the stops to impress even one lady, by singing the most awe-inspiring song, growing the most lustrous tail, or building the tallest and shiniest bower.

Why do females choose showy males? Evolutionary biologists believe that conspicuous displays are signals that those males possess "good genes." If a male has the time, energy, ability, and resourcefulness to build, decorate, and maintain a giant bower, for example, it indicates that he carries genes that have allowed him to thrive. By mixing her own genes with those of the most successful male around, the female passes those desirable traits on to her own offspring.

FLASHING THE CASH

Might conspicuous consumption in humans serve a similar evolutionary function as bowers in bowerbirds and flashy feathers in peacocks? If so, we'd expect to find two things. First, the tendency toward showy resource displays should increase with increased motivation to attract a mate—the prime directive of our mate-acquisition subself. And second, this motivation should be especially likely to produce conspicuous consumption in men but not in women.

In an initial test of this idea, psychologist Jim Roney asked men to fill out a survey rating themselves on a series of traits. Some of the men answered the survey together with a group of other men working on the same questionnaire. Other guys filled out the survey in a room that included several attractive women. Roney found that men's responses changed depending on the room in which they filled out the survey. In the room with women, men said they were more ambitious about their careers and rated attaining wealth as very important to them. Even though the women never talked to the men and could not even see what they wrote on their questionnaires, the mere presence of females apparently indicated to men that mating season was open.

Our own research with Josh Tybur, Jill Sundie, Bob Cialdini, and Geoffrey Miller found that activating men's mate-acquisition subself doesn't simply lead men to value wealth in their hearts—it leads them to want to flaunt their wealth in public. We asked men and women how much money they would spend on things such as a car, a watch, a dinner, a mobile phone, and a vacation. For example: Do you want an inexpensive watch for $25 or one that cost $275, a $50 restaurant dinner or a $300 gourmet feast, a cut-rate $500 European junket or a luxury $3,000 vacation?

Before asking them to make their spending decisions, we activated the mate-acquisition subself for half the participants. We had them write about going on their ideal date, describing in detail their fantasy partner's looks and personality, as well as how they wanted their perfect evening to end. The other half of the subjects were in the control condition; they wrote about pleasant weather.

When the mate-acquisition subself was off duty, men and women did not differ in their inclination to spend. They didn't always want the cheapest products, but they weren't inclined to overspend either. Waking people's inner mate seeker, though, triggered an impulsive spending orgy—but only for men. With the flame of desire lit, men went into show-off mode, craving extravagant cars, flashier mobile phones, expensive vacations, and any other product they could display conspicuously.

It's not that men were consciously aware of a link between their purchasing decisions and their mating motives; they did not, in fact, have any reason to believe that women would see their flashy purchases. Instead, activating the mate-acquisition subself simply led men to want the expensive items. And with mating on their minds, they were more willing to shell out extra money to acquire those conspicuous goodies.

Just as bowerbirds flaunt the blue in their bowers for potential mates, men appear to flaunt the green in their wallets to charm their dates. Does it work? It probably depends on the amount of green in the wallet and the choosiness of the date. Charming a woman used to hanging around with the Kennedys, for example, would probably require some serious display—maybe even an ultraopulent yacht longer than a football field with solid gold bathroom fixtures and barstools covered in whale penis foreskins. We don't know what Jackie Kennedy thought about this eclectically extravagant décor, but we do know that she married Onassis—on his lavishly appointed private island.

PEACOCKS, PORSCHES, AND PAPAS

The fact that a desire to acquire a mate triggers men to flash the cash is consistent with findings that male animals are more likely to conspicuously display their feathers, antlers, or bowers when presented with mating opportunities. Men, it seems, are not always that different from peacocks. When a peahen comes strutting into the vicinity, peacocks instinctively fan out their magnificently grandiose tails. It doesn't even need to be a real peahen—a picture of one will trigger the same show-off response. Men appear to do likewise. Merely sitting in a room with other women—or just thinking about a date—prompts the desire to spend conspicuously.

But while it's tempting to draw analogies between them, are all men really like peacocks? As discussed in the last chapter, human beings play more than one strategy, with some of us being fast and some being slow. Psychologists Jeffry Simpson and Steve Gangestad developed a personality test that can assess the extent to which a man is like a peacock—inclined to invest all his energies into colorful and flashy feathers while contributing little toward helping the female raise the young. In the language of life history theory, peacocks follow a fast strategy. And just as some humans follow a fast strategy, the researchers found that these men are indeed very much like peacocks. Simpson and Gangestad call these fast players "unrestricted" strategists. The unrestricted playboy types are interested in having a good time, with little or no desire to settle down or raise a family. And like peacocks, such men are more promiscuous. They are willing to have sex with women even when they're not in love, and they think it's a fine idea to have ongoing sexual relationships with more than one woman at a time.

But not all men are like this. Simpson and Gangestad found that a substantial proportion of men find promiscuity unfulfilling and even downright unappealing. Unlike peacocks, some men are more "restricted"; they want to find one long-term romantic partner, settle down, and raise a family. These men follow a slow life history strategy.

Our colleague Jill Sundie suspected that conspicuous consumption would be found primarily among fast, peacock-like men. Working with Jill, Josh Tybur, Kathleen Vohs, and Dan Beal, we tested whether putting the mate-acquisition subself in charge would have a different effect on men who are like peacocks and those who aren't.

The findings couldn't have been clearer: priming a desire to attract a mate produced conspicuous consumption only in the fast, peacock-like men. For the marrying kind of fellows following a slow strategy, on the other hand, the same mate-attraction motive did not trigger a desire to put themselves on display. If anything, these men didn't want to draw attention to themselves by going over the top with flashy purchases (if these guys are going to spend big money, they want it to be inconspicuous). By contrast, the fast peacock types went straight for the most blaring products. They didn't even care if the goods were genuine or counterfeit. As long as they looked expensive and attracted attention, these guys wanted to display them. In fact, the effects were strongest after the playboy-style guys thought about a romantic tryst with someone they'd never see again—a one-night stand. As soon as the women indicated they wanted a relationship, these guys started losing their inspiration to spend.

This study shows that if you see a man cruising around in a shiny Porsche, gold plated or otherwise, he's probably of the fast peacock variety. When a man drives a Porsche, Gad Saad and John Vongas find, he actually experiences a surge in testosterone—the hormone involved, across the animal kingdom, in male mating displays, as when a peacock spreads his tail or a bowerbird struts in front of his bower. It's probably a good bet that the guy driving the Porsche is looking for a good time, not for a good wife.

Does conspicuous consumption work? In one study, Jill Sundie and her colleagues compared women's interest in young professional men who drove either a flashy Porsche or a modest Honda. The flashy car impressed women, who indicated that they would rather go out on a date with the guy driving the Porsche. But women weren't blindly seduced by the bling. When asked which man they would rather marry, the luster of the conspicuous car quickly dulled. For long-term commitment, women preferred the less flashy, and likely more reliable, fellow driving the Honda.

THE ULTIMATE DRIVER OF BEHAVIOR

After the "peacocks and Porsches" findings were published, both Jill and Vlad got yet another wave of e-mails, calls, and letters from outraged Porsche owners. These men (and they were all men) argued that their conspicuous consumption had nothing at all to do with the ultimate reason of attracting a mate. They pointed instead to various proximate reasons. Some said they had purchased the cars for their distinctive styling; others bought them because they liked the feel of a Porsche; still others simply enjoyed the experience of cruising with the top down on weekends. As one man put it, he'd owned his Porsche for over two decades and been happily married to his wife for most of that time. Of course, this raises the question why he purchased a Porsche back when he was single and whether it had anything to do with sparking the interest of this attractive woman.

Vlad received one phone call from the president of a European Porsche enthusiasts' club. This guy was clearly concerned, but unlike the others, he wasn't surprised or angered by the findings. Rather, he was distraught about what the study would reveal to the wives of Porsche owners about their husbands. The same fellow later sent Vlad a German Porsche television advertisement that he thought "might be related" to the study. In the ad, a beautiful woman in a long raincoat walks by a shiny new Porsche in a mysterious dark alley. She is struck by the awesome beauty of the car and begins to caress its smooth angles flirtatiously. Finally, unable to resist, she opens her coat to expose her almost naked body to the Porsche.

Not very subtle. But a superb depiction of the ultimate reason for buying a Porsche.

Once again, when we observe people doing seemingly foolish things like throwing away money to have their Porsches or their bathroom fixtures plated in gold, there is often more going on than meets the eye. Although conspicuous consumption might appear to be vain and wasteful, such behavior can serve an important function at a deeper evolutionary level.

Our choices have multiple causes; some obvious, others obscure. We are aware of some of the proximate causes of our behavior. If you've ever purchased a luxury car, you might have spent a lot of time thinking about its eye-popping leather interior or its chrome-plated engine that blasts from zero to sixty in a few milliseconds. And if you bought a hybrid car, you may very well have been thinking about how the environmental benefits outweighed the hefty price tag. But most of the time we are not consciously aware of the underlying ultimate reasons for our choices.

WHEN IT COMES to mating purchases, a person's choices can be very different based on one particularly important biological factor—whether that person is male or female. For example, men use conspicuous consumption to attract mates but women don't. In fact, sex differences go much deeper than conspicuous consumption. If you want to predict where a person is likely to invest his or her limited resources, what he or she is likely to value, and which products he or she is likely to buy, perhaps the most important question to ask is this: Are we are talking about a man or a woman? In the next chapter, we look more closely at how men's and women's decisions differ—and why. We start by exploring a puzzling aspect of human culture: Why do men in some societies pay several years' income for the company of a woman, whereas in other societies a woman's family pays an immense dowry to buy her the company of a man?

8

Sexual Economics: His and Hers

IN MARCH 2008, Eliot Spitzer was forced to resign his position as governor of New York, steeped in scandal over his involvement with the Emperor's Club VIP escort service. Spitzer had racked up over $80,000 in bills for services that are, even in the free-wheeling Empire State, decidedly illegal—as he no doubt knew, having previously served as New York's attorney general. In the media frenzy that followed, reporters discovered that some of the world's wealthiest men had, like Spitzer, paid handsomely for the services of Emperor's Club escorts.

For many of us less tycoonish proletarians, an astonishing part of the scandal was how little escorting $80,000 would buy from this particular enterprise, whose website advertised a "social introduction service for those accustomed to excellence." The website specialized in introducing "gentlemen of exceptional standards" to women who included "fashion models, pageant winners and exquisite students." To make consumers' decisions easier, the website included prices in American dollars, British pounds, and euros, with a wide choice of female companions ranked from three diamonds to seven diamonds, depending on "the model's character and the grace with which she handles public relations/interactions." Alluring photos of the women in high-fashion, though typically low-coverage, outfits drew attention to their stunningly graceful curves, if not their social graces. For the company of a woman ranked with seven diamonds (presumably for having the most character and grace), a fellow would have to shell out $3,100 for just one hour's worth of escorting. If he wanted a twenty-four-hour period of escortship, the bill would be $31,000 (more than enough to buy a fully equipped new Prius). Potential customers interested in something slightly less pricey could settle for a three-diamond model at a mere $1,000 an hour.

What some men pay for an hour's worth of a woman's company, other men pay for a lifetime's. The going rate for a wife in Afghanistan, as reported by the *Guardian,* is £2,000 (about $3,140). Although this might sound like pocket change to one of the Emperor Club's VIPs, it is two years' income for a typical Afghan. Down in sub-Saharan Africa and across many parts of Asia, the cost of a bride likewise runs to more than a man's entire annual income. Most men in those countries will have to save every penny even to be considered as a potential husband, and many still won't have enough to qualify.

Why are men willing to pay so much for the company of a woman? This question is as much about mammalian biology as economics. It's the question at the heart of a thorny issue about whether men's and women's psychologies are the same or different. While the sexes are often more alike than dissimilar, here we examine an important reproductive difference between them. We will see how this simple biological difference in reproduction provides insight into much more than prostitution and marriage. It also shapes how men and women make decisions about which products to buy in a recession, how big a tip to leave at a restaurant, and even how high a credit bill they are willing to run up. To explain how, we next introduce you to the "his" and "hers" versions of our subselves.

WHY DO MEN PAY SO MUCH FOR THE COMPANY OF A WOMAN?

Economist Siwan Anderson studies *bride price*—the payment made by a groom's family to the family of his future bride. Anderson contrasts the bride price with *dowry,* a payment made by a bride's family to the groom's at the time of marriage. While people in Western societies may be more familiar with the concept of dowry, bride price is actually much more prevalent around the world. *Murdock's World Ethnographic Atlas* of 1,167 preindustrial societies shows that bride price is found in fully two-thirds of the world's societies, whereas dowry is found in less than 4 percent.

Why is bride price so prevalent? Anderson believes that bride price has generally served, at least in part, as payment for a woman's fertility. The price of a bride has historically been linked to virginity, with young, healthy virgins commanding the highest prices, and women who already have children often not bringing any bride price at all.

In the language of evolutionary biology, the economics of bride price are linked to the biological principle of *minimum parental investment*. In any mammalian species, humans included, reproduction requires females, at a minimum, to carry an energetically hungry fetus for several months and then nurse it afterward. Males, by contrast, are biologically exempt from paying the high cost of reproduction. The minimum male requirement is a donation of sperm.

Human males don't get a completely free ride, though. Because human babies are born especially helpless, their chances of survival and success in life increase dramatically if the father hangs around to provide resources for the infant and the mother. So before a woman agrees to the possibility of becoming pregnant and incurring the high biological costs of reproduction, she and her family often demand evidence that a potential suitor is willing and able to provide resources. Forking over a substantial portion of his income, whether by paying a bride price or purchasing a diamond engagement ring, is, for the man, like making a down payment, indicating a commitment to stick around and provide resources over the long haul.

In a thought-provoking paper on sexual economics, social psychologists Roy Baumeister and Kathleen Vohs argue that this biological sex difference in reproduction leads to a situation in which men are willing to pay for sex and women set the price—in the form of money, commitment, or other resources. If the man is not willing to commit resources over the long haul, then the woman may demand a high onetime price for her affections, like the escorts at the Emperor's Club. Baumeister and Vohs argue that men are motivated to seek sex at the lowest possible price, whereas women are motivated to get the highest price possible. From this perspective, sex for women is more of a cost, whereas for men it's more of an opportunity.

Consider the minimum standard you would require before you would consider someone as a marriage or dating partner. For example, what is the minimum level of intelligence you would require in a person before you'd consider marrying him or her? Now consider this: Would that standard change if you were only thinking about a sexual partner? For instance, what is the minimum intelligence you would need to consider having a one-night stand with a person (assuming you'd be willing to do such a thing and that no one would ever find out about it)?

When Doug and his colleagues asked college students about their minimum standards for different types of relationships, men and women had very similar standards for a date (seeking at least an average IQ). The sexes also converged in their criteria for a marriage partner (for which only above-average applicants need apply). But for sexual partners, especially one-night stands, men and women parted company. Women would not sleep with a guy unless he scored well above average in intelligence. When a man isn't going to stick around, the woman demands more for the pleasure of her intimate company—sometimes even $31,000 for just one day. But men were willing to have sex with a woman even if she was well below average in intelligence. (Is she able to tie her own shoes? No? Well, that's not really so important.)

There isn't anything peculiarly American about American males' lower standards for sexual partners. David Schmitt and his team of 118 researchers from six different continents found the same pattern in all fifty-two societies they examined. But all of these studies examined only what people were willing to report on questionnaires. What if men and women were offered a real opportunity for a one-night stand? Would they still respond so differently?

A now classic study in the 1980s had a member of the opposite sex approach students on campus and say, "I have been noticing you around campus. I find you to be very attractive." Before the student could recover from the possible shock of this very direct compliment, the person asked, "Would you go to bed with me?"

How would you have reacted to this come-on? If you are a woman, the odds are pretty high you would have said no. In fact, 100 percent of women said no to the request. And it wasn't because the guy was otherwise scary or unattractive. If he instead asked, "Would you go out with me?" over 50 percent of the women said yes.

But if you are a man, we'd bet money on a different outcome. When this total stranger propositioned them for casual sex, over 70 percent of men said yes. In fact, men were more likely to agree to go to bed than to go on a date. Some of the guys even asked, "Do we have to wait till tonight?" And the few men who did say no were simultaneously thankful and apologetic, saying things like, "Oh, thanks for asking, but I can't. I just got engaged."

A decade later, after the AIDS epidemic had become public, the researchers conducted the same study again. Alas, nothing had changed: over 70 percent of men again said, "Sure!" while 0 percent of the women were willing, often reacting with irritation and some variant of "Get lost, creep!"

This sex difference in wariness about having a one-night stand makes sense in terms of the basic biological sex difference in minimum parental investment. If a woman gets pregnant, she will have to pay a high biological cost: she'll have to carry a fetus, then nurse an infant, and then care for a child for years afterward. This is true regardless of whether her pregnancy stems from a one-night encounter with a charming stranger or from the thousandth night of conjugal bliss with her loving, dedicated husband. If a man has a one-night stand, on the other hand, he can recover his caloric investment by eating an extra piece of bacon for breakfast the next morning.

I LOVE YOU . . . SORT OF

Imagine you're a woman and your new romantic partner says, "I love you," for the very first time. How would you react? Would you be thrilled? Or might you be a little suspicious? A man's saying, "I love you," implies a desire to invest more than just the time it takes to im-plant sperm and suggests that he might even stick around to help raise the children. But talk is cheap, and because such verbal commit-ments can be broken, women are often suspicious of the intentions be-hind a man's profession of love.

Women and men have been shown to have different reactions the first time a new partner professes his or her love. The sex difference stems from whether these three words of loving assurance are said be-fore or after the new couple has started having sex. Women are hap-pier to hear "I love you" afterward, whereas men are happier to hear it before the couple becomes intimate.

Why? Perhaps men take a woman's loving words as a signal that he is better positioned to experience carnal lovemaking in the near fu-ture. But after the fact, hearing "I love you" from a woman might sound more like "Don't you dare leave me!" In fact, men of the non-committal "unrestricted" variety (those gold Porsche drivers we met in the last chapter) are rather unhappy to hear "I love you" from a woman after sex has already occurred, perhaps because these fellows were hoping to reap the sexual benefit without having to pay a com-mitment cost.

Josh Ackerman, a professor at MIT who led the "I love you" study, explains that "saying 'I love you' is a negotiation process." When men and women negotiate a relationship, both are trying to avoid a differ-ent evolutionary mistake. For women, it would be a big mistake to im-pulsively trust a partner's declaration of "I love you" and gamble on a sexual relationship without the man's investment. For men, the big mistake would be failure to communicate commitment and potentially lose a sexual relationship.

In fact, the study found that men and women didn't just differ in their reactions to hearing "I love you"; they also differed in who said these words first in a relationship. When Ackerman and his team first surveyed people about their beliefs, most people thought that women tend to be the first to say, "I love you." After all, women are supposed to be mushy romantic types who express their feelings. But in actual relationships, men were first to profess their love 70 percent of the time, saying, "I love you" forty-two days earlier in a relationship than women, on average!

An evolutionary perspective suggests that women are warranted in their wariness when a man claims to be falling in love so quickly. Better to wait and see if he produces other signs of continuing commitment, such as, perhaps, a diamond ring worth a few months' salary.

ARE MEN COMPLETELY NONDISCRIMINATING?

Although many men might be perfectly willing to hop into bed with a complete stranger, most real sexual opportunities do not come without a cost. In the real world, a man rarely meets a woman on campus who offers him a no-cost hour of sex. A guy pursuing a friendly gal in a singles bar might, at the very least, have to pay for a few drinks and spend several hours demonstrating his charm and lack of psychological impediments. And what begins as a potential one-night stand might well turn into a longer relationship and even lead to marriage down the line.

While men have lower standards than women when it comes to sex, men are not completely nondiscriminating. After the Eliot Spitzer scandal, for example, several media sources made the Emperor's Club website available to the public. An inspection of the escorts on the site reveals two features they had in common: youth and beauty. All the highly priced escorts were uniformly physically attractive, and all were in their twenties. The women were probably several decades younger than their wealthy middle-aged male clients.

In *Bringing Down the House*, Ben Mezrich wrote about a group of MIT nerds who won millions playing blackjack in Las Vegas. In researching the book, he interviewed a woman named April who had worked as a stripper at one of Las Vegas's top gentlemen's clubs, where she made several thousand dollars a night as a lap dancer. If she was willing to make additional "house calls," she could earn up to $3,000 an hour. At the time of the interview, however, April was twenty-five years old and explained that she was no longer able to command as high a price for her company. As Mezrich put it, "She was already considered old in her line of work."

Men's preference for youthful and beautiful women is not limited to the patrons of strip clubs and escort services. Social scientists studying people's mate preferences have found that men generally prefer and marry partners younger than themselves, whereas women are interested in somewhat older men. Researchers initially speculated that this difference was linked to gender roles perpetuated by American media. But that explanation did not hold up to careful examination. For starters, men's attraction to younger women is in no way limited to American or even Western society. When Rich Keefe and Doug investigated singles ads and actual marriage ages around the world, including places that had never been exposed to American media, men everywhere preferred women in their early twenties. Even fifteen-year-old boys fantasized about college-age women, who are eighteen to twenty-two years old, despite the fact that the young guys are painfully aware that college women want nothing to do with them.

Why are both older men and teenage boys around the world attracted to women in their early twenties? If you asked a man, he might simply say that women of this age have the most attractive features—a curvaceous figure combined with youthful hair and well-toned skin. But this explanation only provides a surface-level proximate reason. It does not address the deeper question of why the combination of features found in a woman of twenty-two is generally more attractive than the features found in a woman of forty-two, sixty-two, or eighty-two.

From an evolutionary perspective, though, there is a clear reason—women in their early twenties are most fertile. Women at this age not only conceive more easily but also have many more childbearing years remaining. Even if a man says, "I don't want children," his brain is nevertheless wired to light up when he sees a woman whose smooth skin, youthful hair, and rounded hips signal fertility.

The preference for youthful beauty can be seen most clearly in men with enough wealth and status to choose between many possible mates. Multimillionaire Donald Trump has been married three times, when he was thirty-one, forty-four, and fifty-four. He met each of his wives while she was in her twenties and married her shortly thereafter.

King Henry VIII was first married at age seventeen to a woman in her early twenties. He married five other women over the next several decades of his life. His oldest wife, whom he married when he was fifty-one, was herself all of thirty-one on the day of the wedding (he had met her when she was still in her twenties).

Male rulers throughout history, including Roman and Chinese emperors and Middle Eastern sultans, have frequently had hundreds of wives and concubines—and generally all of these men had a preference for young and beautiful virgins. Every year at Swaziland's annual Reed Festival, tens of thousands of young maidens dance topless before King Mswati III, hoping to be chosen as his next wife. Rajinder Singh, the fabulously wealthy Sixth Maharajah of the state of Patiala in India, had 350 wives. There are clear evolutionary benefits to desiring to fornicate with so many young and fertile females. Ismael Ibn Sharif, who ruled Morocco at the turn of the eighteenth century and kept hundreds of wives, had over one thousand recorded children.

The equation of youth + beauty = fertility is even more true in traditional societies than in the developed world. Rich Keefe and Doug found that the tendency for older men to marry younger women was more rather than less pronounced outside North America and Europe. Why? In the United States, Canada, and Europe, women tend to stay beautiful for many years longer than their counterparts in Third World societies, who begin having children earlier and have less access to adequate nutrition, health care, and beauty-enhancing consumer goods. In traditional societies, even Demi Moore and Jennifer Aniston would look their age.

DESIGNING A MATE: HERS VERSUS HIS

Thus far, our discussion of sex differences has been somewhat one-sided: women bear the children, which makes them selective in choosing partners; men expend energy and resources to gain access to women, especially when the women are young and fertile. But if a woman were buying a man, would she be shopping for the same features as a man seeks in a woman or for something different?

Norm Li trained as an economist before earning a PhD in social psychology. He used his economics background to solve an important puzzle regarding men's and women's mate preferences. Some researchers had found big sex differences, with men and women saying they looked for very different characteristics in a mate. But others had found much smaller sex differences. The latter group accused the former of exaggerating the sex differences, arguing that men and women really want more or less the same thing in a mate.

Li suspected that the question of sex differences and similarities had been ignoring a fundamental economic idea: the difference between luxuries and necessities. If, as many previous researchers had been doing, we merely ask, "What would you like in a mate?" we'll get an answer analogous to what we'd get if we asked what you'd like in a car, a house, or a vacation. Whether you are a man or woman, you might say you'd very much like an all-expense-paid week on a secluded, private beach in Hawaii with a charming and sensitive traveling companion who looks like a movie star, followed by a drive home from the airport to your architect-designed home in your sporty new Mercedes. But of course, real people are not in a position to afford everything, so most of us need to settle.

Li wanted to know what would happen if he had men and women work within a more limited (and realistic) budget when it came to mating. He asked men and women to design their ideal mate from a menu that included several desirable characteristics, such as physical attractiveness, social status and resources, warmth and kindness, creativity, and so on. To distinguish those characteristics that were necessities as opposed to luxuries, people were given a budget of "mate dollars" to spend on designing their ideal mate. If they spent more on one feature, they would have less left to spend on other features.

When people had a high mate budget, men and women wanted similar things in a mate: both sexes wanted everything—the equivalent of a kind and affectionate movie star with a PhD, a villa in southern France, and a great sense of humor. But when faced with a more realistic, lower budget, men and women started spending very differently, prioritizing their necessities in distinct ways. Men placed first priority on physical attractiveness, with kindness second and status and resources way down in the list. Women, on the other hand, placed first priority on a man's status and resources, followed by his kindness, with physical attractiveness way down in the list.

This sex difference is, once again, not something peculiar to North America. Like American women, Japanese, Zambian, and Serbian women rate good financial prospects in a mate as more important than do men in those countries. Women everywhere place a great deal of emphasis on a mate's status, ambition, and resources, regardless of his physical attractiveness. Men, by contrast, tend to prefer the good-looking woman regardless of her social class.

WHY DO WOMEN SOMETIMES PAY FOR MEN?

Given that women are the evolutionarily more valuable sex, it makes sense that most of the world's societies impose a bride price, with men paying good money for a young and fertile wife. But then why do several societies have the custom of dowry—a payment made by the bride's family at the time of a wedding? Why would women ever have to pay for men?

An important clue comes from asking which societies have bride price and which have dowry. The more common practice of bride price is found in the majority of traditional societies, which tend to be poor. Dowry only arose more recently with the emergence of large nation-states, such as in China, India, and parts of Europe. In these societies, citizens for the first time in history were able to accumulate substantial wealth, and families were able to pass their accumulated wealth, and thereby their status, on to their children. The increased wealth created a new opportunistic niche for dowry.

But the relatively modern custom of dowry is not the mirror image of bride price. Whereas bride price entails a man paying for sexual access to a fertile woman, dowry does not entail a woman paying for sexual access to a fertile man. As we saw in the college campus study, a woman can have that for free. Instead, dowry involves a woman's family making an investment to ensure that the daughter ends up with a husband who is well positioned to make investments in their grandchildren.

In "Sociology of Bride Price and Dowry," Shalini Randeria and Leela Visaria explain that "dowry is property given *to the bride* by her kin, to take with her to her husband's family." Dowries are essentially resource supplements that a bride receives from her kin to start a new family with her husband, who is required to bring his own resources as well. As Randeria and Visaria explain, dowry is "property which belongs to the woman, and which may be controlled jointly by her husband, who does not have the right to dispose of it." If the couple were to divorce, for example, the dowry would revert to the woman.

In a society where some families have much more status and wealth than others, a woman's family can make an investment in a daughter's future family by paying a dowry that will allow her to secure a husband from one of those wealthy, high-status families. But rather than payment for access to a fertile man, a dowry reflects a woman's family investing in an alliance that promises to provide resources for her and her offspring.

HIS AND HERS MATING SUBSELVES

The recurring argument in this book is that our choices are guided by seven subselves, which take turns steering decision making. Most of the subselves work similarly in men and women, because both sexes needed to solve similar ancestral challenges. When it comes to avoiding disease, for example, men and women need to do similar things to ward off pathogens. But when it comes to mating, men and women face a slightly different set of challenges.

The mating game involves solving two very different evolutionary challenges: acquiring mates and retaining them. As a consequence, we have different subselves assigned to each task. And not only do these subselves influence decisions that go far beyond sex and mating, but they also come in a his and hers version.

SWINGING SINGLES: THE MATE-ACQUISITION GAME

Back during our discussion of home economics, we observed that people use different rules to negotiate in different types of relationships. The decision about who pays for dinner, for example, is different when we're dining out with our family or with our coworkers. When you're trying to woo a new lover, the rules change once again.

Both the man and the woman are trying to show off their positive attributes. Both sexes, for example, become more generous tippers when their mate-acquisition subself has been primed. But while both sexes put on displays of blatant generosity, men and women are actually advertising different things.

Sex differences in the mate-acquisition game stem from the biological principle of minimum parental investment discussed earlier. Singles ads written by a man are more likely to advertise his own status or wealth ("company president," "own home near beach," "make six figures," "enjoy skiing and yachting"), showing off the human equivalent of a peacock's feathers. Women's ads are instead likely to specify that their future partner must meet some minimum level of status or wealth ("college education a must," "must make six figures"). And on the receiving end, men are more likely to respond to ads written by women in the years of peak fertility (perhaps accompanied by an attractive photo), whereas women are more likely to respond to ads that advertise men's income and educational levels.

Long before there were personal ads, of course, men and women did their best to advertise to the opposite sex. Throughout history and across human cultures, young men in their teens and twenties have taken great risks to acquire wealth and status—and to show it off. One consequence of all this showing off is that men are much more likely to die in accidents or conflicts with other men, especially during their teens and twenties, when the competition for mates is fiercest. In Spain, for example, men aged twenty-four to thirty-five are, compared to women of the same age, fully five times more likely to die in accidents and homicides rather than from natural disease processes. In areas where there is especially high income disparity (where the local poor are especially poorer than the local *ricos*), it's even worse—with those desperate young men being six times more likely to die in accidents or violent altercations. And it isn't just a Spanish machismo thing; the exact same pattern is seen in data from eighty-two countries around the globe. Young men everywhere are literally killing themselves for attention and status.

In dozens of our own studies, we have activated men's mate-acquisition subself by having them look at photos of attractive women or imagining going on a date or watching a romantic movie. We repeatedly find that a lustful state of mind leads men to start showing off and competing in various ways: becoming more reckless, adventurous, creative, aggressive, heroic, independent, and inclined to spend money on flashy products. In effect, men motivated to attract a mate turn into peacocks and scream to the world, "Look at me! I stand out from the crowd!"

ALL THE SINGLE LADIES

Women too want to stand out. But instead of showing off their wealth and bravado like men, women advertise something different. When a woman's mate-acquisition subself is running the show, she becomes more agreeable, cooperative, and helpful. Ladies in a romantic frame of mind are more supportive and likelier to go along with the group; they're also eager to assist other people in need. But this veneer of benevolence doesn't mean that mating-minded women are less competitive. Rather, the competition involves being the nicest, the most supportive, and the most helpful.

Recall that both men and women become more generous tippers when their mate-acquisition subself is in charge. Why? For a man, tipping is a way to advertise his wealth. Leaving large bills on a table or making a generous charitable donation shows that a man can afford to give money away. We know that giving money to charity for romance-minded men is about the money because when men are given the opportunity to be helpful in a way that doesn't involve money or heroism, having romance on the mind no longer leads them to be more helpful. Activating the mate-acquisition subself did not lead men to want to go out and pick up trash in the park or do volunteer work. Men seem to ask: What's the point in helping if there is no opportunity to flaunt money or machismo?

For a woman, on the other hand, generous tipping is one way to advertise her caring nature. Leaving a large tip or making a donation can be a way for a woman to demonstrate that she cares about the well-being of others. As long as someone is around to see the act, a mate-attraction motive leads women to become more helpful, regardless of whether it involves money. Mating-minded women are more eager to volunteer to serve soup at a homeless shelter, dedicate their time to teach underprivileged kids to read, or spend the weekends nursing sick people back to health at the hospital. Whereas men want to draw attention to the size of their charitable spending, women want to draw attention to the charitable nature of the spending.

Women seek to stand out in another way that gets to the heart of men's and women's biological difference in reproduction. Unlike men, women's mate-acquisition subself does not lead them to throw caution to the wind and take brazen risks. But there is one telling exception. Women take more risks if doing so enhances their appearance. Women primed with a mate-attraction motive are more willing to take diet pills, for example, even when they know that the pills can cause heart problems later in life. And they are more willing to tan their bodies to enhance their appearance, even when they are aware that doing so can cause skin cancer.

Women go to great lengths to be the fairest in the land and to advertise their beauty. They spend a great deal of time, energy, and money choosing clothes, accessories, and shades of makeup that enhance their attractiveness. Yearly spending on women's fashion apparel in the United States alone is well over $100 billion—more than twice the amount the entire US national government spends on education!

Americans also spend $11 billion per year on medical interventions to improve their looks, and 92 percent of the customers are women. Many women regularly risk infection, disability, and death to have their bodies surgically cut into, invasively rejiggered, and stitched together—all in the hope of enhancing signs of apparent fertility. The most popular cosmetic surgical procedure is breast augmentation, but the options on the menu include everything from facelifts to tummy tucks to the Brazilian butt lift, in which a woman's own fat is transferred to enhance the shape and size of her buttocks. And if surgery sounds too invasive, consider the most popular nonsurgical procedure—a Botox injection, which involves pumping a paralyzing toxin into the facial muscles to reduce wrinkling around the eyes and mouth. Besides all that, women spend additional billions on books, magazines, and fitness classes designed to help them reduce the age-related accumulation of midsection fat and tone their leg muscles to look more like college students.

Social psychologist Sarah Hill has found that women regard money spent on beauty as a necessity rather than a luxury. Hill and her colleagues examined what happens to women's spending on beauty products in economic downturns. Normally during economic recessions, consumer spending decreases, especially on nonessential luxuries. But spending on necessities can actually increase in times of recession. For example, someone who normally eats cheap Top Ramen noodles once a week and homemade gourmet pasta on the other nights might need to start eating Top Ramen daily in a recession, increasing his or her proportionate spending on such inexpensive foods to ensure at least a bare minimum of calories.

When Hill and her colleagues examined women's spending in economic recessions, they found that while economic downturns lead women to spend less on most products, they spend more money on products that enhance appearance. For instance, sales figures from one of the world's biggest cosmetics companies, L'Oreal, showed that during 2008, a year when the rest of the economy was suffering record declines in sales, L'Oreal experienced sales growth of 5.3 percent. Why the seemingly irrational splurging on cosmetics during economic recessions? Because when times are tough, it becomes even more important to attract one of those desirable guys with a good job. Just as economic inequality magnifies men's competitiveness, economic hard times also magnify women's investments in their appearance.

WEDDING BONDS: THE MATE-RETENTION GAME

A while back, one of our wives took a course in which the professor recommended a rational economic approach to resolving conflicts in relationships. The idea was that one spouse should provide rewards to the partner in exchange for getting something he or she desired in return. For example, if the man finds sex more rewarding than does the woman, but she likes to eat in nice restaurants more than he does, the wife could simply make sexual favors contingent on the man shelling out for an upscale meal. The professor's advice followed directly from the model of rational economics. But although this Wall Street approach might make sense in an interaction between a prostitute and a john, we actually don't recommend that you try it at home.

Exchanges between long-term romantic partners are not like those between customers and shopkeepers, but they're also not quite like those during the initial courtship. From an evolutionary perspective, human males and females form partnerships (such as marriage) because those partnerships have historically benefitted their children. Because those children share their parents' genes, mom's and dad's genetic interests become a bit sibling-like. But despite their common genetic incentives, spouses' interests are not identical to those between brothers and sisters. When our sibling goes on a date with a great new romantic partner, we are likely to count this as a benefit; if our spouse became involved with a new lover, on the other hand, we'd likely count this as a substantial loss and sufficient grounds to terminate the relationship completely.

Divorces in particular highlight that blood is thicker than wedding wine. When romantic pairs split up, formerly loving couples who once comfortably shared million-dollar homes begin to fight bitterly over every compact disc, fork, spoon, and folding chair. Many families continue to support and care about their prodigal sons, but there's typically not much love lost between former spouses, and any exchanges of resources that do occur often involve both sides feeling cheated.

The rules for marriage partners also differ in another way from the initial rules for dating partners. Although women tend to be choosier than men when it comes to short-term relationships (recall women's higher standards for a one-night stand), men and women are more alike than different when it comes to marriage partners. Men looking for a marriage partner want every bit as many IQ points as women do. This makes sense in terms of human evolution. It is possible for a man to have offspring in the typical mammalian style—with very little investment (some of our male ancestors benefitted greatly from having lots of one-night stands). But our species differs from 95 percent of other mammals in that human males typically stay around and contribute resources after their young are born. Sometimes men even stay around for the rest of their lives, faithfully bringing home their paychecks, fixing leaks in the roof, and taking out the garbage. Thus, when it comes to getting married, as compared to having an affair, men are in for a much higher commitment of resources. Hence, men up their standards considerably for marriage partners.

JEALOUSY: HIS AND HERS

Although men and women are more similar than different when it comes to their standards for marriage partners, wedding bonds and parenthood don't completely erase all sex differences. Even after a couple has a child, there remains a nagging biological wrinkle called *paternal uncertainty*. Barring one of those movie-plot exchanges of babies in the nursery, a woman has no doubts about whether a given child is hers or not. For a man, however, there is never complete certainty. Even if his wife has been completely faithful, as in the vast majority of cases, the man does not know this for certain unless he can be sure he was with her every minute of that fateful ovulatory cycle nine months ago. Studies show that somewhere between 3 and 10 percent of children are not the biological descendants of the man listed as the father on their birth certificate. To add legal insult to this genetic injury, a divorced man is, in many jurisdictions, required to continue making child-support payments, even if DNA tests establish that he is not the biological father of a child born during his marriage.

Paternal uncertainty leads to an interesting sex difference in the triggers for jealousy. Imagine that the person with whom you've been seriously involved has become interested in someone else. What would make you more upset: (1) your partner falls in love with and forms a deep emotional attachment to the other person, or (2) your partner has sexual intercourse one night with that other person?

When evolutionary psychologist David Buss and his colleagues asked this question, they found that men and women had very different reactions. Approximately 80 percent of women said they would be more upset to discover that their man had formed an emotional attachment to another woman. For men, the findings were reversed. Although guys did not find it especially pleasant to think about their woman forming an emotional attachment, the majority of men said they would be even more distressed to discover a sexual infidelity. Other researchers have found the same sex difference in Korea, Japan, Germany, the Netherlands, and Sweden. In fact, even though men are more likely to be unfaithful in a relationship, it is a woman's sexual infidelity that is more likely to lead to divorce. And it gets a lot more serious than that—around the world, jealousy is a common cause of homicide, with men being more than four times as likely to kill over jealousy.

On the other side of the equation, although a woman does not have to worry about unintentionally raising someone else's child, she does stand to lose her husband's resource contributions if he falls in love with another woman. Given that the average man will jump into bed with a strange woman who approaches him on a college campus, a wife may appreciate that her partner's sexual tryst does not necessarily mean he's deeply committed to the other woman. Although she will likely be far from thrilled by her husband's philandering, she may have considerably more concerns about his emotional attachments. The emotional attachment is a stronger indicator that he might divert resources from his current family to the other woman. The psychology of men's and women's jealousy seems to have been shaped by subtle biological differences in reproduction. And as we discuss next, those subtle differences can even affect your credit score.

SEXUAL SUPPLY AND DEMAND

Macon and Columbus, Georgia, are two cities less than a hundred miles apart. They share a similar history and economic climate. Yet the residents of the two cities have drastically different spending habits. The good folks down in Columbus carry massive credit card debt, averaging $3,479 more per person than their fellow Georgians over in Macon. Why the big difference? An important clue comes from a second difference between the two cities. Whereas in fiscally responsible Macon there are only 0.78 single men for every woman, in debt-strapped Columbus there are 1.18 single men for every woman.

In their classic book *Too Many Women?*, Marcia Guttentag and Paul Secord argue that fluctuations in sex ratios—the ratio of adult men to women in a particular geographical location—have dramatic effects on sexual behaviors. When there are more women, as happens during and after major wars, there is more promiscuity, people get married later, and more children are born out of wedlock. When there are more men, on the other hand, guys start getting more committal, marrying earlier, running around less, and investing more in their families.

All this makes sense in terms of basic mating economics. When women are scarce, they call the shots, demanding that men commit more time and resources to them alone. But when men are scarce and have easy access to multiple women, guys are less willing to commit to any single woman, and women must consequently lower their demands. Guttentag and Secord even argue that shifting sex ratios in the population had a lot to do with the sexual revolution and "free love" ethos of the 1960s and 1970s in the United States. During this time of sexual experimentation, there were more women than men.

If you've ever seen the reality television programs *The Bachelor* or *The Bachelorette*, you've observed the behavioral consequences of an imbalanced sex ratio. On *The Bachelor*, where twenty-five women spend several weeks vying for one man's hand in marriage, the women become catty and malicious toward each other, while growing more promiscuous and more tolerant of their man's promiscuity. The ladies are visibly annoyed as they watch their "boyfriend" make out with other women and even share an overnight "fantasy suite" with three different ladies on consecutive nights. But when the sex ratio dictates that the man can call the shots, there is little the women can do.

In contrast, on *The Bachelorette*, where twenty-five men vie to propose to one lucky lady, the men are chivalrous and refined in front of their potential girlfriend, telling her how much they want to settle down and start a family. Meanwhile the boys brutishly get into fistfights with each other when she's not around. The sex ratio's effect on violence is no laughing matter. In India, sex ratios vary greatly among different regions, and a 1 percent change in sex ratio is associated with a 5 percent change in the murder rate! Homicides increase dramatically when women are scarce.

How does all of this relate to credit card debt in Georgia? Because there are more available guys in Columbus, each guy has to compete harder for one of those scarce women. One way to do that is to spend money, buy flashier cars, and take dates out to more expensive restaurants. When Vlad and his team calculated sex ratios in 134 cities across America, they found a striking relationship between the sex ratio, the number of credit cards people owned, and the average debt a person had. The fewer the women in a city, the higher the debt and the more credit cards people had.

Although the results were consistent with mating economics, it was not certain whether it was men or women who were spending more. So the team moved to the laboratory to conduct more rigorous studies. College students were shown photographs of crowds of other students. Some saw photographs in which the majority of people were men; others saw photos in which the majority were women. Then people in the study were presented with an actual opportunity to get $20 tomorrow or $35 in a month. Sex ratio did not affect women's choices, but men who had seen a lone woman surrounded by other men became more impulsive and chose immediate payoffs. Never mind that the more delayed option presented a much better investment opportunity (you try to find an investment that yields 75 percent interest per month). When women were scarce, men wanted money now.

In another study, people read a news article from the *Chicago Tribune* describing the local population as either having more single men or more single women. One headline read, for example, "Fewer Women for Every Man." Other people read a story that reversed the headline to say there were fewer men for every woman. After reading the article, people indicated how much money they would save each month from a paycheck, as well as how much money they would borrow on a credit card for immediate expenditures.

When women were scarce, men cut their savings by 42 percent. If the men felt that they still didn't have enough money for things they needed now, they increased their credit card debt by 84 percent. And where did the money go? To the women, of course. When women were scarce, men paid more for Valentine's Day gifts and more for engagement rings ($278 more, in fact). On the other side of the equation, women who felt they were scarcer were in fact harder to impress. After they'd just read that there were lots of single men in the area, they fully expected those hopeful fellows to spend more on gifts and engagement rings.

The financial consequences of sex ratio are on full display in Las Vegas—a city with 1.16 men for every woman, one of the most male-skewed cities in America. Las Vegas often lures men (and their wallets) with the promise of an abundance of females, but in reality casino floors are flush with many more men than women. And when a man in a casino is surrounded by many other men and only a few ladies, he is most likely to lay down the big bets from which casinos profit.

The effects of sex ratios extend beyond the casino floor or even the United States. China, for example, currently has a surplus of 40 million extra single men. As a consequence, the practice of bride price has been returning to China in full force. Some areas have seen a four-fold increase in bride price in the last decade, and half of the men in the countryside can no longer even afford a bride, which sometimes costs as much as three hundred cows. Men from Asian countries with a shortage of women are now paying large sums of money for wives from other countries such as Vietnam. In turn, the men in Vietnam are beginning to feel the need for more resources, just like the good ole boys down in Columbus, Georgia.

BLOKES, SHEILAS, AND WALLETS

Maybe you've never bought a spouse for £2,000 or engaged the services of an "elite social introduction service" for $31,000 a night. But it's nearly certain that your decisions have been affected by whether your mating subself is of the his or hers type.

If you're a typical woman, you have probably spent more dollars than you'd care to count on makeup, hair products, and stylish clothes, all designed to make you appear more like the prototypical fertile member of our species. And without your even being aware of it, your spending patterns have likely been influenced by your own ovulatory cycles and by the economy's financial cycles (as when women boost their spending on beauty products during an economic decline).

If you're a typical man, you have spent countless dollars buying drinks, flowers, and dinners to woo women. If you haven't conspicuously thrown away money on flashy cars, expensive watches, and drinks for the house, then maybe you've quietly purchased tasteful gifts for that special woman to whom you want to prove your commitment. Your spending patterns have been influenced not only by daily fluctuations in your testosterone levels but also by the local ratio of blokes to sheilas. And although much of this has been happening outside your awareness, it has reflected the operation of a brain designed to make these decisions in a way that is, ultimately, deeply rational.

OUR TOUR OF the rational animal's habitat has so far included visits with a wide cast of colorful characters, including the studded rocker Elvis Presley, the fast-spending rapper MC Hammer, the technological visionary Steve Jobs, and a high-priced Las Vegas lap dancer named April. Our journey in search of humankind's deeper nature has taken us around the world, from Amazonia to Zambia, with stops in Macon, Georgia, and a gentleman's club in Albuquerque, New Mexico. Next we bring it all back home, revisiting each of the subselves inside your head and paying special attention to the various parasites who are trying to sneak in there every day. As we'll see, these parasites try to turn your own subselves against you, exploiting your otherwise smart evolutionary biases to sell you products, solicit your contributions, and otherwise take you for a ride.

9

Deep Rationality Parasites

THE EUROPEAN CUCKOO, whose distinctive call is immortalized in the sound of the cuckoo clock, would not qualify for a good-parenting award. Whereas most birds sit patiently on their eggs to keep them warm and protected, the cuckoo simply deposits its precious offspring-to-be in a total stranger's nest. To trick a bird of another species into caring for its young, the cuckoo first slyly removes an egg from the unsuspecting host's nest, replacing it with one of its own, which often closely mimics the pilfered egg's appearance.

But the scam doesn't end there. As soon as the young cuckoo hatches, its first act is to dispose of any other eggs in the nest, leaving itself as the sole occupant. With the disappearance of their rightful young, the foster parents are now free to devote all their care and attention to their new only child. The hoodwinked parents, commonly a pair of tiny reed warblers, don't appear to notice they are rearing an impostor, which quickly grows to twice the size of its providers. Meanwhile, loving mommy and daddy work like Sisyphus around the clock to keep up with the voracious appetite of the gigantic young cuckoo.

The cuckoo is an especially nefarious social parasite, deviously exploiting the adaptive tendencies of its fellow birds for its own gain. But parasitism isn't a rarity in the animal kingdom. Virtually every successful organism attracts the company of leeches, moochers, stowaways, and manipulators seeking to take advantage of its evolutionary success.

Humans are likewise not exempt from parasites, and our free riders range from microscopic one-celled organisms to other human beings.

Fellow-person parasites often take the form of the various profiteers lurking in our midst, some of whom are adorned in religious robes, political sashes, or freshly pressed business suits. But rather than hiding eggs in our nests, these miscreants seek to swipe our nest eggs.

Consider Bernard Madoff, the former chairman of the NASDAQ stock exchange, who orchestrated the largest financial fraud in US history, bilking investors out of $18 billion (not to be confused with $18 million, which, though still a fortune, would be a thousand times less). Just as cuckoos exploit the adaptive instincts of their fellow birds, Madoff exploited those of his fellow man. In the same way a cuckoo tricks unsuspecting birds by producing eggs that resemble those laid by their victims, Madoff preyed on people with whom he shared common bonds of affinity and religion. A well-respected member of a tightknit Jewish community, Madoff targeted fellow in-group members such as Steven Spielberg, Elie Wiesel, Mort Zuckerman, and Frank Lautenberg, as well as Yeshiva University and the Women's Zionist Organization of America. Operating as an insider, Madoff approached individuals of his faith with special offers. Although people are naturally suspicious of anything that sounds too good to be true, a common heritage with Madoff provided a reason to trust that he was offering an inside deal. This sense of tribal affinity also made it difficult to ask hard questions. Interrogating a fellow member of the inner circle for hard information is like demanding receipts from your beloved Aunt Mildred—you just don't question family. But rather than helping members of the inner circle, who were told their investments were worth $65 billion, old Bernie tricked them into funding the escapades of the Madoff clan.

The reasons people give their savings to those they shouldn't trust are surprisingly similar to the reasons they spend money on things they don't need, can't afford, or don't even really want. Just as in all species there is an arms race between successful organisms and parasites, the same is true for each of our subselves, which are locked in a race with outsiders who seek to take advantage of them. Whether masquerading in the form of helpful individuals, caring politicians, or friendly corporations, these manipulators seek to profit from our evo-lutionary needs by using our ancient wisdom against us. But by discov-ering what they don't want us to know, we can defend ourselves from nefarious malfeasance.

THE EXPLOITATION CONTINUUM

Exploitation doesn't sound like something most people want to be a part of. But it is not always a one-way street. Sometimes the exploiter gives back. Take the relationship between a clown fish and a sea anemone. The clown fish takes advantage of the sea anemone by loi-tering near its poisonous tentacles for safety. But the clown fish re-turns the favor by eating tiny parasites that can harm the sea anemone. The clown fish gets safety and a meal, while the sea anemone gets a much-needed cleaning. Everybody wins. Biologists call this kind of two-way exploitation *symbiotic mutualism*, with each party benefitting the other.

In other cases the exploiter doesn't provide much of a benefit to its host, as when a beetle looking for greener pastures hitches a ride on the back of a bison. Biologists use the term *commensalism* to de-scribe this one-sided relationship, in which one party benefits and the other is neither significantly helped nor harmed. The sticky ties be-tween the remora fish and the whale shark exemplify such relation-ships. Remoras, which have an adhesive disk on the surface of their heads, attach themselves to whale sharks, which tend to be sloppy eaters. When food floats away from the shark's mouth, the small remora unhitches itself and collects the floating scraps of seafood. In this hanger-on relationship, the remora wins, but the shark neither wins nor loses.

But sometimes the exploiter hurts its relationship partner, as when a mosquito or a tick takes a portion of its mammalian host's blood supply. Biologists call this relationship *parasitism*, meaning that one party benefits while the other is harmed. Most parasites have some built-in limits to their greed, since their own welfare depends on the host's survival. If parasites get too greedy, the host might die, as when overzealous viruses kill the organism that provides their meal ticket.

But even nature's checks and balances can't always restrain the immense greed of some parasites, which can literally suck the life right out of their hosts. The digger wasp, for example, paralyzes a caterpillar and then lays its eggs in the caterpillar's still-living body, which provides a source of food when the wasp eggs hatch. The wasp benefits—but the caterpillar is obliterated.

As with animals, other people can exploit us in mutually beneficial ways, as when a clothing advertisement uses our natural responsiveness to beauty to draw attention to a new line of threads that might actually make us more attractive. At other times, human parasites might exploit us in ways that are only a little costly, as when a waiter pretends to give us inside information about the benefits of a more expensive bottle of wine, when its main advantage is that it will allow him to extract a slightly bigger tip. But sometimes human parasites prey on our evolutionary tendencies to suck the life savings right out of us, as pyramid schemers like Bernie Madoff do to their investors.

Let's consider how our ancestral needs open us up to exploitations, from the beneficial to the malignant, by exploring our love-hate relationships with Madison Avenue, Wall Street, and Hollywood Boulevard. Along the way, we'll probe the secret relationships between shoe companies, Hallmark cards, jewelry tycoons, and our occasionally bedazzled subselves.

WHY WE BUY

The word "marketer" doesn't have a positive connotation for most people. It may instead call to mind those advertising hucksters who broadcast "New and Improved!!!" in fluorescent orange letters all over shiny new packaging for a product that was perfectly fine to begin with. But not all Madison Avenue types are bad. Marketers can sometimes be quite helpful—by identifying what people need and then helping them satisfy those needs.

If you are yearning for a car that lessens your carbon footprint, for example, good marketers are eager to identify that desire, make sure such cars are manufactured, and then inform you about the new car's availability and special features. Although marketers are technically exploiting consumers, this exploitation is often mutually beneficial, like the symbiotic relationship between a clown fish and a sea anemone. You want an environmentally friendly car, and marketers want to help you find the vehicle that best meets your needs.

If you have a product or service to market, an evolutionary perspective highlights something very useful: people everywhere have the same evolutionary needs, and those fundamental needs have a profound influence on their decisions.

From Alabama to Zanzibar, all humans need to affiliate with friends, get respect, keep themselves safe from the bad guys, avoid disease, attract a mate, maintain a loving relationship, and care for family. Even if people claim that some of these needs have no effect on their personal choices, we know that all human brains are wired to pursue these ancestral goals. Whether you are aware of it or not, even your desire for that environmentally friendly car may well have been stoked by deeper motives having nothing to do with saving the planet or even gas money (remember the study on "going green to be seen").

Each year people collectively spend billions of dollars on products and services that help fulfill each of our evolutionary needs. The need to affiliate contributes to a $160 billion mobile phone industry (that number is for the United States alone), serving the affiliative need of people so motivated to stay in touch that they text their friends while driving into oncoming traffic (r u kidding!? 2 gd 2 B true! . . . WTF! . . . crash :<). The need for status inspires people to accumulate such giant mounds of stuff that it has spawned an entire new industry whose sole purpose is to store our excess material goodies—the $22.6 billion self-storage industry. The need to keep ourselves safe from the bad guys contributes to the $29 billion home-security industry that rigs our dwelling with alarms to keep away the villains (fence not included in the $29 billion figure—that goes to the $7 billion fencing industry). And the need to avoid pathogens contributes to a $27 billion soap and detergent industry, designed to keep our homes, clothes, and bodies scrubbed clean of all those nasty little microbes.

And if you're all cleaned up and looking for a mate, you might feel inspired to make a contribution to the billion-dollar Internet dating industry or one of the other multi-billion-dollar industries that provide snazzy duds, cosmetics, cologne, cleansing creams, grooming, and gym memberships to make us look good for those dates. Once you meet someone special, the need to hang on to that mate is facilitated by the $70 billion wedding industry (throw in a few billion extra for the honeymoon industry). And if you're not yet broke, the need to care for kin contributes to additional billions spent on relatives young and old, encompassing the $57 billion senior home-care industry and the $21 billion toy industry, which includes princess dolls and action figures based on Walt and Roy O. Disney's classic movies (but the costs of Disney amusements parks, Disney resort hotels, Disney movies, Disney music, the Disney channel, and Disney cruises are not included and go on a separate tab).

The need for friends, safety, status, lovers, and families leads us to fork money over to manufacturers that make products to satisfy these ancestral desires, and the manufacturers fork over a share to the marketers, who make sure we're aware of the options and where to purchase them. So far, so good—everybody wins. But even symbiotic relationships can sometimes enter a grey area. At what point does the relationship between manufacturers, marketers, and consumers cross the line from symbiosis to parasitism? And how can you tell the difference?

GETTING PEOPLE TO PAY MORE AND BUY MORE

If you make a living selling something, the principles of economics suggest that you should seek to sell as many units as you can for the highest possible price. This is much easier said than done, of course. Of all the businesses started in the United States, 34 percent disappear within the first two years, and 56 percent are gone within four. For any would-be capitalist tycoon, the critical questions are how to get people to buy your product in the first place and then how to get people to pay more for your product. From an evolutionary perspective, both problems have a surprisingly simple solution.

Let's say you open a shoe company called the Corner Cobbler, and you're trying to figure out how much to charge for your shoes. If you used the most common pricing strategy, called cost plus, you would take the cost of producing the shoes and add some extra on top for profit. But shoes can be expensive to produce, and you may quickly learn that most people are not willing to pay this much for your product, which has the unglamorous function of allowing them to step on things without hurting the soles of their feet—the utilitarian purpose of a shoe. Yet those same people are willing to pay a lot more for the same pair of shoes if they believe this footwear will help them fulfill some additional social need, such as looking cool and attaining status in the eyes of others. If shoe companies want to charge people more for the shoes they are hawking, they would do well to persuade consumers that their shoes are not just shoes. This way, they might be able to charge $150 for a shoe that costs only $15 to produce, even if consumers are fully aware that the status-enhancing leather foot coverings are not really any better at protecting their toes than another pair selling for half the price.

Exploiters of our evolutionary needs can compel consumers to pay more for products that seem to fulfill those needs, regardless of the products' actual utilitarian function. This is precisely what makes Madison Avenue so effective. The explosion of advertising in the twentieth century didn't just inform people about products; it transformed those products into something much greater than the sum of their parts. When was the last time you saw a car ad touting, "The Model S is really effective at getting you from point A to point B"? You rarely see such ads because modern cars are intentionally hyped as being about so much more than mere transportation. They are instead status symbols, family fun rooms, sexy-curved muscle sculptures, places to bond with friends, and protective steel armor systems that will keep us safe in any situation.

Cars are not unique in this regard. Modern clothing is about more than keeping your corporeal person protected from the elements, housing is about more than having a roof over your head, and even food is rarely about the physiological need to eat. If it were, advertising would proclaim, "Come to the Olive Garden—we've got your calories right here!" or "If you're looking to fill your stomach up efficiently, look no further than Red Lobster." To coax us into paying premiums for basic products, companies have persuaded us that we're not paying for just a shrimp, just a car, or just a shirt. These products are instead so much more valuable because they help fulfill deeper ancestral needs.

Let's return to your Corner Cobbler shoe business. By making it seem like your shoes can fulfill the need for status, you can charge a higher price. Perhaps you'll want to change your name to The Pampered Paw. But your goal to sell as many shoes as possible is going to come up against another inherent obstacle: the raw number of consumers. Shoes last a while, and people only need so many pairs. Or do they?

A hundred years ago, an average American had around two pairs of shoes—one for everyday wear and a nice Sunday pair. Given the utilitarian function of shoes to protect the feet, having just a couple pairs was sufficient to meet this need. But what if shoes could help fulfill multiple needs? And more importantly, what if different pairs of shoes were required to fulfill each of those needs?

Some shoes, for example, can help you achieve status at work or on the playground (think Bruno Magli or Michael Jordan). Others can help us achieve mating goals (think Manolo Blahnik stilettos). Others can help you be healthier, like those North Face trail runners or Sketchers Shape Ups. And then, of course, there are shoes for wearing when casually hanging out with friends, and yet other kinds of cozy footwear for wearing at home with the family, and still others for when you need serious protection from the elements.

Has the shoe industry's diversification motivated the average Joe and Jane to buy more shoes? Shoe betcha! A typical American man today owns five pairs of shoes, while a woman owns eleven. When it comes to more affluent individuals, *Time* magazine reports that higher-stepping men own an average of twelve pairs, and upscale women own an average of twenty-seven, with 19 percent owning more than fifty pairs of shoes, inching closer to former Philippine first lady and fanatical shoe aficionado Imelda Marcos. This is good news for your shoe business. Rather than being limited to a best-case scenario in which every person owns a pair of shoes, now you can sell every person seven pairs. After all, each of your evolutionary needs is fundamentally important, and each of your subselves must have its shoe needs covered.

Across many industries, exploiters of our evolutionary needs have successfully persuaded consumers that we need different variants of essentially the same product. As with shoes, these different variants are often targeted to our different subselves. Consider greeting cards. How often do you need to "greet" people? It turns out that Americans feel compelled to greet people quite a bit, as reflected in the $7.5 billion greeting card industry. Companies like Hallmark have helped institutionalize holidays and "special occasions" that require greeting, and many of these greetings are directed specifically at our different subselves. Happy Mate Acquisition—It's Valentine's Day! Happy Mate Retention—It's Our Anniversary! Happy Disease Avoidance—Get Well Soon! Happy Status Striving—Congratulations! Happy Affiliation—oops, did you forget to send those "Thank You!" cards? Better get the "I'm Sorry!" ones. Happy Kin Care—We're Expecting! Which card—It's a Boy! or It's a Girl!—is appropriate for the baby shower? And you'd better not forget to greet that woman who cared for you— Happy Mother's Day! And don't forget to send another special Hallmark greeting to dad on Father's Day!

If you want to greet people properly, though, you should really send a gift as well. Perhaps some flowers or candies, or maybe something a little more practical, like a gift card for Amazon or iTunes. Special occasions and holidays are also festive times, and it would be downright insensitive of us if we didn't let our friends and neighbors know just how festive we feel by buying some decorations—at Easter, Halloween, Thanksgiving, and, of course, the bedecked behemoth of them all, Christmas. The monthlong holiday season between Thanksgiving and Christmas is a veritable orgy of spending—to the tune of $165 billion a year. There is a reason why the Friday after Thanksgiving is called Black Friday; this is when many retailers turn a profit and move their ledger books from the red into the black, thanks to the millions of shoppers who want to spend their money so badly that they wait in lines outside the store throughout the night.

Is this symbiotic mutualism or parasitism? Do both companies and consumers benefit by inspiring shoppers to purchase more shoes, more greeting cards, and more presents for an ever-increasing number of holidays and special occasions?

Rather than genuinely fulfilling our evolutionary needs, many of these purchases might instead simply make us feel like those needs are being met. This is because the companies and marketers that stand to profit from our spending often pander to our ancestral cravings by recasting whatever product they're pushing to make it appeal to an otherwise disconnected evolutionary need. You need to attract a mate? How about some new shoes! You need to gain some status? How about some new shoes!

On nature's exploitation continuum, the relationship between consumers and the companies who target them is often less symbiotic and perhaps more commensal—the middle ground between symbiotic mutualism and parasitism. Many companies are like remora fish, attaching themselves to our wallets and snatching up the dollars that drop out during our sometimes sloppy spending. It certainly beats being paralyzed so that someone can lay eggs in our flesh for their offspring to feed on, right? Well, as we discuss next, that's what "they" would like you to think.

SWIMMING (AND SPENDING) IN INFESTED WATERS

The yellow tang is a brightly colored fish that resides in the tropical reefs of the Indian Ocean. When it needs a deep-sea cleaning, the yellow tang looks for its symbiotic buddy, the cleaner wrasse. The tang recognizes its symbiotic partner by the bright lateral stripe running down the length of its body. But before the yellow tang will grant access to its sensitive gills and mouth, the cleaner wrasse must first perform a secret dance to win the tang's trust, like entering a PIN number into the fish's neurological automatic bank teller machine.

This code system normally works out well, except that near the same reef lurks another small fish called the saber-toothed blenny, which is almost identical in size and appearance to the cleaner wrasse. It even sports the same shiny stripe down its back. If approached by a yellow tang, the blenny also knows the secret dance, which gives it complete access to the most private parts of the big fish. But once allowed in, instead of providing a service, the blenny uses its saber-like teeth to rip a chunk of flesh from the unsuspecting client. Rather than helping the yellow tang rid itself of parasites, the saber-toothed blenny is a parasite—in disguise.

Like the saber-toothed blenny, human social parasites often try to make themselves look like the good guys, and they even know all the right moves to gain our trust. But once you let them in, they'll rip you off by taking a bite out of your wallet. Let's look at the ways in which our evolutionary tendencies can open us up to exploitation by those lurking social parasites.

HOW MUCH WOULD YOU PAY FOR A ROCK?

The first known diamond engagement ring was commissioned for Mary of Burgundy by the Archduke Maximilian of Austria in 1477. Later, the Victorians regularly exchanged "regards" rings set with birthstones. But diamonds were almost unheard of by most people until the 1930s, when the De Beers group deployed a two-tentacled strategy unabashedly intended to exploit us.

De Beers was founded as a mining operation in 1888, after an 83.5-carat diamond was found in present-day Kimberley, South Africa. Financed by the Rothschild family, the company began consolidating smaller outfits and quickly grew into a small empire. In 1927, Ernest Oppenheimer, a German immigrant who had previously founded another mining company backed by financier J. P. Morgan, managed to wrest control of De Beers and truly maximize its exploitative prowess.

Oppenheimer, concerned that new diamond mines were being discovered throughout Africa, worried that the increased supply would swamp the market and force prices down. Some experts today believe that if gem prices were determined by a free open market, a diamond might fetch between $2 and $30. But chances are that either you or someone who loves you has been compelled to pay substantially more for this lump of compressed coal—and you can thank De Beers.

To keep prices high, Oppenheimer solidified De Beers into a diamond cartel. After gaining control of 90 percent of the world's diamond production and distribution, De Beers began to artificially limit

the supply—thus the "rarity"—of diamonds. This is important because people are inherently attracted to objects and opportunities that
are scarce. Robert Cialdini, our mentor and author of *Influence,* spent
several years going underground to study the scams used by insurance
salesmen, used car dealers, and cult leaders. He found that many of
these hustlers exploit people's desire for goodies they think are scarce.
By manipulating perceived scarcity, the De Beers parasite could now
draw people in like flies to a neon light, extracting ever-more money
from its human hosts.

The scarcity ploy was certainly exploitative, but it's what came next
that makes De Beers truly a deep rationality parasite. In addition to
controlling supply and distribution, De Beers oversaw another critical
part of the diamond business: marketing. "A gemstone is the ultimate
luxury product. It has no material use," Oppenheimer confessed.
"Men and women desire to have diamonds not for what they can do
but for what they desire." But De Beers needed to manufacture this
desire—to fabricate the yearning specifically for diamonds. To spin a
yarn that would turn a rock into one of the most valuable commodities
on earth, it turned to Madison Avenue.

In 1947, Frances Gerety was a young copywriter working for De
Beers's advertising agency, N. W. Ayer & Son. Although Gerety herself
never married, she had a big impact on millions of other marriages by
coining the phrase "a diamond is forever." *Advertising Age* magazine
named it the single best advertising slogan of the twentieth century.
The eminently memorable phrase was the centerpiece of campaigns
featuring ethereal women longing for eternal love, symbolized by a
diamond engagement ring. While perpetuating the mythology of love
surrounding diamonds, the "diamond is forever" slogan was also clev-
erly designed to ensure that women hung on to their diamonds for
the rest of their lives ("I never hated a man enough to give him his
diamonds back," Zsa Zsa Gabor once noted).

The notion of keeping diamonds forever was aimed to prevent a
secondary market for used diamonds. The trick was to persuade
people that to really have special meaning, your diamond should be
untouched by another woman (you try giving your bride-to-be a used

diamond ring originally intended for another female stranger). By maintaining that true love could only be expressed through a brand-new diamond ring, De Beers managed to maintain control of the diamond trade at the wholesale level, enabling retailers to sell diamonds at a high price without competition from secondary markets.

De Beers had orchestrated the perfect parasitic coup. After making its product artificially scarce, its marketing strategy perpetually activated the subself most vulnerable to scarcity: the mate-acquisition subself. As described in an earlier chapter, this subself particularly fancies scarce and rare objects, being drawn to restaurants "off the beaten path" and "limited-edition" goodies.

Only thirty years after the launch of the "diamond is forever" campaign, a diamond ring was considered not simply a luxury but a necessity in the modern engagement ritual. By the 1960s, 80 percent of American brides-to-be were demanding, and getting, a diamond; today that number remains similar, with the average engagement ring costing $3,200 (De Beers's original marketing suggested that a man should spend the equivalent of one month's income on an engagement ring, but it later readjusted the monetary value of a woman's love, increasing the price to two months' income). De Beers did not limit its appetite for profit to America. Countries like Japan, which never had a tradition of romantic marriage, made diamonds a tough sell for brides. But De Beers persuaded even Japanese mate-acquisition subselves to part with their money for some shiny coal. Whereas in 1967 only 5 percent of brides in Japan wore a diamond, this percentage had increased to 77 percent by 1990.

A RING FOR EVERY SUBSELF

De Beers stuffed its coffers by exploiting our mate-acquisition subself, through both marketing and manipulative business practices. But the jewelry industry today would not be a $150 billion juggernaut if it had settled for only one of our subselves. An engagement ring can be put on only one finger, and jewelry makers couldn't help but notice that we have ten fingers, nine of which remained unprofitably naked.

Thankfully, there is now a different ring—or some piece of jewelry—for every available finger, wrist, ankle, toe, neck, belly button, ear, nose, eyebrow, cheek, chin, nipple, and lip (both above and below the waist).

Now that a woman's fourth finger on the left hand was taken, De Beers moved to conquer the fourth finger on the right hand by exploiting women's status subself. "Your left hand says we. Your right hand says me," De Beers explains in its marketing. After all, what better way for modern women to show their independence than by buying their own diamond rings? (In addition to, not instead of, the engagement ring, of course.) The jewelry maker Kwiat offers a line of right-hand rings for around $5,000, but you can also scoop one up at Walmart, whose Keepsake Independence ("a shining symbol of your feminine spirit") retails for $389.

Of course, not only women express their status through jewelry. Even if a fellow doesn't yearn to look like Mr. T, who regularly wore twenty pounds of gold chains around his neck, men of all sorts spend serious money on bling fashioned from costly gems and metals. In a professional sports championship, for example, the real trophy is the ring given to each player. One football player described the ideal ring as the "ten table ring," meaning that people in a restaurant could see the ring from ten tables away in every direction. The Green Bay Packers 2011 Super Bowl rings certainly met this goal—each contained more than one hundred diamonds.

Now that you have announced your status and your deep feelings for your loved one, you will need to retain your mate by finding a way to ensure that he or she continues to love you. But how? De Beers has a handy suggestion: "Say you'd marry her all over again with a diamond anniversary ring." If you really want to prove your enduring love, that special anniversary ring comes with a matching diamond necklace, earrings, and bracelet. And if giving your loved one diamonds for your anniversary is becoming too blasé and predictable, De Beers also offers the "eternity ring" (a symbol of continuing affection and appreciation) and the "trilogy ring" (representing the past, present, and future of a relationship). De Beers can really kill a lot of birds with one stone—or rock, in their case.

Jewelry solves more than the needs of mate acquisition, mate re-tention, and status. There are friendship bracelets, best-friend neck-laces, and forever-friends rings to keep us in touch with our BFFs, not to mention class rings to keep us all connected with the old crowd from County High School or State U. If you're a parent, what better way to express your love than with a graduation ring for your child, who should likewise buy his or her parents some jewelry for any one of the many special occasions throughout the year (Tiffany & Co. offers a special Mother's Day butterfly brooch for $7,900, but if you're feeling strapped for cash, you could just pick up a Tiffany "Yours Mom" heart charm for only $1,275). And to bling out the self-protection subself, "intuitive jewelry artist" Robyn A. Harton offers a collection of afford-able jewelry to protect us from negative energy, crime, radiation, in-jury, demons, and the "evil eye," as well as pieces for "all-purpose general protection."

Jewelry also becomes a surprising elixir that can fight disease, as when a necklace or bracelet stores important medical information or when we derive special healing powers from an energy bracelet. Zepter Luxury International, for example, offers magnetic jewelry to heal us from "all types of ailments from arthritis to circulation prob-lems, migraine headaches to frozen shoulders." Although it might seem silly to think that a piece of jewelry can make people healthier or feel better, the reality is that millions of people are desperate to find ways to fulfill the evolutionary need of disease avoidance. And whichever direction they turn, there's usually some kind of parasite eager to take their money.

A PILL WITH THAT, SIR?

Recent decades have witnessed an infestation in American homes. Rather than taking traditional forms like vermin or locusts, these crit-ters take the form of pills. From Abilify, Adderall, and Ambien to Zofran, Zoloft, and Zyprexa, prescription drugs have invaded our bathroom cabinets like squirmy centipedes in basement walls. Whereas in 1929 the average American filled less than two prescrip-tions per year, by 2006 each child got four, each adult got eleven, and each senior citizen got twenty-eight. The 2012 United Healthcare prescription drug catalog offered choices from among 1,080 different pills, with yearly sales in the United States totaling $307 billion—almost enough money to pave the entire US interstate system in gold.

Given all the pills people are popping, you'd think there was some serious new affliction going around. And there is! A massive outbreak of pharmaceutical parasites exploiting our ancestral tendencies.

Part of the dramatic pharmaceutical growth stems from the explosion of direct-to-consumer advertising (the "ask your doctor" ads). These ads attempt to bypass the power of the traditional middleman in the pill business (the doctor) by empowering us regular folks to play doctor ourselves. Instead of waiting for your doctor to diagnose you with something, the ads bait you into performing self-diagnoses and encourage you to prescribe your own treatment.

This is like sending your disease-avoidance subself—your inner compulsive hypochondriac—to the candy store, where every twitch, hiccup, or social aberration can be alleviated with a scoop into yet another bin full of colorful pills. Tired? Moody? Coughing? Sneezing? Depressed? Anxious? Hyper? Cholesterol too high? Cholesterol too low? Can't get it up? Can't get it down? Whatever ails you, there is a pill that promises to meet your need. "Do you fall asleep at night and wake up in the morning?" comedian Chris Rock recalls hearing in one ad, then quips, "Yeah, I got that." Need help with your sleep? No worries, here's a little something to help you fall asleep, and another pill to stay asleep, and a little something extra to help you wake up in the morning. And if you're a little anxious about all the pills you're taking, here is something else to calm you down a bit.

It's true that drug companies produce some drugs that can treat serious illnesses and save or prolong lives. But make no mistake about it: they are in the business of peddling pills. And like our friends in the diamond business, pharmaceutical corporations make money by selling more rather than less of their product. Although purported to help us, prescription drugs are ironically the fourth-leading cause of death in the United States. Adverse reactions from properly prescribed and properly administered drugs cause about 106,000 deaths per year. A person is ten times more likely to die from taking legal medication than from experimenting with dangerous illegal drugs, which kill about ten thousand people per year. Perhaps the war on drugs should be redirected.

Even if you're uncertain whether pharmaceutical companies are the good guys or the bad guys, you'd probably agree that those who blatantly counterfeit medicines are definitely on the parasitic end of the exploitation continuum. The malicious fake-meds industry rakes in an estimated $75 billion a year—that's more money than the profits made from heroin and cocaine.

Counterfeit drugs look like the real thing but contain no active in- gredients. They oftentimes kill by failing to treat life-threatening ill- nesses, most notably in developing nations where recent setbacks in treating malaria, HIV/AIDS, and tuberculosis have been attributed to counterfeit medical supplies. But lethal additives and seemingly harmless fillers can also cause drugs to act differently in a patient's system, potentially resulting in death. Not only is it not much fun when that asthma medicine doesn't contain any active ingredients, but it's even less fun when a familiar-looking headache medication lands you in the emergency room.

WHAT "THEY" DON'T WANT YOU TO KNOW ABOUT

Given so many shady dealings in the world of modern medicine, it's easy to become cynical and a little paranoid when it comes to pharma- ceuticals. If you're convinced that real or fake pill pushers are out to get your money, you'll be glad to know there are like-minded people who can help.

Meet Kevin Trudeau. Like a growing number of people, Trudeau believes that the drug companies are hiding and suppressing informa- tion about natural ways to cure disease. He asserts that even if you're sick, you don't need all those pills the drug companies are hawking. What you need instead is Trudeau's book *Natural Cures "They" Don't Want You to Know About*. The book reveals how you can "easily cure" not only arthritis, acid reflux, phobia, depression, obesity, chronic fatigue syndrome, attention deficit disorder, and diabetes but also multiple sclerosis, lupus, AIDS, cancer, herpes, and muscular dystrophy. This might sound too good to be true, but take a look at Trudeau on television in his infomercials, being interviewed by paid actors who are constantly astounded by the effectiveness of his cures.

Some naysayers have criticized Trudeau for having absolutely no medical training. But his proponents would argue that this simply proves that he is not a pawn of the pharmaceutical companies. Trudeau has also been criticized for his inability to provide evidence to back up many of his claims. For example, he cites a twenty-five-year research study involving a natural cure for diabetes at the University of Calgary. Critics have been outraged that the study doesn't seem to exist. What critics fail to understand, according to Trudeau, is that the university had no choice but to destroy its findings to prevent reprisals from the pharmaceutical industry.

The book "they" don't want you to know about has so far sold over 5 million copies, and you can receive your own copy for a mere $29.95 plus $11.95 shipping (oh, and another $19.95 handling fee "they" don't want you to know about, a "free" newsletter subscription that will result in an additional $30 charge, and constant harassment by Trudeau's henchmen, who will call you daily to sell you additional products, as well as more harassment by all the other swindlers who will get your contact information from a "mooch list" that Trudeau will sell them).

But wait—that's not all! It turns out that Trudeau is somewhat of a modern miracle worker, capable of fulfilling many more needs than just curing your medical ailments. His other books include *Debt Cures "They" Don't Want You to Know About* and *The Money-Making Secrets "They" Don't Want You to Know About,* as well as *Your Wish Is Your Command* (a fourteen-CD lecture from an undisclosed location in the Swiss Alps that will give you the "hidden key" to take complete control of your personal and financial wishes). And there is also the perennial best seller *Free Money "They" Don't Want You to Know About*. This last book will direct you to a search engine that will charge $18 per search to find your "free money." And if you earn more than $500 a month, you won't qualify for 89 percent of the programs "they" don't want you to know about, which are just government grants some people are too lazy to Google.

Trudeau also doesn't want you to know about his extensive criminal record. After getting out of prison for fraud and larceny, Trudeau entered the fight against obesity by joining forces with Nutrition for Life, which the attorney general of Illinois together with seven other states successfully prosecuted as a pyramid scheme. Trudeau's literary inspiration came in 2004, when the Federal Trade Commission (FTC) made him the only person in history to be banned for life from selling anything on television (he had been pitching multiple products that included a "hair farming system" that was supposed to "finally end baldness in the human race" and a "breakthrough that in 60 seconds can eliminate addictions"). The FTC only allowed him to promote his own books via infomercials, which are supposedly under the protection of the First Amendment. But that hasn't been working out so well either—in 2011 Trudeau was fined $37.6 million for defrauding the public. Trudeau claims that "they" are scheming to keep his books off of shelves, so better get one quickly, because they're bound to be scarce soon.

PROTECTION FROM DEEP RATIONALITY PARASITES

From con men to company men, many conspirators seek to exploit our deeply rational tendencies. Some of us don't mind being exploited some of the time, especially when the exploiters are symbiotic partners who give as well as take. But many of us are duped into being on the short end of one-way parasitic relationships, which can lead to a loud sucking sound coming straight from our wallets. Like the cuckoo or the saber-toothed blenny, human social parasites take advantage of our ancestrally successful biases.

How can you determine if you're dealing with a symbiotic partner intent on helping you or a social parasite bent on exploiting you? It can be difficult. Bernie Madoff's clients, for example, didn't know they were being duped until it was too late. Social parasites are expert deceivers, carefully diverting our attention and strategically concealing information. But you can do three things to protect yourself.

Know Thy Enemy

If you begin to feel like something is a little fishy, ask a simple question: Is the other person really what he or she appears to be? Exploiters like Bernie Madoff and Kevin Trudeau will often tell you that they are just like you. But before taking them at their word, it pays to look a little closer. The cuckoo also attempts to have the egg it sneaks into another bird's nest mimic the eggs of the intended foster parent. But the cuckoo's egg will rarely be completely identical to that of the targeted bird. If the victimized bird were to take a closer look, it would recognize the fake. In fact, many successfully spot the parasitic egg and throw it out of the nest before any damage can be done. Likewise for us humans. Even if someone seems to be just like you, unless he is your identical twin, your interests don't completely overlap. Taking a closer look at an opportunity that seems too good to be true will likely reveal that it is. If it still sounds like a great deal, ask what the other person gains from your benefit. If the answer is the feeling of satisfaction from helping you, this is a clear warning that you're dealing with a bad egg.

Know Thy Situation

If you are feeling compelled to spend a lot of money, sign on the dotted line, or make some big decision, ask yourself, Have I been primed to feel this way right now? Exploiters will often first prime in their unsuspecting targets the specific subself most vulnerable to their pitch. Before trying to sell you a "rare" diamond ring costing two months of your salary, for example, a deep rationality parasite might activate your mate-acquisition subself, for which the opportunity to part with thousands of dollars for a scarce rock might seem perfectly reasonable. But the same decision might seem ludicrous to your other six selves, who are being shut out of the current decision-making process by a manipulative exploiter. Even if at that moment it feels like the smartest decision in the world, the best advice is to wait and sleep on it. By giving yourself a little more time, you enable your other subselves to weigh on the decision. What seemed like a no-brainer one day might look foolish the next. And by waiting, you'll avoid being played for a fool.

Know Thyself

Finally, if you find yourself really wanting something you can't afford, ask yourself a deeper question: What evolutionary need is this purchase attempting to fulfill? The answer will often come back to one of our seven subselves. For instance, your yearning for that expensive family trip to Disney World likely reflects a need to be a good parent, and that pricey diamond anniversary ring reflects a need to be a good spouse. Realizing that our material desires reflect deeper evolutionary needs provides an important insight: before maxing out your credit card, consider alternative ways to achieve the same evolutionary need. Usually there will be plenty of options. Rather than taking your kids to Disney World, you might equally meet your need to be a good parent by spending some quality time with them (one of our wives is fond of noting that "love" is spelled T-I-M-E not C-A-S-H). And rather than buying expensive jewelry as an anniversary gift, you might equally meet your need to be a good spouse by telling your partner a heartfelt "I love you" and writing a thoughtful note to express exactly why he or she means so much to you. Our brains are wired not to seek material goods but to fulfill evolutionary needs. And just like our wise ancestors, we are fully capable of fulfilling those needs without draining our bank accounts.

Conclusion

Mementos from Our Tour

IN THESE PAGES, we have traveled widely in time and space, from the depths of the Amazon jungle to the crowded streets of New York, meeting rock stars, topless dancers, and Silicon Valley billionaires along the way. We've cruised into Memphis, Tennessee, in Elvis Presley's diamond-encrusted Cadillac and considered the cost of brides in Afghanistan. During the exotic wildlife portion of the tour, we had close encounters with loss-averse capuchin monkeys, conspicuous bowerbirds, suicidal turtles, and unscrupulously parasitic cuckoos.

As we look over the photos of our nine-day trip, which particular memories do we want to carry around with us in our wallets?

- Here's a picture to help us remember the first day of our journey: It's Joe Kennedy Sr. in a tuxedo performing a dazzling trick jump on a skateboard, with a beautiful Hollywood actress looking on. The note on the back reminds us of the insight we gained on that initial leg of the tour: Although our decisions may sometimes appear irrationally foolish on the surface, they are often deeply rational—the products of decision-making mechanisms designed to boost our evolutionary fitness.

- Here's a snapshot to help us remember day two: Martin Luther King Jr. addressing a large crowd in Birmingham, Alabama, while his evil twin is backstage with his arm around Eve Black (the dangerously fun-loving and flirtatious woman afflicted with multiple personality disorder). The associated insight: We all have multiple subselves—each with different and sometimes conflicting priorities.

- Snapshot number three shows ousted Disney Company CEO Michael Eisner coldly handing Walt Disney an itemized bill for Mickey Mouse's wardrobe, lodging, and feeding expenses. The insight there: The market-pricing rules of Wall Street economics apply to only a small portion of our important everyday decisions, most of which involve family, friends, and long-term exchange partners to whom we apply very different sets of rules.

- Our fourth Polaroid shows Zambia's president Levy Mwanawasa at the post office, using a magic marker to scrawl "return to sender" on a giant bin full of genetically modified food from the United States. The caption: Our minds are built like smoke detectors, biased in ways that sometimes lead us to miss opportunities but that would have helped our ancestors avoid possible dangers.

- In the fifth snapshot we see several shirtless members of an Amazon tribe accepting an honorary degree from Harvard for their successful performance on a test of logical reasoning. The takeaway: When seemingly difficult problems are framed in ancestrally relevant terms, we don't need fancy educations to look like savants.

- Next we see a colorful action shot of MC Hammer dancing in a yellow vest and parachute pants in front of his repossessed mansion. This one isn't imaginary; it comes from an ad for Nationwide Insurance, along with an appropriate caption: "Life comes at you fast." The insight here: Different people follow different life history strategies, with some taking a fast and others a slow approach to accumulating and expending economic resources.

- To remember the seventh segment, picture Leonardo Di-Caprio driving a brand-new, conspicuously green Prius to his luxurious solar-panel-covered mansion, as he publicly proclaims his altruistic motivation to help the environment. The takeaway of this leg of our journey: The conscious reasons for our decisions and their ultimate evolutionary functions may be very different.

- From the eighth day of our trip, here's a grainy picture shot with a hidden camera of New York governor Eliot Spitzer handing a bag full of eighty thousand $1 bills to a beautiful and scantily clad young woman. The caption: When it comes to one of the most important evolutionary markets, men and women are exchanging very different natural resources.

- And finally, we have a photo from the last leg of our journey showing a colorful cuckoo bird wearing a diamond ring, perched on investment swindler Bernie Madoff's shoulder. The insight there: Evolutionary successes attract parasites; some are symbiotic, but others are exploitative tricksters taking advantage of our evolutionary needs.

THREE LESSONS ABOUT THE RATIONAL ANIMAL

If one of our children were looking over this photo album, he or she might ask, "What are the three life lessons I should take away from all this, Daddy?" (we both have analytic and inquisitive kids). Here's what we'd say:

Lesson 1: Don't assume other people are morons.

The recently prevalent view of decision making—of people making haphazard and irrationally biased decisions—doesn't fully capture how people make important everyday choices. Decisions are almost always biased and sometimes even foolish, but if you dig a little deeper, those biases and seeming irrationalities often make good evolutionary sense.

Behavioral economists have uncovered a host of ways in which people's decisions can be oversimplified, self-defeating, and biased. If you read about this research, it's easy to chuckle at the foibles of human nature. And it turns out that we humans suffer from one especially strong bias: we secretly believe that it's *other people* who are the fools, whereas we are thoughtfully brilliant geniuses. The theory that people are eminently rational applies to us, but the theory that people are irrational applies to them.

But the more deeply we look, the more we realize that people's decisions, though sometimes foolish and irrational at the surface, are often driven by subconscious programs that make deeper evolutionary sense. Even if the person making the decision can't explain the evolutionary logic behind it, humans have evolved to make decisions in ways that are typically good for their evolutionary interests. So you shouldn't assume that you yourself are an omniscient Econ, and it will serve you well not to assume that other people are self-defeating morons.

This is not to say that our evolutionary tendencies will always steer us correctly. Deep rationality is geared to the ancestral, not the modern, world. In many ways, we've designed the modern world to reflect our ancestral needs (we use our iPhones and automobiles to keep in touch with friends and families, for example). But there is sometimes a mismatch between our evolved inclinations and the current environment, as when those Bernie Madoff–style parasites exploit our inclinations toward familial trust. An evolutionary perspective helps us identify where we should expect these kinds of mismatches and how to work around our automatic reactions when they might get us into trouble. So respect your inner chimp, but also read *Consumer Reports*.

Lesson 2: Rational self-interest is not in your self-interest.

The classic economic model of decision making presumes a mind designed to maximize self-interest. It applies well to interchanges involving Wall Street traders or consumers buying used cars from strangers, but is surprisingly inappropriate in describing how most people make most of their important decisions.

Contrary to what many psychologists and economists used to believe, market economics is the wrong way to approach most of the decisions you make on a day-to-day basis. This applies not only to your interactions with friends, family, and most of the people you know and care about, but also to your decisions on the job. Your workday life will be a lot more livable if you do not deal with your bosses, workers, or peers like you'd deal with a stranger haggling over the price of a used car. Even research on economic games finds that students trained in economics actually make less money, shooting themselves in the foot with selfish choices that irritate other people who would otherwise cooperate with them. Merely calling a game the "Wall Street game" led people in one experiment to cooperate less and walk away with fewer rewards in their pockets.

Instead of asking what your friends, neighbors, and business associates can do for you, try asking what you can do to make them more like family. You may find they enjoy doing business with you more than they would if you negotiated hard over every nickel and dime on the restaurant bill.

Lesson 3: Don't leave home without consulting your other selves.

There is no single utility-maximizing banker inside your head. People instead have at least seven different subselves. Each subself calculates costs and benefits according to different evolutionary priorities, and each takes turns steering our conscious decisions in subconscious ways.

Just as it is incorrect to assume that there is an omniscient Wall Street banker inside your head, it's equally incorrect to assume that there is a single decision maker of any stripe. There's more than one you in there. There's an affiliation subself, who shares and shares alike with friends and colleagues; a status subself, who plays to win; and a disease-avoidance subself, who will pass up possible rewards to avoid unwanted microbial gifts.

Three other subselves are dedicated to very different parts of the reproductive game. The mate-acquisition subself, especially the "his" model, is concerned with getting a date and is willing to take a lot of risks and throw away resources. The mate-retention subself, on the other hand, is careful to sit on the nest egg and inclined to treat other nest mates using a generous exchange rule: the love you take is equal to the love you make. The kin-care subself is the most generous of all, giving with little or no expectation of return, and feeling especially rewarded when family members are happy and doing well.

The self-protection subself, on the other hand, is the one most likely to look carefully under the hood before closing a deal, and it is this subself that comes closest to using a set of rules familiar to our friends on Wall Street.

Our different subselves come out automatically when we are around different people, and they can also be awakened by specific threats and opportunities. However, we can exercise at least some control over their appearance, as we saw in many of the studies we discussed, in which people made very different decisions depending on which subself had been activated beforehand. In those experiments, researchers primed the different subselves by having people look at images that pertained to a particular subself, or watch a romantic or scary movie, or imagine themselves in a vividly threatening or promising situation.

But you can voluntarily wake up different subselves yourself. How? By imagining a mental Rolodex album filled with photos of your best friends, your spouse, your children, someone you find sexy, someone who scares you, someone who is sick, or someone you really admire. By purposefully pulling one of those photos into consciousness at the right moment, you can awaken a sleeping subself with a vested interest in your current decision.

Imagine you're about to make a risky decision that has potentially long-lasting consequences. Maybe an attractive salesperson is trying to get you to sign on the dotted line for a shiny, pearl-encrusted Cadillac Eldorado with gold hubcaps, or a beautiful model you just met in a hotel bar in Cartagena is asking whether you'd like to be escorted somewhere. If you're single and as rich as Elvis, maybe there's no need to hesitate. But if you think maybe you might regret the decision in the morning, it's time to pull out that picture of your preschool-age daughter and activate your more conservative kin-care subself.

All of your subselves can be suckered by sneaky parasites, such as when De Beers entices each one to seek a diamond ring of its own. But your subselves can also work in your favor, as when Southwest Airlines activated the kin-care subself to make working for the corporation feel like a family affair. By consulting the right subself in the right situation, you can exercise more control over the important decisions in your life.

THESIS, ANTITHESIS, CONSILIENCE

Everyone likes a street fight. Throughout this book, we've taken a bit of a fighting stance with regard to rational and behavioral economists. But now it's time to make peace among the Wall Street number crunchers, the foible-hunting experimenters in their lab coats, and the khaki-wearing Darwinians. Most importantly, it is critical that we not leave you with the impression that we believe the proponents of the two earlier positions are now lying fatally injured by the roadside, while the evolutionary psychologist rides triumphant into the sunset as the movie credits roll.

We came not to bury the rational or the behavioral economists, but to stand on their shoulders. Rational economists have developed a powerful set of theories about how individuals can optimally allocate resources and how markets can function more efficiently. They have introduced a host of elegant ideas and beautifully precise mathematical models. We believe that those models will be even more precise if rational economists overcome their traditional aversion to asking where people's preferences come from, why different people have different preferences, and why people's preferences change in important ways depending on the evolutionarily relevant context. By considering those questions in light of what we are learning about evolutionary biology and cognitive science, economists can boost the explanatory power and elegance of their models and better contribute to a complete explanation of human decision making.

On the shoulders of rational economists stand behavioral economists, who have expanded our understanding of decision making in important ways. By carefully studying how individuals actually make decisions and identifying important biases and shortcuts people use in the process, behavioral economists have revolutionized our understanding of the connections between psychology and economics. To date, though, the behavioral revolutionaries have yet to come up with a new structure with which to replace the classic rationalist's castle. It is time to move beyond the list of grievances against the mind's limitations and to delve more deeply into the eminently sensible links between evolution and decision making.

To fully understand the present, it is essential to understand the past. By connecting our modern behaviors to their ancestral roots, the next generation of thinkers will be able to stand on the shoulders of earlier giants, focusing their binoculars on a richer panoramic view of the awe-inspiring landscape of human decision making.

WHAT'S IN IT FOR *MOI*?

At the book's opening, we mentioned J. K. Rowling, the British woman who penned the Harry Potter books. The series sold over 400 million copies and catapulted Rowling onto the Forbes list of billionaires, until her penchant for giving away money landed her back in the land of mere multimillionaires. Perhaps the two of us wrote this book about economic decision making because we were hoping to cash in on people's interest in money, imagining long lines of people, credit cards in hand, camping out overnight outside the local bookstore to await our sequel: *The Rational Animal Unravels the Secret of the Philosopher's Stone!* And watch for the Hollywood movie, starring

George Clooney as Doug Kenrick and Daniel Craig as Vlad Griskevicius! That would be, as Brits like Rowling say, rather brilliant, allowing Doug to upgrade from his anticipated retirement hut in Ecuador and Vlad to buy a lifetime supply of Bubblicious pink watermelon bubble gum for his relatives on the farms back in Lithuania. But alas, we'd better wait for a while before we make a down payment on an English estate in Rowling's new neighborhood, or start writing $15 million checks to our favorite charities.

Yet we do already share one commonality with J. K. Rowling. And you probably do too. That commonality is the secret of Rowling's success. Whether we're British, Bostonian, or Bangladeshi, whether our sex chromosomes are XY or XX, and whether we're seven years old or seventy, we all love a mystery.

A couple of years back, Doug read all 4,091 pages of the seven Harry Potter books to his seven-year-old son, who devoured every word. As each night's reading session came to a close, the mesmerized little tyke would plead, "Please, Daddy, just a few more pages!" What he didn't know was that dad wanted to read a few more pages too. What kept us, and hundreds of millions of other readers, entranced was Rowling's masterful ability to keep up the mystery. Every time Harry Potter and his friends Hermione Granger and Ron Weasley solved one puzzle, another, even more intriguing mystery arose.

The topic of mystery brings us back to the real reason that we wrote this book. Science is all about solving mysteries. And the question of what underlies our own human choices is one of the greatest mysteries of all time. It's a wonderfully complex plot, and the scientists who have been investigating it have traced a labyrinth of clues— from evolutionary biology, cognitive psychology, anthropology, and economics. What makes science so appealing, and what keeps the scientific detectives so incredibly excited, is the fact that resolving one puzzle opens up new and more intriguing mysteries.

The mystery of human behavior is part of the same plot as why peacocks flaunt their feathers, why squirrels altruistically sacrifice themselves, and why cuckoos exploit unsuspecting neighbors. The reasons behind your choices are part of the same thread that links the choices of jungle dwellers in the Amazon, hunter-gatherers in Africa, and chic urbanites hunting for fame and fortune in the jungles of Manhattan. Uncovering these connections and piecing together the clues will help us all become wiser decision makers. But most of the threads in this grand story have yet to be unraveled. Our hope is that some of the people who read this book will be inspired to pick up a Sherlock Holmes–style magnifying glass, join the other detectives working the case, and help solve the mystery of the human mind. The next clue is waiting just around the corner.

Acknowledgments

Every time we watch the credits roll at the end of a movie, we're always astounded by the number of people it takes to turn an idea into a complete film. Books are no different. Scores of individuals behind the scenes helped us turn a few raw ideas into a book.

Before we ever put pen to paper, our thinking was shaped by years of thought-provoking conversations about economic decision making with our colleagues and collaborators Bob Cialdini, Steve Neuberg, Jill Sundie, Norm Li, Mark Schaller, Noah Goldstein, Vaughn Becker, Andy Delton, Tess Robertson, Josh Ackerman, Jeff Simpson, Adam Cohen, Josh Tybur, Joe Redden, Jessica Li, Lani Shiota, Kristina Durante, Sarah Hill, Becca Neel, Andrew White, Jenessa Shapiro, Chad Mortensen, and Lionel Nicastle. Each of these brilliant folks helped sharpen our thinking about the topic and teach old dogs some new tricks. We are likewise indebted to our colleagues and students at Arizona State University and the University of Minnesota, who both supported and challenged us, preventing us from getting lazy and forcing us to think harder.

Our thinking about the evolutionary roots of decision making was enlightened by the great work of our many brilliant and highly productive colleagues, including Martie Haselton, Leda Cosmides, John Tooby, David Buss, Martin Daly, Margo Wilson, Robert Frank, Mark van Vugt, X. T. Wang, Jon Maner, Peter Todd, Geoffrey Miller, Rob Kurzban, Athena Aktipis, Daniel Nettle, Gerd Gigerenzer, Gad Saad, Steve Gangestad, Bill von Hippel, Andreas Wilke, Bruce Ellis, Jay Belsky, Steven Pinker, Dan Barrett, Dan Fessler, Deb Lieberman, Carlos Navarrete, and A. J. Figueredo. Your creative work inspired many fruitful ideas.

Although we have spent most of our writing careers working on scientific journal articles, both of us were inspired to branch out after taking a graduate seminar in scientific writing taught by one of our favorite science writers, John Alcock.

Your reading experience throughout this book has been thoroughly improved not only by his teachings but by multiple colleagues and friends who read various versions of this book and provided detailed feedback, including Josh Ackerman, Mark Bergen, Robert Cialdini, Andy Delton, Kristina Durante, Sarah Hill, George John, Akshay Rao, Joe Redden, Jeff Simpson, David Lundberg Kenrick, Geoffrey Miller, Josh Tybur, Kevin Upton, Bram Van den Bergh, Kathleen Vohs, Jianfeng Yu, and Dong Zee. We are also thankful to several doctorate students who provided insightful feedback on the book, including Stephanie Cantu, Michael Covey, Chiraag Mittal, Nick Olson, and Ethan Young.

Doug's thinking about evolution and behavior was powerfully influenced by years of fascinating conversations with his friends Rich Keefe, Ed Sadalla, and Mark Schaller, often conducted during long walks or delicious meals. Speaking of delicious meals, Carol Luce not only provided five-star sustenance while Doug was working on this book, but also accompanied that fine cuisine with insightful intellectual nourishment and various tips for cooking and preparing the ideas presented in these pages. David Lundberg Kenrick has not only become Doug's other intellectual companion but has also used his extensive video-production skills to help bring some of these ideas to cinematic life (as you can see if you search on YouTube for "How Mating and Self-Protection Motives Alter Loss Aversion" or "Kenrick–The Rational Animal"). Dave's younger brother, Liam, helped Doug learn about J. K. Rowling by encouraging him to carefully read all the Harry Potter books, which also helped ameliorate any inclination to write in the style of a scientific journal article. Grandma Jean Luce also found other things to entertain Liam, generously freeing Doug up to write anything at all.

Vlad is indebted to Elliot Aronson and Anthony Pratkanis for inspiring him to pursue social psychology and to Bob Cialdini and Doug Kenrick (before he was a coauthor) for teaching him how to think both inside and outside the box. Vlad's parents, Antanas and Danute, gave him the invaluable gifts of opportunity and trust, providing him the opportunity to pursue whatever he wanted, while always trusting that he would figure things out. And big brother Agnius encouraged him to boldly explore the universe of ideas. Vlad is also appreciative for years of friendship with Gil Koresh, Paul Zahka, Anuranjan Singh, Brennan Diamond, Darren Weiss, Taylor Umlauf, and Josh Sorkin, who provided companionship and many life lessons during road trips, spring-training games, and garage-band practices. Particular thanks to Gil, who was always there for a walk and a deep conversation. Vlad hopes to continue those deep conversations with his growing kids, Greta, Nora, and Nicholas, who constantly provide a new life perspective and a reminder to take joy in life's little things. Speaking of the kids, Nana Charynanne provided endless hours of much-appreciated loving care. And, of course, Vlad is deeply indebted and thankful to his loving and devoted wife, Jenny, who selflessly does countless things every day that enable him to keep his sanity and provide him time to write. I love you.

Both Doug and Vlad are also deeply grateful to our supportive editor, T. J. Kelleher; our production editor, Sandra Beris; and our agent, Jim Levine.

Notes

INTRODUCTION: CADILLACS, COMMUNISTS, AND PINK BUBBLE GUM

The opening quote comes from Bertrand Russell's 1950 book *Unpopular Essays*.

For information on Elvis's various Cadillacs, see "Elvis's Cadillacs" (http://elvis cadillacs.tripod.com). Elvis spent $100,000 on the custom Cadillac in 1960, which is the equivalent of spending $785,400 today. It was equipped with various other luxury features besides the diamond-dusted paint job and gold-plated hub-caps, including a refrigerator and a ten-disk record changer (there were no CDs back then).

According to d'Estries (2012), J. K. Rowling had given away $160 million in charitable donations by 2012. The $15 million check was written to a multiple sclerosis treatment center at the University of Edinburgh (D'Zurilla 2010). Her mother had died at age forty-five from complications related to multiple sclerosis.

Besides being husband to 365 wives, Rajinder Singh was the first man in India to own a car or airplane; he was also an international polo champion. One of his many wives was an Irish-born British subject, which caused quite a stir in Britain in the 1890s (see Collins and LaPierre [1975] and Wikipedia, "Rajinder Singh").

For more on Ray Otero, see Feuer (2008).

The Rational Animal

For a more academic treatment of the contrast between our position and earlier economic models, see Kenrick et al. (2009) and Kenrick et al. (2012).

CHAPTER 1: RATIONALITY, IRRATIONALITY, AND THE DEAD KENNEDYS

For more on Joe Kennedy and his family, see Goodwin (1987) and Collier and Horowitz (1984). *The Kennedy Curse* was written by Edward Klein (2003).

Rational Man: People as Econs

For a basic introduction to the assumptions of classic rational economics, see any introductory economics textbook, such as Bronfenbrenner, Sichel, and Gardner (1990). As David Friedman notes, economics "starts from the assumption that individuals have objectives and tend to choose the correct way to achieve them" (1996, 3). In his classic work on economic rationality, John Stuart Mill proposed that a human being could be arbitrarily defined as "a being who inevitably does that by which he may obtain the greatest amount of necessaries, conveniences, and luxuries, with the smallest quantity of labour and physical self-denial with which they can be obtained" (1836/1874). For an entertaining application of the assumption that all our choices reflect rational decisions, see Levitt and Dubner's *Freakonomics* (2005).

Irrational Man: People as Morons

See Grady (1999) for the argument that the curse of the Kennedys is due to their own reckless risk taking.

For the scientific origins of loss aversion, see Kahneman and Tversky (1979) and Tversky and Kahneman (1981). To further explore the roots of behavioral economics, see Simon (1955, 1956).

For accessible books on behavioral economics, see Ariely's *Predictably Irrational* (2008), Thaler and Sunstein's *Nudge* (2008), and Kahneman's *Thinking Fast and Slow* (2011).

Deep Rationality: Humans as Animals

For evolutionary examinations of economics and decision making, see Aktipis and Kurzban (2004), Saad (2007), Gandolfi, Gandolfi, and Barash (2002), Cosmides and Tooby (1994), Kanazawa (2001), and Kenrick et al. (2009).

For more general introductions to evolutionary psychology, see Buss (2005), Confer et al. (2010), Crawford and Krebs (2008), Dunbar and Barrett (2009), Gangestad and Simpson (2007), and Kenrick (2011).

Loss Aversion in Monkeys and Men

For the study of loss aversion in monkeys, see Lakshminarayanan, Chen, and Santos (2008).

For more on how monkeys and humans share the same decision biases, see Lakshminarayanan, Chen, and Santos (2011).

For more on human ancestral conditions, see Carroll (2009).

For more on the evolution of loss aversion in humans, see Li et al. (2012) and Winterhalder (2007).

Proximate Versus Ultimate Reasons for Behavior

For the scientific origins of proximate and ultimate explanations in biology, see Tinbergen (1963).

For a more detailed discussion of proximate and ultimate explanations in humans, see Kenrick, Griskevicius, et al. (2010) and Alcock (2013, ch. 10).

The Subconscious Influence of the Ovulatory Cycle

For the ovulation and spending study, see Durante et al. (2011).

For the ovulation and stripping study, see Miller, Tybur, and Jordan (2007).

The Kennedys and the Biology of Risk

For the skateboarding study, see Ronay and von Hippel (2010).

For studies showing that the presence of a woman increases men's risk taking at card games, see Baker and Maner (2008, 2009).

For the study showing men take more risks in the presence of an ovulating woman, see Miller and Maner (2011a).

For the study showing that smelling T-shirts worn by ovulating women increases men's testosterone levels, see Miller and Maner (2010).

CHAPTER 2: THE SEVEN SUBSELVES

For more on the life of Martin Luther King Jr., see Branch's (1988) Pulitzer Prize–winning account of the civil rights leader and his place in history.

Selves Within the Self

For the classic *The Three Faces of Eve,* see Thigpen and Cleckley (1957).

For good descriptions of the split-brain studies, see Gazzaniga (1985) and Sperry (1968).

For the book on our evolved psychological systems or modules, see Kurzban (2010). For a more scientific analysis, see Barrett and Kurzban (2006).

Primed for Persuasion

For a general introduction to the idea of subselves, see Kenrick (2011).

For the advertising study, see Griskevicius et al. (2009).

How Many Subselves Are There?

For more scientific detail on these subselves, see Kenrick, Li, and Butner (2003), Kenrick, Neuberg, et al. (2010), Kenrick, Griskevicius, et al. (2010), and Griskevicius and Kenrick (forthcoming).

For the touching study at the University of Groningen, see Gazzola et al. (2012).

Self-Protection Subself: The Night Watchman

For more about the dangers of ancestral life, see Pinker (2011).

For statistics on crime and violence in modern times, see Federal Bureau of Investigation (2011).

For more on how a self-protection motive influences psychology and behavior, see Ackerman et al. (2006), Becker et al. (2007, 2010), Maner et al. (2005), Neuberg, Kenrick, and Schaller (2011), Schaller, Park, and Mueller (2003), and Ohman and Mineka (2001).

For the car preferences study, see Griskevicius et al. (2006).

Disease-Avoidance Subself: The Compulsive Hypochondriac

For more on the behavioral immune system, see Schaller and Park (2011).

For more on how a disease-avoidance motive influences psychology and behavior, see Ackerman et al. (2009), Miller and Maner (2011b), Mortensen et al. (2010), and Neuberg, Kenrick, and Schaller (2011).

For the pregnancy study, see Navarrete, Fessler, and Eng (2007).

Affiliation Subself: The Team Player

For the importance of friendship in hunter-gatherers, see Hill and Hurtado (1996).

For more on how the affiliation motive influences psychology and behavior, see Baumeister and Leary (1995), Maner, DeWall, et al. (2007), and Mead et al. (2011).

Status Subself: The Go-Getter

For more on the study of stress and dominance in baboons, see Sapolsky (2002).

For more on the benefits of status on human health, see Marmot (2004).

For more on status and luxury fever, see Frank (1999).

For the idea of gaining status via dominance versus prestige, see Henrich and Gil-White (2001) and Cheng et al. (2013).

For the effects of status motives on aggression, see Griskevicius, Tybur, et al. (2009).

Mate-Acquisition Subself: The Swinging Single

For more on how many human behaviors are related to mate acquisition, see Miller (2000).

For some research comparing mating preferences in homosexuals and heterosexuals, see Bailey et al. (1994) and Kenrick et al. (1995). As discussed in Kenrick (2011), homosexuality raises some interesting puzzles from an evolutionary perspective, but male homosexual preferences paradoxically provide strong support for the two central ideas of this book: that the ultimate causes of our behavior are often not conscious and that the mind is organized in a modular fashion. If male homosexuals were acting "rationally" in a traditional sense, they would seek partners their own age or perhaps follow society's standards for what constitutes an attractive man (older with high status). Instead, homosexual men are interested in young, physically attractive men, even when those men do not reciprocate their interest and even though these cues would be associated with women in the years of peak fertility rather than deemed stereotypically "masculine" characteristics.

For the car preferences study, see Griskevicius et al. (2006).

Mate-Retention Subself: The Good Spouse

For more on marriage and parenting in humans, see Geary (2000).

For more on how mate-retention motives influence psychology and behavior, see Maner, Gailliot, et al. (2007) and Maner et al. (2009).

Kin-Care Subself: The Nurturing Parent

For more on parenting in traditional societies, see Geary (2000) and Hill and Hurtado (1996).

For how much it costs to raise children, see Lino (2010).

For more on how kin-care motives influence behavior, see Glocker et al. (2009) and Hrdy (1999).

Remembering the Seven Subselves by Climbing the Developmental Pyramid

For more on the developmental pyramid, see Kenrick, Griskevicius, et al. (2010).

Reversing Loss Aversion

For loss aversion as a specific numerical constant, see Thaler et al. (1997).

For the study demonstrating how different fundamental motives reverse loss-aversion patterns, see Li et al. (2012).

CHAPTER 3: HOME ECONOMICS VERSUS WALL STREET ECONOMICS

For more on Walt Disney, the Walt Disney Company, and Michael Eisner, see Stewart (2005) and Thomas (1976, 1998).

For more on the ideas presented in this chapter, see Kenrick, Sundie, and Kurzban (2008).

Playing Games

For the origins of the prisoner's dilemma, see Rapaport and Chammah (1965).

For more on actual behavior in economic games, such as the ultimatum game, across cultures, see Henrich et al. (2005) and Camerer (2003).

Home Economics: The Kinship Game

For the study on economic games with twins, see Segal and Hershberger (1999). For more on twins, see Segal (2000) and Segal and Harris (2008).

For more on the principle of inclusive fitness (also known as *kin selection*), see Hamilton (1964) and Burnstein, Crandall, and Kitayama, 1994.

For a discussion of selective altruism toward kin in ground squirrels, see Sherman (1981). For a discussion of nepotism in white-fronted bee-eaters, see Emlen, Wrege, and Demong (1995).

For the family inheritance findings, see Smith, Kish, and Crawford (1987).

For findings on stepchildren and adopted children, see Daly and Wilson (1998).

Home Economics Versus Corporate Economics

For the evolutionary prisoner's dilemma study, see Kenrick et al. (2006) and Kenrick, Sundie, and Kurzban (2008).

For more on game theory and human evolution, see Hagen and Hammerstein (2006).

For more on sibling rivalry, see Trivers (1974).

Team Payoffs: The Affiliation Game

For Alan Fiske's models of exchange, see Fiske (1992).

For more on the relationship between Steve Jobs and Steve Wozniak, see Isaacson (2011).

For more on "equality matching" and the evolution of reciprocal altruism, see Trivers (1971) and Axelrod and Hamilton (1981).

For more on the study about exchanging different types of rewards, see Foa and Foa (1980) and Turner, Foa, and Foa (1971).

Pyramid Play: The Status Game

For more on the evolution of leadership and followership, see Van Vugt, Hogan, and Kaiser (2008) and Van Vugt and Ahuja (2010).

For more on how people behave differently depending on whether they have high or low status, see Rucker, Galinsky, and Dubois (2012).

Foxhole Economics: The Self-Protection Game

For more on Genghis Khan and the city of Nishapur, see Weatherford (2005).

Is Market Economics Any Way to Run a Business?

For more information on Frederick Winslow Taylor, see Gabor (2000).

Bringing Home Economics to Wall Street

For the trust game study, see DeBruine (2002).

A Family Company

For more on family companies, see Nicholson (2008).

The quote about Southwest being like a family comes from Grubbs-West (2005). For more on Southwest Airlines, see Smith (2004) and Freiberg and Freiberg (1996).

CHAPTER 4: SMOKE DETECTORS IN THE MIND

For more on the Zambia aid story, see Lewin (2007) and BBC News (2002).

Defective Brains and *Does Adaptive = Accurate?*

For a more detailed discussion of errors and biases from an evolutionary perspective, see Haselton et al. (2009).

For auditory looming in humans, see Neuhoff (1998, 2001). For auditory looming in rhesus monkeys, see Ghazanfar, Neuhoff, and Logothetis (2002).

Not All Errors Are Created Equal and *Money Up in Smoke*

For more on the smoke detector principle and human biases, see Haselton and Nettle (2006) and Nesse (2005).

The Behavioral Immune System: In the Mind of Your Disease-Avoidance Subself

For more on the behavioral immune system, see Schaller and Park (2011) and Schaller and Duncan (2007).

For the condom study, see Tybur et al. (2011).

For the study on the behavioral and physical immune systems, see Schaller et al. (2010).

Revisiting Zambian Aid and Mutant French Fries

For the story on McDonald's pulling mutant french fries, see Martin (2000).

For more on the safety of genetically modified foods, see World Health Organization, "20 Questions on Genetically Modified Foods."

Sex Detectors: In the Mind of Men's Mate-Acquisition Subselves

For more on sexual pheromones in moths, see Wyatt (2003).

For more on men's sexual-overperception bias, see Haselton and Buss (2000) and Maner et al. (2003).

Sexy Bad Boy Delusions: In the Mind of Women's Mate-Acquisition Subselves

For how ovulation leads women to see sexy cads as good dads, see Durante, Griskevicius, Simpson, et al. (2012).

Reason for Optimism: In the Mind of Your Status Subself

For more on Steve Jobs, see Isaacson (2011).

For further reading on overconfidence and better-than-average effects, see Alicke, Dunning, and Kruger (2005), Hoorens (1993), Larrick, Burson, and Soll (2007), Moore and Healy (2008), and Weinstein (1980).

For the study on the evolutionary basis of overconfidence, see Johnson and Fowler (2011).

For the study of overconfidence, competence, and leadership, see Anderson et al. (2012).

Born to Be Biased

For data on beliefs about marriage, see Arnett and Schwab (2012).

CHAPTER 5: MODERN CAVEMEN

For more on the Shiwiar, see Sugiyama (2004a, 2004b).

For the Shiwiar and performance on logic tests, see Sugiyama, Tooby, and Cosmides (2002).

Logically Deficient Minds and *Communicating on Our Natural Frequency*

For medical errors, see Vohs and Frances Luce (2010).

For the "Linda problem," see Tversky and Kahneman (1983).

Why Can't Johnny Do the Math? and *Communicating on Our Natural Frequency*

For cancer study and natural frequencies, see Gigerenzer et al. (2007).

Detecting Cheaters

For the workings of cheater detection, see Cosmides (1989) and Cosmides and Tooby (1992).

Erasing Errors by Engaging the Affiliation Subself

For the Asian disease problem, see Tversky and Kahneman (1981).

For the revised version of the disease problem, see Wang (1996a, 1996b).

How to Help Suicidal Turtles (and Irrational Humans)

For suicidal turtles, see Scott (2009).

CHAPTER 6: LIVING FAST AND DYING YOUNG

For more on MC Hammer, see Wikipedia, "MC Hammer."

For the *Sports Illustrated* article, see Torre (2009).

For *The Millionaire Next Door,* see Stanley and Danko (1996).

Life History Theory

For more detailed discussions of life history theory, see Kenrick and Luce (2000), Kaplan and Gangestad (2005), Roff (2002), Stearns (1992), Hill and Kaplan (1999), and Chisholm (1993).

The Three Stages

For more on the three stages, see Kenrick, Griskevicius, et al. (2010).

For risky behavior in the mating stage, see Wilson, Daly, and Pound (2002).

For the study on testosterone, see Dabbs and Morris (1990).

For the studies on violence, homicide, and "trivial altercations," see Daly and Wilson (1988) and Wilson and Daly (1985).

For average ages of becoming a first-time parent, see Griskevicius et al. (2011).

For the hockey and aggression study, see Palmer (1993).

For testosterone dropping after marriage and the birth of a child, see Gettler et al. (2011) and Gettler, McDade, and Kuzawa (2011).

The Age of Entrepreneurism

For the testosterone and investing study, see Coates and Herbert (2008).

For testosterone injections in New York, see Abraham (2012).

For entrepreneurs peaking by age twenty-five, see Arrington (2011).

For the mergers and acquisitions study, see Levi, Li, and Zhang (2010).

For the testosterone and negotiation study, see Burnham (2007).

For the successful entrepreneurs study, see Wadhwa et al. (2009).

Fast Versus Slow Strategies

For the original marshmallow study, see Mischel, Ebbesen, and Zeiss (1972).

For the relationship between the marshmallow study and later behavior, see Shoda, Mischel, and Peake (1990).

High Risk, No Reward

For more on Ray Otero, see Feuer (2008).

For more on the New York State Lottery, see DiNapoli (2008).

Fast and Slow People

For more on fast and slow life history strategies, see Griskevicius et al. (2013), Nettle (2010), and Figueredo et al. (2009).

For reproductive timing statistics, see Mathews and Hamilton (2005).

Raised to Run

For the influence of childhood environment on life history strategies, see Ellis et al. (2009), Belsky, Steinberg, and Draper (1991), and Del Giudice (2009).

For the study of local mortality levels in 170 countries, see Low et al. (2008).

For the Chicago neighborhood study, see Wilson and Daly (1997).

For the study of violent crime in the United States, see Griskevicius et al. (2011).

For the effect of childhood environment on the timing of puberty and menstruation, see Belsky, Houts, and Fearon (2010) and Ellis (2004).

For influence of the first five years of life, see Simpson et al. (2012).

For the marshmallow and unpredictable environment study, see Kidd, Palmen, and Aslin (2013).

Win, Crash, or Burn

For the very informal rock star study, see Dial the Truth Ministries, "Premature Death of Rock Stars." Note that this is not a scientific study and likely underestimates how long rock stars live.

For monkey studies, see Rosenblum et al. (2001) and Andrews and Rosenblum (1991).

For studies on how stress influences life history strategies, see White et al. (forthcoming) and Griskevicius et al. (2011a, 2011b, 2013).

Off to the Races

For more on Ray Otero, see Feuer (2008).

CHAPTER 7: GOLD PORSCHES AND GREEN PEACOCKS

For the gold Porsche, see Russia (2008).

For *The Theory of the Leisure Class,* see Veblen (1899).

For more about "grillz," see Nelly's 2006 song of the same name.

Why Do We Throw Money Away?

For more on conspicuous consumption across cultures and time, see Bird and Smith (2005), Godoy et al. (2007), Sundie et al. (2011), and Veblen (1899).

For more about an economic take on conspicuous consumption, see De Fraja (2009).

Are We Out of Touch with the Causes of Our Own Behavior?

For more on how people don't know the reasons for their decisions, see Nisbett and Wilson (1977).

For the "Why People Really Buy Hybrids" study, see Klein (2007).

For the "going green to be seen" study, see Griskevicius, Tybur, and Van den Bergh (2010).

For the automobile culture quote, see Schneider (2004).

For more on the Sextons' work, see Dubner (2011).

For more on who's getting the first Fisker Karma, see Autoblog (2011).

For more on *Consumer Reports* and the Fisker Karma, see O'Toole (2012).

Multiple Explanations for the Same Behavior

For the scientific origins of proximate and ultimate explanations in biology, see Tinbergen (1963).

For a more detailed discussion of proximate and ultimate explanations in humans, see Kenrick, Griskevicius, et al. (2010) and Alcock (2013).

Bower Power

For more on bowerbird displays, see Borgia (1985) and Miller (2000).

Flashing the Cash

For more on the study of women's influence on young men, see Roney (2003).

For the study of how mate-acquisition motives influence conspicuous consumption, see Griskevicius et al. (2007).

Peacocks, Porsches, and Papas

For the personality test, see Simpson and Gangestad (1991). For a fuller discussion of the concept, see Gangestad and Simpson (2000).

For the study of conspicuous consumption in peacock-like men, see Sundie et al. (2011).

For the conspicuous consumption and testosterone study, see Saad and Vongas (2009).

The Ultimate Driver of Behavior

To find the German Porsche ad, see YouTube, "Hot Girl Flashes Porsche 911."

For more on evolution and consumer behavior, see Miller (2009) and Saad (2007, 2011).

CHAPTER 8: SEXUAL ECONOMICS: HIS AND HERS

For more on the Eliot Spitzer scandal, see Wikipedia, "Eliot Spitzer Prostitution Scandal."

For more on the Emperor's Club escorts, see *Huffington Post* (2008).

For more on the prices for brides, see Beaumont (2007) and Tertilt (2005).

Why Do Men Pay So Much for the Company of a Woman?

For more on bride price, see Anderson (2007).

For more on the principle of minimum parental investment, see Trivers (1972).

For the sexual-economics study, see Baumeister and Vohs (2004).

For the study of men's and women's minimum standards for mates and dates, see Kenrick et al. (1990, 1993).

For men's lower standards for women for sex across cultures, see Schmitt (2005) and Schmitt et al. (2003).

For the "Would you go to bed with me?" study, see Clark and Hatfield (1989).

I Love You . . . Sort Of

For the "I love you" study, see Ackerman, Griskevicius, and Li (2011).

Are Men Completely Nondiscriminating?

For *Bringing Down the House,* see Mezrich (2002).

For age preferences in mates across cultures, see Kenrick and Keefe (1992).

For teenagers' age preferences in mates, see Kenrick et al. (1996).

Designing a Mate: Hers Versus His

For the "design a mate" study, see Li et al. (2002).

For more on gender differences and similarities in mate preferences, see Buss (1989) and Li and Kenrick (2006).

Why Do Women Sometimes Pay for Men?

For more on dowry and bride price, see Randeria and Visaria (1984), Anderson (2007), and Rajamaran (1983).

Swinging Singles: The Mate-Acquisition Game

For more on men's and women's singles ads, see Kenrick and Keefe (1992), Rajecki, Bledsoe, and Rasmussen (1991), Wiederman (1993), and Baize and Schroeder (1995).

For the studies of different causes of mortality, see Kenrick and Gomez-Jacinto (2013).

For more on how men behave when mate-acquisition motives are activated, see Baker and Maner (2008), Griskevicius et al. (2006a, 2006b, 2007, 2009), Iredale, Van Vugt, and Dunbar (2008), Wilson and Daly (2004), and Van der Bergh, Dewitte, and Warlop (2008).

All the Single Ladies

For how mate acquisition leads women to become agreeable, see Griskevicius, Goldstein et al. (2006).

For the tipping study, see Griskevicius et al. (2007).

For the study on women taking risks to look beautiful, see Hill and Durante (2011).

For the study on how beauty for women is a necessity, see Hill et al. (2012).

Wedding Bonds: The Mate-Retention Game

For the study on men's high standards for marriage partners, see Kenrick et al. (1990).

Jealousy: His and Hers

For the research on sex differences in jealousy, see Buss et al. (1999) and Sagarin (2005).

For cross-cultural replication, see Buunk et al. (1996), Buss et al. (1999), and Wiederman and Kendall (1999).

Sexual Supply and Demand

For the Georgia statistics and for how sex ratio influences men's spending, see Griskevicius et al. (2012).

For *Too Many Women?*, see Guttentag and Secord (1983).

For more on sex ratio in different countries, see Hesketh (2009), Francis (2011), Belanger and Tran (2011), and Hudson and den Boar (2005).

For more on sex ratio and women's behavior, see Durante, Griskevicius, Cantu, et al. (2012).

CHAPTER 9: DEEP RATIONALITY PARASITES

For more about cuckoos and reed warblers, see Davies and Brooke (1988) and Alcock (2013).

For more about Bernie Madoff, see Kirtzman (2009).

The Exploitation Continuum

For more information about the distinct forms of mutualism and parasitism between different species, see Boucher (1985), Hoeksma and Bruna (2000), and Hirsch (2004).

Getting People to Pay More and Buy More

For data on business failure from the Bureau of Labor Statistics, see Knaup (2005).

For the statistics on shoe ownership among the affluent, see *Time* (2006).

Swimming (and Spending) in Infested Waters

For a discussion of aggressive mimicry in blennies and wrasses, see Wickler (1966) and Cheney and Cote (2005).

For a discussion of scarcity and the parallels between animal parasites and humans, see Cialdini (2008).

How Much Would You Pay for a Rock?

For a discussion of Ernest Oppenheimer and De Beers, see Kanfer (1993).

A Pill with That, Sir?

For the statistics on drug prescriptions, see Schondelmeyer (2007).

For the statistics on drug deaths, see Null et al. (2011).

For more on the fake-medicine industry, see World Health Organization, "Growing Threat from Counterfeit Medicines."

CONCLUSION: MEMENTOS FROM OUR TOUR

Lesson 2: Rational Self-Interest Is Not in Your Self-Interest.

For the research on the effects of merely calling a strategic interaction the "Wall Street game," see Liberman, Samuels, and Ross (2004).

References

Abraham, Tamara. 2012. "Is Testosterone the New Drug of Choice on Wall Street? How Traders Are Using Male Hormone Booster Shots to Maintain a Competitive Edge." *Daily Mail,* February 10, http://www.dailymail.co.uk/femail/article -2099372/Is-testosterone-new-drug-choice-Wall-Street-How-traders-using -male-hormone-booster-shots-maintain-competitive-edge.html.

Ackerman, J. M., D. V. Becker, C. R. Mortensen, T. Sasaki, S. L. Neuberg, and D. T. Kenrick. 2009. "A Pox on the Mind: Disjunction of Attention and Memory in the Processing of Physical Disfigurement." *Journal of Experimental Social Psychology* 45: 478–485.

Ackerman, J. M., V. Griskevicius, and N. P. Li. 2011. "Let's Get Serious: Communicating Commitment in Romantic Relationships." *Journal of Personality and Social Psychology* 100: 1015–1026.

Ackerman, J. M., J. R. Shapiro, S. L. Neuberg, D. T. Kenrick, D. V. Becker, V. Griskevicius, J. K. Maner, and M. Schaller. 2006. "They All Look the Same to Me (Unless They're Angry): From Out-Group Homogeneity to Out-Group Heterogeneity." *Psychological Science* 17: 836–840.

Aktipis, C. A., and R. Kurzban. 2004. "Is *Homo Economicus* Extinct? Vernon Smith, Daniel Kahneman and the Evolutionary Perspective." In *Advances in Austrian Economics,* edited by R. Koppl, 7:135–153. Amsterdam: Elsevier.

Alcock, J. 2013. *Animal Behavior: An Evolutionary Approach.* 10th ed. Sunderland, MA: Sinauer Associates.

Alicke, Mark D., D. A. Dunning, and J. I. Kruger. 2005. *The Self in Social Judgment.* New York: Psychology Press.

Anderson, C., S. Brion, D. M. Moore, and J. A. Kennedy. 2012. "A Status-Enhancement Account of Overconfidence." *Journal of Personality and Social Psychology* 103: 718–735.

Anderson, S. 2007. "The Economics of Dowry and Brideprice." *Journal of Economic Perspectives* 21, no. 4 (fall): 151–174.

Andrews, M. W., and L. A. Rosenblum. 1991. "Attachment in Monkey Infants Raised in Variable-Demand and Low-Demand Environments." *Child Development* 62: 686–693.

Ariely, D. 2008. *Predictably Irrational*. New York: HarperCollins.

Arnett, J. J., and J. Schwab. 2012. "The Clark University Poll of Emerging Adults." Clark University, December 2012, http://www.clarku.edu/clarkpoll/pdfs/Clark_Poll_Peer%20Inst.pdf.

Arrington, Michael. 2011. "Internet Entrepreneurs Are Like Professional Athletes, They Peak Around 25." TechCrunch, April 30, http://techcrunch.com/2011/04/30/internet-entrepreneurs-are-like-professional-athletes-they-peak-around-25.

Autoblog. 2011. "First Fisker Karma Headed to Leonardo DiCaprio, Colin Powell and Al Gore Soon After." Autoblog, July 13, http://www.autoblog.com/2011/07/13/first-fisker-karma-headed-to-leonardo-dicaprio-colin-powell-and.

Axelrod, R., and W. D. Hamilton. 1981. "The Evolution of Cooperation." *Science* 211: 1390–1396.

Bailey, J. M., S. Gaulin, Y. Agyei, and B. A. Gladue. 1994. "Effects of Gender and Sexual Orientation on Evolutionarily Relevant Aspects of Human Mating Psychology." *Journal of Personality and Social Psychology* 66: 1081–1093.

Baize, H. R., and J. E. Schroeder. 1995. "Personality and Mate Selection in Personal Ads: Evolutionary Preferences in a Public Mate Selection Process." *Journal of Social Behavior and Personality* 10: 517–536.

Baker, M., and J. K. Maner. 2008. "Risk-Taking as a Situationally Sensitive Male Mating Strategy." *Evolution and Human Behavior* 29: 391–395.

———. 2009. "Male Risk-Taking as a Context-Sensitive Signaling Device." *Journal of Experimental Social Psychology* 45: 1136–1139.

Barrett, H. C., and R. Kurzban. 2006. "Modularity in Cognition: Framing the Debate." *Psychological Review* 113: 628–647.

Baumeister, R. R., and M. R. Leary. 1995. "The Need to Belong: Desire for Interpersonal Attachments as a Fundamental Human Motivation." *Psychological Bulletin* 117: 497–529.

Baumeister, Roy F., and Kathleen D. Vohs. 2004. "Sexual Economics: Sex as Female Resource for Social Exchange in Heterosexual Interactions." *Personality and Social Psychology Review* 8, no. 4: 339–363.

BBC News. 2002. "Famine-Hit Zambia Rejects GM Food Aid." BBC News, October 29, http://news.bbc.co.uk/2/hi/africa/2371675.stm.

Beaumont, P. 2007. "Starving Afghans Sell Girls of Eight as Brides." *Guardian*, January 6, http://www.guardian.co.uk/world/2007/jan/07/afghanistan.peter-beaumont.

Becker, D. V., U. S. Anderson, S. L. Neuberg, J. K. Maner, J. R. Shapiro, J. M. Ackerman, M. Schaller, and D. T. Kenrick. 2010. "More Memory Bang for the Attentional Buck: Self-Protection Goals Enhance Encoding Efficiency for Potentially Threatening Males." *Social Psychological and Personality Science* 1: 182–189.

Becker, D. V., D. T. Kenrick, S. L. Neuberg, K. C. Blackwell, and D. M. Smith. 2007. "The Confounded Nature of Angry Men and Happy Women." *Journal of Personality and Social Psychology* 92: 179–190.

Belanger, D., and G. L. Tran. 2011. "The Impact of Transnational Migration on Gender and Marriage in Sending Communities of Vietnam." *Current Sociology* 59: 59–77.

Belsky, J., R. M. Houts, and R. M. P. Fearon. 2010. "Infant Attachment Security and Timing of Puberty: Testing an Evolutionary Hypothesis." *Psychological Science* 21: 1195–1201.

Belsky, J., L. Steinberg, and P. Draper. 1991. "Childhood Experience, Interpersonal Development, and Reproductive Strategy: An Evolutionary Theory of Socialization." *Child Development* 62: 647–670.

Bird, Rebecca Bliege, and Eric Alden Smith. 2005. "Signaling Theory, Strategic Interaction, and Symbolic Capital." *Current Anthropology* 46, no. 2: 221–248.

Borgia, Gerald. 1985. "Bower Quality, Number of Decorations and Mating Success of Male Satin Bowerbirds (*Prilonorhynchus violaceus*): An Experimental Analysis." *Animal Behavior* 33: 266–271.

Boucher, D. H., ed. 1985. *The Biology of Mutualism*. New York: Oxford University Press.

Branch, T. 1988. *Parting the Waters: America in the King Years, 1954–63*. New York: Simon and Schuster.

Bronfenbrenner, M., W. Sichel, and W. Gardner. 1990. *Economics*. 23rd ed. Boston: Houghton Mifflin.

Burnham, Terence C. 2007. "High-Testosterone Men Reject Low Ultimatum Game Offers." *Proceedings of the Royal Society B* 274: 2327–2330.

Burnstein, E., C. Crandall, and S. Kitayama. 1994. "Some Neo-Darwinian Decision Rules for Altruism: Weighing the Cues for Inclusive Fitness as a Function of the Biological Importance of the Decision." *Journal of Personality and Social Psychology* 67: 773–789.

Buss, D. M. 1989. "Sex Differences in Human Mate Preferences: Evolutionary Hypotheses Tested in 37 Cultures." *Behavioral and Brain Sciences* 12: 1–49.

———. 2005. *The Handbook of Evolutionary Psychology*. New York: Wiley.

Buss, D. M., T. K. Shackelford, L. A. Kirkpatrick, J. C. Choe, H. K. Lim, M. Hasegawa, T. Hasegawa, and K. Bennett. 1999. "Jealousy and the Nature of Beliefs About Infidelity: Test of Competing Hypotheses About Sex Differences in the United States, Korea, and Japan." *Personal Relationships* 6: 125–150.

Buunk, B. P., A. Angleitner, V. Oubaid, and D. M. Buss. 1996. "Sex Differences in Jealousy in Evolutionary and Cultural Perspective: Tests from the Netherlands, Germany, and the United States." *Psychological Science* 7: 359–363.

Camerer, C. F. 2003. *Behavioral Game Theory: Experiments in Strategic Interaction*. New York: Russell Sage Foundation.

Carroll, S. B. 2009. *Remarkable Creatures: Epic Adventures in the Search for the Origin of Species*. Orlando, FL: Houghton Mifflin Harcourt.

Cheney, K. L., and I. M. Cote. 2005. "Frequency-Dependent Success of Aggressive Mimics in a Cleaning Symbiosis." *Proceedings of the Royal Society B* 272: 2635–2639.

Cheng, J. T., J. L. Tracy, T. Foulsham, A. Kingstone, and J. Henrich. 2013. "Two Ways to the Top: Evidence that Dominance and Prestige Are Distinct Yet Viable Avenues to Social Rank and Influence." *Journal of Personality and Social Psychology* 104: 103–125.

Chisholm, J. S. 1993. "Death, Hope, and Sex: Life-History Theory and the Development of Reproductive Strategies." *Current Anthropology* 34: 1–24.

Cialdini, R. B. 2008. *Influence: Science and Practice*. 5th ed. Boston: Allyn and Bacon.

Clark, R. D., and E. Hatfield. 1989. "Gender Differences in Receptivity to Sexual Offers." *Journal of Psychology and Human Sexuality* 2: 39–55.

Coates, J. M., and J. Herbert. 2008. "Endogenous Steroids and Financial Risk Taking on a London Trading Floor." *Proceedings of the National Academy of Sciences* 105: 6167–6172.

Collier, P., and D. Horowitz. 1984. *The Kennedys: An American Drama*. New York: Warner/Simon and Schuster.

Collins, L., and D. LaPierre. 1975. *Freedom at Midnight*. New York: Simon and Schuster.

Confer, J. C., J. A. Easton, D. S. Fleischman, C. D. Goetz, D. M. Lewis, C. Perilloux, and D. M. Buss. 2010. "Evolutionary Psychology: Controversies, Questions, Prospects, and Limitations." *American Psychologist* 65: 110–126.

Cosmides, L. 1989. "The Logic of Social Exchange: Has Natural Selection Shaped How Humans Reason? Studies with the Wason Selection Task." *Cognition* 31: 187–276.

Cosmides, L., and J. Tooby. 1992. "Cognitive Adaptations for Social Exchange." In *The Adapted Mind: Evolutionary Psychology and the Generation of Culture*, edited by J. Barkow, L. Cosmides, and J. Tooby, 163–228. New York: Oxford University Press.

———. 1994. "Better Than Rational: Evolutionary Psychology and the Invisible Hand." *American Economic Review* 84: 327–332.

Crawford C., and D. Krebs, eds. 2008. *Foundations of Evolutionary Psychology*. New York: Lawrence Erlbaum Associates.

D'Estries, M. 2012. "J. K. Rowling's Charity Giving Knocks Her Off Forbes' Billionaires List." Mother Nature Network, March 13, http://www.mnn.com/lifestyle/arts-culture/blogs/jk-rowlings-charity-giving-knocks-her-off-forbes-billionaires-list.

D'Zurilla, Christie. 2010. "J. K. Rowling Donates $15.4 Million to Multiple Sclerosis Research." *Los Angeles Times,* August 31, http://latimesblogs.latimes.com/gossip/2010/08/multiple-sclerosis-jk-rowling-donates-to-ms-research.html.

Dabbs, J. M., and R. Morris. 1990. "Testosterone, Social Class, and Antisocial Behavior in a Sample of 4,462 Men." *Psychological Science* 1: 209–211.

Daly, M., and M. Wilson. 1988. *Homicide*. New York: Aldine de Gruyter.

Daly, Martin, and Margo Wilson. 1998. *The Truth About Cinderella*. New Haven, CT: Yale University Press.

Davies, N. B., and M. de L. Brooke. 1988. "Cuckoos Versus Reed Warblers: Adaptations and Counteradaptations." *Animal Behavior* 36: 262–284.

De Fraja, Gianni. 2009. "The Origin of Utility: Sexual Selection and Conspicuous Consumption." *Journal of Economic Behavior and Organization* 72: 51–69.

DeBruine, L. M. 2002. "Facial Resemblance Enhances Trust." *Proceedings of the Royal Society B* 269, no. 1498: 1307–1312.

Del Giudice, M. 2009. "Sex, Attachment, and the Development of Reproductive Strategies: Economic Uncertainty and Life History Strategies." *Behavioral and Brain Sciences* 32: 1–21.

Dial the Truth Ministries. n.d. "Premature Death of Rock Stars." Dial the Truth Ministries, http://www.av1611.org/rockdead.html.

DiNapoli, T. P. 2008. "2008 Comptroller's Report of the Financial Condition of New York State." Office of the State Comptroller, http://www.osc.state.ny.us/finance/finreports/fcr08.pdf.

Dubner, Stephen J. 2011. "Hey Baby, Is That a Prius You're Driving?" Freakonomics, July 7, http://www.freakonomics.com/2011/07/07/hey-baby-is-that-a-prius-you%E2%80%99re-driving.

Dunbar, Robin, and Louise Barrett. 2009. *Oxford Handbook of Evolutionary Psychology*. Oxford: Oxford University Press.

Durante, K. M., V. Griskevicius, S. M. Cantu, J. A. Simpson, and J. M. Tybur. 2012. "Sex Ratio and Women's Careers: Does a Scarcity of Men Lead Women to Choose Briefcase over Baby?" *Journal of Personality and Social Psychology* 103: 121–134.

Durante, K. M., V. Griskevicius, S. E. Hill, C. Perilloux, and N. P. Li. 2011. "Ovulation, Female Competition, and Product Choice: Hormonal Influences on Consumer Behavior." *Journal of Consumer Research* 37: 921–934.

Durante, K. M., V. Griskevicius, J. A. Simpson, S. M. Cantu, and N. P. Li. 2012. "Ovulation Leads Women to See Sexy Cads as Good Dads." *Journal of Personality and Social Psychology* 103: 292–305.

Ellis, B. J. 2004. "Timing of Pubertal Maturation in Girls." *Psychological Bulletin* 130: 920–958.

Ellis, B. J., A. J. Figueredo, B. H. Brumbach, and G. L. Schlomer. 2009. "Fundamental Dimensions of Environmental Risk: The Impact of Harsh vs. Unpredictable Environments on the Evolution and Development of Life History Strategies." *Human Nature* 20: 204–268.

Emlen, S. T., P. H. Wrege, and N. J. Demong. 1995. "Making Decisions in the Family: An Evolutionary Perspective." *American Scientist* 83: 148–157.

Federal Bureau of Investigation. 2011. "Crime in the United States: 2011." FBI.gov, http://www.fbi.gov/about-us/cjis/ucr/crime-in-the-u.s/2011/crime-in-the-u.s.-2011.

Feuer, A. 2008. "Thousands Later, He Sees Lottery's Cruelty Up Close." *New York Times,* August 21, http://www.nytimes.com/2008/08/22/nyregion/22super.html?_r_1.

Figueredo, A. J., G. Vásquez, B. H. Brumbach, J. A. Sefcek, B. R. Kirsner, and W. J. Jacobs. 2005. "The K-Factor: Individual Differences in Life History Strategy." *Personality and Individual Differences* 39, no. 8: 1349–1360.

Fiske, A. P. 1992. "The Four Elementary Forms of Sociality: Framework for a Unified Theory of Social Relations." *Psychological Review* 99: 689–723.

Foa, E. B., and U. G. Foa. 1980. "Resource Theory: Interpersonal Behavior as Exchange." In *Social Exchange: Advances in Theory and Research,* edited by K. J. Gergen, M. S. Greenberg, and R. H. Willis, 77–94. New York: Plenum Press.

Francis, A. M. 2011. "Sex Ratios and the Red Dragon: Using the Chinese Communist Revolution to Explore the Effect of the Sex Ratio on Women and Children in Taiwan." *Journal of Population Economics* 24: 813–837.

Frank, Robert. 1999. *Luxury Fever.* Princeton, NJ: Princeton University Press.

Freiberg, K. L., and J. A. Freiberg. 1996. "Nuts! Southwest Airlines Crazy Recipe for Business and Personal Success." New York: Broadway Books.

Friedman, D. 1996. *Hidden Order: The Economics of Everyday Life.* New York: HarperCollins.

Gabor, A. 2000. *The Capitalist Philosophers.* New York: Times Business.

Gandolfi, Arthur, Anna S. Gandolfi, and David P. Barash. 2002. *Economics as an*

Evolutionary Science: From Utility to Fitness. Piscataway, NJ: Transaction Publishers.

Gangestad, S. W., and J. A. Simpson. 2000. "The Evolution of Human Mating: Trade-Offs and Strategic Pluralism." *Behavioral and Brain Sciences* 23: 573–644.

Gangestad, S. W., and J. A. Simpson, eds. 2007. *The Evolution of Mind: Fundamental Questions and Controversies*. New York: Guilford Press.

Gazzaniga, M. 1985. *The Social Brain: Discovering the Networks of the Mind*. New York: Basic Books.

Gazzola, Valeria, Michael L. Spezio, Joset A. Etzel, Fulvia Castelli, Ralph Adolphs, and Christian Keysers. 2012. "Primary Somatosensory Cortex Discriminates Affective Significance in Social Touch." *Proceedings of the National Academy of Sciences* 109: 9688–9689.

Geary, D. C. 2000. "Evolution and the Proximate Expression of Human Paternal Investment." *Psychological Bulletin* 126: 55–77.

Gettler, L. T., A. B. Feranil, T. W. McDade, and C. W. Kuzawa. 2011. "Longitudinal Evidence That Fatherhood Decreases Testosterone in Human Males." *Proceedings of the National Academy of Sciences* 108, no. 29: 16194–16199.

Gettler, L. T., T. W. McDade, and C. W. Kuzawa. 2011. "Cortisol and Testosterone in Filipino Young Adult Men: Evidence for Co-regulation of Both Hormones by Fatherhood and Relationship Status." *American Journal of Human Biology* 23, no. 5: 609–620.

Ghazanfar, A. A., J. G. Neuhoff, and N. K. Logothetis. 2002. "Auditory Looming Perception in Rhesus Monkeys." *Proceedings of the National Academy of Sciences USA* 99, no. 24: 15755–15757.

Gigerenzer, G., W. Gaissmaier, E. Kurz-Milcke, L. M. Schwartz, and S. Woloshin. 2007. "Helping Doctors and Patients to Make Sense of Health Statistics." *Psychological Science in the Public Interest* 8: 53–96.

Glocker, M. L., D. D. Langleben, K. Ruparel, J. W. Loughead, R. C. Gur, and N. Sachser. 2009. "Baby Schema in Infant Faces Induces Cuteness Perception and Motivation for Caretaking in Adults." *Ethology* 115: 257–263.

Godoy, Ricardo, Victoria Reyes-Garcia, Tomas Huanca, William R. Leonard, Thomas McDade, Susan Tanner, Vincent Vadez, and Graig Seyfried. 2007. "Signaling by Consumption in a Native Amazonian Society." *Evolution and Human Behavior* 28: 124–134.

Goodwin, D. K. 1987. *The Fitzgeralds and the Kennedys: An American Saga*. New York: Simon and Schuster.

Grady, S. 1999. "Kennedy Curse Is a Product of the Kennedy Hubris." *Lawrence Journal-World*, July 20, 6B.

Griskevicius, V., J. A. Ackerman, S. M. Cantu, A. W. Delton, T. E. Robertson, J. A.

Simpson, M. E. Thomson, and J. M. Tybur. 2013. "When the Economy Falters Do People Spend Or Save? Responses to Resource Scarcity Depend on Childhood Environments." *Psychological Science* 24: 197–205.

Griskevicius, V., R. B. Cialdini, and D. T. Kenrick. 2006. "Peacocks, Picasso, and Parental Investment: The Effects of Romantic Motives on Creativity." *Journal of Personality and Social Psychology* 91: 63–76.

Griskevicius, V., A. W. Delton, T. E. Robertson, and J. M. Tybur. 2011a. "The Environmental Contingency of Life History Strategies: Influences of Mortality and Socioeconomic Status on Reproductive Timing." *Journal of Personality and Social Psychology* 100: 241–254.

Griskevicius, V., J. M. Tybur, A. W. Delton, and T. E. Robertson. 2011b. "The Influence of Mortality and Socioeconomic Status on Risk and Delayed Rewards: A Life History Theory Approach." *Journal of Personality and Social Psychology* 100, 1015–1026.

Griskevicius, V., N. J. Goldstein, C. R. Mortensen, R. B. Cialdini, and D. T. Kenrick. 2006. "Going Along Versus Going Alone: When Fundamental Motives Facilitate Strategic (Non)conformity." *Journal of Personality and Social Psychology* 91: 281–294.

Griskevicius, V., N. J. Goldstein, C. R. Mortensen, J. M. Sundie, R. B. Cialdini, and D. T. Kenrick. 2009. "Fear and Loving in Las Vegas: Evolution, Emotion, and Persuasion." *Journal of Marketing Research* 46: 385–395.

Griskevicius, V., and D. T. Kenrick. Forthcoming. "Fundamental Motives: How Evolutionary Needs Influence Consumer Behavior." *Journal of Consumer Psychology*.

Griskevicius, V., J. M. Tybur, J. A. Ackerman, A. W. Delton, T. E. Robertson, and A. E. White. 2012. "The Financial Consequences of Too Many Men: Sex Ratio Effects on Saving, Borrowing, and Spending." *Journal of Personality and Social Psychology* 102: 69–80.

Griskevicius, V., J. M. Tybur, S. W. Gangestad, E. F. Perea, J. R. Shapiro, and D. T. Kenrick. 2009. "Aggress to Impress: Hostility as an Evolved Context-Dependent Strategy." *Journal of Personality and Social Psychology* 96: 980–994.

Griskevicius, V., J. M. Tybur, J. M. Sundie, R. B. Cialdini, G. F. Miller, and D. T. Kenrick. 2007. "Blatant Benevolence and Conspicuous Consumption: When Romantic Motives Elicit Strategic Costly Signals." *Journal of Personality and Social Psychology* 93: 85–102.

Griskevicius, V., J. M. Tybur, and B. Van den Bergh. 2010. "Going Green to Be Seen: Status, Reputation, and Conspicuous Conservation." *Journal of Personality and Social Psychology* 98: 392–404.

Grubbs-West, L. 2005. *Lessons in Loyalty: How Southwest Airlines Does It—an Insider's View*. Dallas, TX: Cornerstone Leadership Institute.

Guttentag, M., and P. F. Secord. 1983. *Too Many Women? The Sex Ratio Question.* Beverly Hills, CA: Sage Publications.

Hagen, E. H., and P. Hammerstein. 2006. "Game Theory and Human Evolution: A Critique of Some Recent Interpretations of Experimental Games." *Theoretical Population Biology* 69: 339–348.

Hamilton, W. D. 1964. "The Genetical Evolution of Social Behavior." *Journal of Theoretical Biology* 7: 1–52.

Haselton, M. G., G. A. Bryant, A. Wilke, D. A. Frederick, A. Galperin, W. Frankenhuis, and T. Moore. 2009. "Adaptive Rationality: An Evolutionary Perspective on Cognitive Bias." *Social Cognition* 27: 733–763.

Haselton, M. G., and D. M. Buss. 2000. "Error Management Theory: A New Perspective on Biases in Cross-Sex Mind Reading." *Journal of Personality and Social Psychology* 78: 81–91.

Haselton, M. G., and D. Nettle. 2006. "The Paranoid Optimist: An Integrative Evolutionary Model of Cognitive Biases." *Personality and Social Psychology Review* 10, no. 1: 47–66.

Henrich, J., and F. J. Gil-White. 2001. "The Evolution of Prestige: Freely Conferred Status as a Mechanism for Enhancing the Benefits of Cultural Transmission." *Evolution and Human Behavior* 22: 165–196.

Henrich, Joseph, Robert Boyd, Samuel Bowles, Colin Camerer, Ernst Fehr, Herbert Gintis, Richard McElreath, Michael Alvard, Abigail Barr, Jean Ensminger, Kim Hill, Francisco Gil-White, Michael Gurven, Frank Marlowe, John Q. Patton, Natalie Smith, and David Tracer. 2005. "'Economic Man' in Cross-Cultural Perspective: Behavioral Experiments in 15 Small-Scale Societies." *Behavioral and Brain Sciences* 28, no. 6: 795–815.

Hesketh, T. 2009. "Too Many Males in China: The Causes and Consequences." *Significance* 6: 9–13.

Hill, K., and A. M. Hurtado. 1996. *Aché Life History: The Ecology and Demography of a Foraging People.* Hawthorne, NY: Aldine de Gruyter.

Hill, K., and H. Kaplan. 1999. "Life History Traits in Humans: Theory and Empirical Studies." *Annual Review of Anthropology* 28: 397–438.

Hill, S. E., C. Rodeheffer, V. Griskevicius, K. M. Durante, and A. E. White. 2012. "Boosting Beauty in an Economic Decline: Mating, Spending, and the Lipstick Effect." *Journal of Personality and Social Psychology* 103: 275–291.

Hill, Sarah E., and Kristina M. Durante. 2011. "Courtship, Competition, and the Pursuit of Attractiveness: Mating Goals Facilitate Health-Related Risk-Taking and Strategic Risk Suppression in Women." *Personality and Social Psychology Bulletin* 37: 383–394.

Hirsch, A. M. 2004. "Plant-Microbe: A Continuum from Commensalism to Parasitism." *Symbiosis* 37: 345–363.

Hoeksma, J. D., and E. M. Bruna. 2000. "Pursuing the Big Questions About Interspecific Mutualism: A Review of Theoretical Approaches." *Oecologia* 125: 321–330.

Hoorens, Vera. 1993. "Self-Enhancement and Superiority Biases in Social Comparison." *European Review of Social Psychology* 4, no. 1: 113–139.

Hrdy, S. B. 1999. *Mother Nature: A History of Mothers, Infants, and Natural Selection.* New York: Pantheon.

Hudson, Valerie M., and Andrea M. den Boar. 2005. *Bare Branches: The Security Implications of Asia's Surplus Male Population.* Cambridge, MA: MIT Press.

Huffington Post. 2008. "Emperors Club: All About Eliot Spitzer's Alleged Prostitution Ring." *Huffington Post,* October 18, updated May 25, 2011, http://www.huffingtonpost.com/2008/03/10/emperors-club-all-about-e_n_90768.html.

Iredale, W., M. Van Vugt, and R. I. M. Dunbar. 2008. "Showing Off in Humans: Male Generosity as a Mating Signal." *Evolutionary Psychology* 6, no. 3: 386–392.

Isaacson, Walter. 2011. *Steve Jobs.* New York: Simon and Schuster.

Johnson, D. D. P., and J. H. Fowler. 2011. "The Evolution of Overconfidence." *Nature* 477: 317–320.

Kahneman, Daniel. 2011. *Thinking Fast and Slow.* New York: Farrar, Straus and Giroux.

Kahneman, Daniel, and Amos Tversky. 1979. "Prospect Theory: An Analysis of Decision Under Risk." *Econometrica* 47: 263–291.

Kanazawa, S. 2001. "De Gustibus Est Disputandum." *Social Forces* 79: 1131–1163.

Kanfer, S. 1993. *The Last Empire: De Beers, Diamonds, and the World.* New York: HarperCollins.

Kaplan, H., and S. Gangestad. 2005. "Life History Theory and Evolutionary Psychology." In *The Handbook of Evolutionary Psychology,* edited by David M. Buss, 68–95. New York: John Wiley and Sons.

Kenrick, D. T. 2011. *Sex, Murder, and the Meaning of Life: A Psychologist Investigates How Evolution, Cognition, and Complexity Are Revolutionizing Our View of Human Nature.* New York: Basic Books.

Kenrick, D. T., C. Gabrielidis, R. C. Keefe, and J. Cornelius. 1996. "Adolescent's Age Preferences for Dating Partners: Support for an Evolutionary Model of Life-History Strategies." *Child Development* 67: 1499–1511.

Kenrick, D. T., and L. Gomez-Jacinto. 2013. "Economics, Sex, and the Emergence of Society: A Dynamic Life History Model of Cultural Variation." In *Advances in Culture and Psychology,* edited by M. Gelfand, C. Y. Chiu, and Y. Y. Hong. Vol. 3. New York: Oxford University Press.

Kenrick, D. T., V. Griskevicius, S. L. Neuberg, and M. Schaller. 2010. "Renovating the Pyramid of Needs: Contemporary Extensions Built upon Ancient Foundations." *Perspectives on Psychological Science* 5: 292–314.

Kenrick, D. T., V. Griskevicius, J. M. Sundie, N. P. Li, Y. J. Li, and S. L. Neuberg. 2009. "Deep Rationality: The Evolutionary Economics of Decision-Making." *Social Cognition* 27: 764–785.

Kenrick, D. T., G. R. Groth, M. R. Trost, and E. K. Sadalla. 1993. "Integrating Evolutionary and Social Exchange Perspectives on Relationships: Effects of Gender, Self-Appraisal, and Involvement Level on Mate Selection Criteria." *Journal of Personality and Social Psychology* 64: 951–969.

Kenrick, D. T., N. L. Li, and J. Butner. 2003. "Dynamical Evolutionary Psychology: Individual Decision Rules and Emergent Social Norms." *Psychological Review* 110: 3–28.

Kenrick, D. T., Y. J. Li, A. E. White, and S. L. Neuberg. 2012. "Economic Subselves: Fundamental Motives and Deep Rationality." In *Social Thinking and Interpersonal Behavior: The 14th Sydney Symposium of Social Psychology,* edited by J. Forgas, K. Fiedler, and C. Sedikides, 23–43. New York: Psychology Press.

Kenrick, D. T., and C. L. Luce. 2000. "An Evolutionary Life-History Model of Gender Differences and Similarities." In *The Developmental Social Psychology of Gender,* edited by T. Eckes and H. M. Trautner, 35–63. Hillsdale, NJ: Erlbaum.

Kenrick, D. T., and R. C. Keefe. 1992. "Age Preferences in Mates Reflect Sex Differences in Human Reproductive Strategies." *Behavioral and Brain Sciences* 15: 75–133.

Kenrick, D. T., R. C. Keefe, A. Bryan, A. Barr, and S. Brown. 1995. "Age Preferences and Mate Choice Among Homosexuals and Heterosexuals: A Case for Modular Psychological Mechanisms." *Journal of Personality and Social Psychology* 69: 1166–1172.

Kenrick, D. T., S. L. Neuberg, V. Griskevicius, M. Schaller, and D. V. Becker. 2010. "Goal-Driven Cognition and Functional Behavior: The Fundamental Motives Framework." *Current Directions in Psychological Science* 19: 63–67.

Kenrick, D. T., E. K. Sadalla, G. Groth, and M. R. Trost. 1990. "Evolution, Traits, and the Stages of Human Courtship: Qualifying the Parental Investment Model." *Journal of Personality* 53: 97–116.

Kenrick, D. T., F. Sanabria, J. M. Sundie, and P. R. Killeen. 2006. *When Dilemmas Disappear: How Fitness Interdependencies Transform Strategic Games.* Unpublished manuscript.

Kenrick, D. T., J. M. Sundie, and R. Kurzban. 2008. "Cooperation and Conflict Between Kith, Kin, and Strangers: Game Theory by Domains." In *Foundations of Evolutionary Psychology: Ideas, Issues and Applications,* edited by C. Crawford and D. Krebs, 371–382. Mahwah, NJ: Erlbaum.

Kidd, C., H. Palmen, and R. N. Aslin. 2013. "Rational Snacking: Young Children's Decision-Making on the Marshmallow Task Is Moderated by Beliefs About Environmental Reliability." *Cognition* 126: 109–114.

Kirtzman, A. 2009. *Betrayal: The Life and Lies of Bernie Madoff.* New York: Harper-Collins.

Klein, E. 2003. *The Kennedy Curse.* New York: St. Martin's Press.

Klein, Jonathan. 2007. "Why Do People Really Buy Hybrids." The Topline Strategy Group, http://www.cleanenergycouncil.org/files/Topline_Strategy_Report_Why_People_Really_Buy_Hybrids.pdf.

Knaup, A. 2005. "Survival and Longevity in the Business Employment Dynamics Data." *Monthly Labor Review* (May): 50–56.

Kurzban, Robert. 2010. *Why Everyone (Else) Is a Hypocrite: Evolution and the Modular Mind.* Princeton, NJ: Princeton University Press.

Lakshminarayanan, V., M. K. Chen, and L. R. Santos. 2008. "Endowment Effect in Capuchin Monkeys (*Cebus apella*)." *Philosophical Transactions of the Royal Society B: Biological Sciences* 363: 3837–3844.

———. 2011. "The Evolution of Decision-Making Under Risk: Framing Effects in Monkey Risk Preferences." *Journal of Experimental Social Psychology* 47, no. 3 (May): 689–693.

Larrick, R. P., K. A. Burson, and J. B. Soll. 2007. "Social Comparison and Confidence: When Thinking You're Better Than Average Predicts Overconfidence (and When It Does Not)." *Organizational Behavior and Human Decision Processes* 102, no. 1: 76–94.

Levi, Maurice, Kai Li, and Feng Zhang. 2010. "Deal or No Deal: Hormones and Completion of Mergers and Acquisitions." *Management Science* 56: 1462–1483.

Levitt, S., and S. J. Dubner. 2005. *Freakonomics: A Rogue Economist Explores the Hidden Side of Everything.* New York: William Morrow.

Lewin, Alexandra C. 2007. "Zambia and Genetically Modified Food Aid." In *Food Policy for Developing Countries: Case Studies,* edited by Per Pinstrup-Andersen, Fuzhi Cheng, Søren Elkjær Frandsen, Arie Kuyvenhoven, and Joachim von Braun, 1–12. Ithaca, NY: Cornell Library's Center for Innovative Publishing.

Li, N. P., J. M. Bailey, D. T. Kenrick, and J. A. W. Linsenmeier. 2002. "The Necessities and Luxuries of Mate Preferences: Testing the Tradeoffs." *Journal of Personality and Social Psychology* 82: 947–955.

Li, N. P., and D. T. Kenrick. 2006. "Sex Similarities and Differences in Preferences for Short-Term Mates: What, Whether, and Why." *Journal of Personality and Social Psychology* 90: 468–489.

Li, Y. J., D. T. Kenrick, V. Griskevicius, and S. L. Neuberg. 2012. "Economic Decision Biases and Fundamental Motivations: How Mating and Self-Protection Alter Loss Aversion." *Journal of Personality and Social Psychology* 102: 550–561.

Liberman, V., S. M. Samuels, and L. Ross. 2004. "The Name of the Game: Predictive Power of Reputations Versus Situational Labels in Determining Prisoner's Dilemma Game Moves." *Personality and Social Psychology Bulletin* 30: 1175–1185.

Lino, M. 2010. "Expenditures on Children by Families, 2009." United States Department of Agriculture Center for Nutrition Policy and Promotion, http://www.cnpp.usda.gov/Publications/CRC/crc2009.pdf.

Low, B. S., A. Hazel, N. Parker, and K. B. Welch. 2008. "Influences on Women's Reproductive Lives: Unexpected Ecological Underpinnings." *Cross Cultural Research* 42: 201–219.

Maner, J. K., C. N. DeWall, R. F. Baumeister, and M. Schaller. 2007. "Does Social Exclusion Motivate Interpersonal Reconnection? Resolving the 'Porcupine Problem.'" *Journal of Personality and Social Psychology* 92: 42–55.

Maner, J. K., M. T. Gailliot, D. A. Rouby, and S. L. Miller. 2007. "Can't Take My Eyes Off You: Attentional Adhesion to Mates and Rivals." *Journal of Personality and Social Psychology* 93: 389–401.

Maner, J. K., D. T. Kenrick, D. V. Becker, A. W. Delton, B. Hofer, C. J. Wilbur, and S. L. Neuberg. 2003. "Sexually Selective Cognition: Beauty Captures the Mind of the Beholder." *Journal of Personality and Social Psychology* 85: 1107–1120.

Maner, J. K., D. T. Kenrick, S. L. Neuberg, D. V. Becker, T. Robertson, B. Hofer, A. Delton, J. Butner, and M. Schaller. 2005. "Functional Projection: How Fundamental Social Motives Can Bias Interpersonal Perception." *Journal of Personality and Social Psychology* 88: 63–78.

Maner, J. K., S. L. Miller, D. A. Rouby, and M. T. Gailliot. 2009. "Intrasexual Vigilance: The Implicit Cognition of Romantic Rivalry." *Journal of Personality and Social Psychology* 97: 74–87.

Marmot, M. 2004. *Status Syndrome: How Your Social Standing Directly Affects Your Health and Life Expectancy*. London: Bloomsbury.

Martin, Annika K. 2000. "Why McDonald's Pulled Frankenfries from Menu." CNN.com, April 28, http://archives.cnn.com/2000/US/04/28/fries4_28.a.tm/index.html.

Mathews, T. J., and B. E. Hamilton. 2009. "Delayed Childbearing: More Women Are Having Their First Child Later in Life." National Center for Health Statistics Data Brief 21. Centers for Disease Control and Prevention, August, http://www.cdc.gov/nchs/data/databriefs/db21.pdf.

Mead, N. L., R. F. Baumeister, T. F. Stillman, C. D. Rawn, and K. D. Vohs. 2011.

"Social Exclusion Causes People to Spend and Consume in the Service of Af-filiation." *Journal of Consumer Research* 37: 902–919.

Mezrich, Ben. 2002. *Bringing Down the House: The Inside Story of Six M.I.T. Students Who Took Vegas for Millions*. New York: Free Press.

Mill, J. S. 1836/1874. "On the Definition of Political Economy, and on the Method of Investigation Proper to It." In *Essays on Some Unsettled Questions of Political Economy*. 2nd ed. London: Longmans, Green, Reader and Dyer. Originally published in *London and Westminster Review*, October 1836.

Miller, G. F. 2000. *The Mating Mind: How Sexual Choice Shaped the Evolution of Human Nature*. London: Heinemann.

Miller, G. F. 2009. *Spent: Sex, Evolution and Consumer Behavior*. New York: Penguin/Putnam.

Miller, G. F., J. M. Tybur, and B. D. Jordan. 2007. "Ovulatory Cycle Effects on Tip Earnings by Lap-Dancers: Economic Evidence for Human Estrus?" *Evolution and Human Behavior* 28: 375–381.

Miller, S. L., and J. K. Maner. 2010. "Scent of a Woman: Male Testosterone Responses to Female Olfactory Ovulation Cues." *Psychological Science* 21: 276–283.

———. 2011a. "Ovulation as a Mating Prime: Subtle Signs of Female Fertility Influence Men's Mating Cognition and Behavior." *Journal of Personality and Social Psychology* 100: 295–308.

———. 2011b. "Sick Body, Vigilant Mind: The Biological Immune System Activates the Behavioral Immune System." *Psychological Science* 22: 1467–1471.

Mischel, Walter, Ebbe B. Ebbesen, and Antonette Raskoff Zeiss. 1972. "Cognitive and Attentional Mechanisms in Delay of Gratification." *Journal of Personality and Social Psychology* 21, no. 2: 204–218.

Moore, D. A., and P. J. Healy. 2008. "The Trouble with Overconfidence." *Psychological Review* 115, no. 2: 502–517.

Mortensen, C. R., D. V. Becker, J. M. Ackerman, S. L. Neuberg, and D. T. Kenrick. 2010. "Infection Breeds Reticence: The Effects of Disease Salience on Self-Perceptions of Personality and Behavioral Avoidance Tendencies." *Psychological Science* 21: 440–447.

Navarrete, C. D., D. M. T. Fessler, and S. J. Eng. 2007. "Elevated Ethnocentrism in the First Trimester of Pregnancy." *Evolution and Human Behavior* 28, no. 1: 60–65.

Nesse, R. M. 2005. "Natural Selection and the Regulation of Defenses: A Signal Detection Analysis of the Smoke Detector Principle." *Evolution and Human Behavior* 26: 88–105.

Nettle, D. 2010. "Dying Young and Living Fast: Variation in Life History Across English Neighborhoods." *Behavioral Ecology* 21: 387–395.

Neuberg, S. L., D. T. Kenrick, and M. Schaller. 2011. "Human Threat Management Systems: Self-Protection and Disease Avoidance." *Neuroscience and Biobehavioral Reviews* 35: 1042–1051.

Neuhoff, J. G. 1998. "A Perceptual Bias for Rising Tones." *Nature* 395, no. 6698: 123–124.

———. 2001. "An Adaptive Bias in the Perception of Looming Auditory Motion." *Ecological Psychology* 13, no. 2: 87–110.

Nicholson, Nigel. 2008. "Evolutionary Psychology and Family Business: A New Synthesis for Theory, Research, and Practice." *Family Business Review* 21: 103–118.

Nisbett, R., and T. Wilson. 1977. "Telling More Than We Can Know: Verbal Reports on Mental Processes." *Psychological Review* 84: 231–259.

Null, G., M. Feldman, D. Rasio, and C. Dean. 2011. *Death by Medicine*. Edinburg, VA: Axios Press.

O'Toole, James. 2012. "*Consumer Reports* Slams Fisker Karma." CNN.com, September 25, http://money.cnn.com/2012/09/25/autos/fisker-karma-consumer-reports/index.html.

Ohman, A., and S. Mineka. 2001. "Fears, Phobias, and Preparedness: Toward an Evolved Module of Fear and Fear Learning." *Psychological Review* 108: 483–522.

Palmer, C. T. 1993. "Anger, Aggression, and Humor in Newfoundland Floor Hockey—an Evolutionary Analysis." *Aggressive Behavior* 19: 167–173.

Pinker, S. 2011. *The Better Angels of Our Nature: The Decline of Violence in History and Its Causes*. London: Penguin Books.

Rajamaran, I. 1983. "Economics of Bride-Price and Dowry." *Economic and Political Weekly* 18: 275–279.

Rajecki, D. W., S. B. Bledsoe, and J. L. Rasmussen. 1991. "Successful Personal Ads: Gender Differences and Similarities in Offers, Stipulations, and Outcomes." *Basic and Applied Social Psychology* 12: 457–469.

Randeria, S., and L. Visaria. 1984. "Sociology of Bride-Price and Dowry." *Economic and Political Weekly* 15: 648–652.

Rapaport, A., and A. M. Chammah. 1965. *Prisoner's Dilemma*. Ann Arbor: University of Michigan Press.

Roff, D. A. 2002. *Life History Evolution*. Sunderland, MA: Sinauer.

Ronay, R., and W. von Hippel. 2010. "The Presence of an Attractive Woman Elevates Testosterone and Physical Risk Taking in Young Men." *Social Psychological and Personality Science* 1: 57–64.

Roney, James R. 2003. "Effects of Visual Exposure to the Opposite Sex: Cognitive Aspects of Mate Attraction in Human Males." *Personality and Social Psychology Bulletin* 29, no. 3: 393–404.

Rosenblum, L. A., C. Forger, S. Noland, R. C. Trost, and J. D. Copland. 2001.

"Response of Adolescent Bonnet Macaques to an Acute Fear Stimulus as a Function of Early Rearing Conditions." *Developmental Psychobiology* 39: 40–45.

Rucker, D. D., A. D. Galinsky, and D. Dubois. 2012. "Power and Consumer Behavior: How Power Shapes Who and What Consumers Value." *Journal of Consumer Psychology* 22: 352–368.

Russell, B. 1950. *Unpopular Essays*. London: George Allen and Unwin.

Russia. 2008. "The Golden Porsche." English Russia, July 4, http://english russia.com/2008/07/04/the-golden-porsche.

Saad, G. 2007. *The Evolutionary Bases of Consumption*. Mahwah, NJ: Lawrence Erlbaum Associates Publishers.

———. 2011. *The Consuming Instinct*. Amherst, NY: Prometheus Books.

Saad, G., and J. G. Vongas. 2009. "The Effect of Conspicuous Consumption on Men's Testosterone Levels." *Organizational Behavior and Human Decision Processes* 110: 80–92.

Sagarin, B. J. 2005. "Reconsidering Evolved Sex Differences in Jealousy: Comment on Harris." *Personality and Social Psychology Review* 9: 62–75.

Sapolsky, R. M. 2002. *A Primate's Memoir: A Neuroscientist's Unconventional Life Among the Baboons*. New York: Scribner.

Schaller, M., and L. A. Duncan. 2007. "The Behavioral Immune System: Its Evolution and Social Psychological Implications." In *Evolution and the Social Mind: Evolutionary Psychology and Social Cognition*, edited by J. P. Forgas, M. G. Haselton, and W. von Hippel, 293–307. New York: Psychology Press.

Schaller, M., G. E. Miller, W. M. Gervais, S. Yager, and E. Chen. 2010. "Mere Visual Perception of Other People's Disease Symptoms Facilitates a More Aggressive Immune Response." *Psychological Science* 21: 649–652.

Schaller, M., and J. H. Park. 2011. "The Behavioral Immune System (and Why It Matters)." *Current Directions in Psychological Science* 20: 99–103.

Schaller, M., J. H. Park, and A. Mueller. 2003. "Fear of the Dark: Interactive Effects of Beliefs About Danger and Ambient Darkness on Ethnic Stereotypes." *Personality and Social Psychology Bulletin* 29: 637–649.

Schmitt, D., and 118 members of the International Sexuality Description Project. 2003. "Universal Sex Differences in the Desire for Sexual Variety: Tests from 52 Nations, 6 Continents, and 13 Islands." *Journal of Personality and Social Psychology* 85, no. 1: 85–104.

Schmitt, D. P. 2005. "Sociosexuality from Argentina to Zimbabwe: A 48-Nation Study of Sex, Culture, and Strategies of Human Mating." *Behavioral and Brain Sciences* 28: 247–311.

Schneider, Greg. 2004. "Toyota's Prius Proving to Be the Hotter Ride in Hybrids." *Washington Post*, August 23, http://www.washingtonpost.com/wp-dyn/articles/A24832–2004Aug22.html.

Schondelmeyer, S. 2007. "Viewpoint: Is the Growth in Our Drug Tab Sustainable? Drug Topics, March 19, http://drugtopics.modernmedicine.com/drug-topics/Special+Reports/Viewpoint-Is-the-growth-in-our-drug-tab-sustain-abl/ArticleStandard/Article/detail/411533.

Scott, Annie. 2009. "W Fort Lauderdale Saves Turtles from Suicide." Gadling, August 4, http://www.gadling.com/2009/08/04/w-fort-lauderdale-saves-turtles-from-suicide.

Segal, N. 2000. *Entwined Lives: Twins and What They Tell Us About Human Behavior.* New York: Plume.

Segal, N. L., and V. A. Harris. 2008. "Bereavement-Related Responses Following the Loss of an MZ or DZ Twin." *Behavior Genetics* 38: 647.

Segal, N. L., and S. L. Hershberger. 1999. "Cooperation and Competition in Adolescent Twins: Findings from a Prisoner's Dilemma Game." *Evolution and Human Behavior* 20: 29–51.

Sherman, P. W. 1981. "Kinship, Demography, and Belding's Ground Squirrel Nepotism." *Behavioral Ecology and Sociobiology* 8: 251–259.

Shoda, Yuichi, Walter Mischel, and Philip K. Peake. 1990. "Predicting Adolescent Cognitive and Self-Regulatory Competencies from Preschool Delay of Gratification: Identifying Diagnostic Conditions." *Developmental Psychology* 26, no. 6: 978–986.

Simon, H. A. 1955. "A Behavioral Model of Rational Choice." *Quarterly Journal of Economics* 69: 99–118.

———. 1956. "Rational Choice and the Structure of the Environment." *Psychological Review* 63: 129–138.

Simpson, J. A., and S. W. Gangestad. 1991. "Individual Differences in Sociosexuality: Evidence for Convergent and Discriminant Validity." *Journal of Personality and Social Psychology* 60: 870–883.

Simpson, J. A., V. Griskevicius, S. I. Kuo, S. Sung, and W. A. Collins. 2012. "Evolution, Stress, and Sensitive Periods: The Influence of Unpredictability in Early Versus Late Childhood on Sex and Risky Behavior." *Developmental Psychology* 48: 674–686.

Smith, G. 2004. "An Evaluation of the Corporate Culture of Southwest Airlines." *Measuring Business Excellence* 8: 26–33.

Smith, M., B. Kish, and C. Crawford. 1987. "Inheritance of Wealth as Human Kin Investment." *Ethology and Sociobiology* 8, no. 3: 171–182.

Sperry, R. W. 1968. "Hemisphere Deconnection and Unity in Conscious Awareness." *American Psychologist* 23: 723–733.

Stanley, Thomas, and William Danko. 1996. *The Millionaire Next Door*. New York: Pocket Books.

Stearns, S. 1992. *The Evolution of Life Histories*. Cambridge: Oxford University Press.

Stewart, J. B. 2005. *Disney War*. New York: Simon and Schuster.

Sugiyama, L. S. 2004a. "Illness, Injury, and Disability Among Shiwiar Forager-Horticulturalists: Implications of Health-Risk Buffering for the Evolution of Human Life History." *American Journal of Physical Anthropology* 123: 371–389.

———. 2004b. "Patterns of Shiwiar Health Insults Indicate that Provisioning During Health Crises Reduces Juvenile Mortality." In *Socioeconomic Aspects of Human Behavioral Ecology: Research in Economic Anthropology*, edited by M. Alvard, 23: 377–400. New York: Elsevier.

Sugiyama, L. S., J. Tooby, and L. Cosmides. 2002. "Cross-Cultural Evidence of Cognitive Adaptations for Social Exchange Among the Shiwiar of Ecuadorian Amazonia." *Proceedings of the National Academy of Sciences* 99: 11537–11545.

Sundie, J. M., D. T. Kenrick, V. Griskevicius, J. M. Tybur, K. D. Vohs, and D. J. Beal. 2011. "Peacocks, Porsches, and Thorstein Veblen: Conspicuous Consumption as a Sexual Signaling System." *Journal of Personality and Social Psychology* 100: 664–680.

Tertilt, M. 2005. "Polygyny, Fertility, and Savings." *Journal of Political Economy* 113: 1341–1371.

Thaler, R. H., A. Tversky, D. Kahneman, and A. Schwartz. 1997. "The Effect of Myopia and Loss Aversion on Risk Taking: An Experimental Test." *Quarterly Journal of Economics* 112: 647–661.

Thaler, Richard, and Cass Sunstein. 2008. *Nudge: Improving Decisions About Health, Wealth, and Happiness*. New Haven, CT: Yale University Press.

Thigpen, C. H., and H. M. Cleckley. 1957. *The Three Faces of Eve*. New York: McGraw-Hill.

Thomas, B. 1976. *Walt Disney: An American Original*. New York: Simon and Schuster.

———. 1998. *Building a Company: Roy O. Disney and the Creation of an Entertainment Empire*. New York: Hyperion.

Time. 2006. "Time Style and Design Poll." *Time,* March 5, http://www.time.com/time/arts/article/0,8599,1169863,00.html.

Tinbergen, N. 1963. "On the Aims and Methods of Ethology." *Zeitschrift für Tierpsychologie* 20: 410–433.

Torre, Pablo S. 2009. "How (and Why) Athletes Go Broke." *Sports Illustrated,* March 23, http://sportsillustrated.cnn.com/vault/article/magazine/MAG1153364/1/index.htm.

Trivers, R. L. 1971. "The Evolution of Reciprocal Altruism." *Quarterly Review of Biology* 46: 35–37.

———. 1972. "Parental Investment and Sexual Selection." In *Sexual Selection and the Descent of Man, 1871–1971*, edited by B. Campbell, 136–179. Chicago: Aldine.

———. 1974. "Parent-Offspring Conflict." *American Zoologist* 14: 249–264.

Turner, J. L., E. B. Foa, and U. G. Foa. 1971. "Interpersonal Reinforcers: Classification, Interrelationship, and Some Differential Properties." *Journal of Personality and Social Psychology* 19: 168–180.

Tversky, A., and D. Kahneman. 1981. "The Framing of Decisions and the Psychology of Choice." *Science* 211: 453–458.

———. 1983. "Extension Versus Intuitive Reasoning: The Conjunction Fallacy in Probability Judgment." *Psychological Review* 90, no. 4: 293–315.

Tybur, J. M., A. D. Bryan, R. E. Magnan, and A. E. Caldwell Hooper. 2011. "Smells Like Safe Sex: Olfactory Pathogen Primes Increase Intentions to Use Condoms." *Psychological Science* 22: 478–480.

Van den Bergh, B., S. Dewitte, and L. Warlop. 2008. "Bikinis Instigate Generalized Impatience in Intertemporal Choice." *Journal of Consumer Research* 35: 85–97.

Van Vugt, M., and A. Ahuja. 2010. *Selected: Why Some People Lead, Why Others Follow, and Why It Matters: The Evolutionary Science of Leadership*. London: Profile Books/New York: Harper.

Van Vugt, M., R. Hogan, and R. Kaiser. 2008. "Leadership, Followership, and Evolution: Some Lessons from the Past." *American Psychologist* 63: 182–196.

Veblen, Thorstein. 1899. *The Theory of the Leisure Class*. New York: Penguin.

Vohs, Kathleen D., and Mary Frances Luce. 2010. "Judgment and Decision Making." In *Advanced Social Psychology: The State of the Science*, edited by Roy F. Baumeister and Eli J. Finkel, 733–756. New York: Oxford University Press.

Wadhwa, V., H. Krisztina, R. Aggarwal, and A. Salkever. 2009. "Anatomy of an Entrepreneur: Family Background and Motivation." Kauffman Foundation, http://www.kauffman.org/uploadedfiles/researchandpolicy/thestudyofentrepreneurship/anatomy%20of%20entre%20071309_final.pdf.

Wang, X. T. 1996a. "Domain-Specific Rationality in Human Choices: Violations of Utility Axioms and Social Contexts." *Cognition* 60: 31–63.

———. 1996b. "Framing Effects: Dynamics and Task Domains." *Organizational Behavior and Human Decision Processes* 68: 145–157.

Weatherford, J. 2005. *Genghis Khan and the Making of the Modern World*. New York: Random House.

Weinstein, N. D. 1980. "Unrealistic Optimism About Future Life Events." *Journal of Personality and Social Psychology* 39, no. 5: 806–820.

White, A. E., Y. J. Li, V. Griskevicius, D. T. Kenrick, and S. L. Neuberg. Forthcoming. "Putting All Your Eggs in One Basket: Life History Strategies, Bet Hedging, and Diversification." *Psychological Science.*

Wickler, W. 1966. "Mimicry in Tropical Fishes." *Philosophical Transactions of the Royal Society B* 251: 473.

Wiederman, M. W. 1993. "Evolved Gender Differences in Mate Preferences: Evidence from Personal Advertisements." *Ethology and Sociobiology* 14: 331–352.

Wiederman, M. W., and E. Kendall. 1999. "Evolution, Sex, and Jealousy: Investigation with a Sample from Sweden." *Evolution and Human Behavior* 20: 121–128.

Wikipedia. n.d. "Eliot Spitzer Prostitution Scandal." Wikipedia, http://en.wikipedia.org/wiki/Eliot_Spitzer_prostitution_scandal.

———. n.d. "MC Hammer." Wikipedia, http://en.wikipedia.org/wiki/MC_Hammer.

———. n.d. "Rajinder Singh." Wikipedia, http://en.wikipedia.org/wiki/Rajinder_Singh.

Wilson, M., and M. Daly. 1985. "Competitiveness, Risk Taking, and Violence: The Young Male Syndrome." *Ethology and Sociobiology* 6: 59–73.

———. 1997. "Life Expectancy, Economic Inequality, Homicide, and Reproductive Timing in Chicago Neighborhoods." *British Medical Journal* 314: 1271–1274.

Wilson, M., M. Daly, and N. Pound. 2002. "An Evolutionary Psychological Perspective on the Modulation of Competitive Confrontation and Risk Taking." In *Hormones, Brain and Behavior,* edited by Donald W. Pfaff, Arthur P. Arnold, Susan E. Fahrbach, Anne M. Etgen, and Robert T. Rubin, 5: 381–408. San Diego, CA: Academic Press.

Wilson, Margo, and Martin Daly. 2004. "Do Pretty Women Inspire Men to Discount the Future?" *Biology Letters* 271: S177–S179.

Winterhalder, B. 2007. "Risk and Decision-Making." In *Oxford Handbook of Evolutionary Psychology*, edited by R. Dunbar and L. Barrett, 433–446. Oxford: Oxford University Press.

World Health Organization (WHO). n.d. "20 Questions on Genetically Modified Foods." WHO, http://www.who.int/foodsafety/publications/biotech/20questions/en/index.html.

———. n.d. "Growing Threat from Counterfeit Medicines." WHO, http://www.who.int/bulletin/volumes/88/4/10–020410/en/index.html.

Wyatt, T. D. 2003. *Pheromones and Animal Behavior: Communication by Smell and Taste*. Cambridge: Cambridge University Press.

YouTube. n.d. "Hot Girl Flashes Porsche 911 Banned Commercial Funny 2013 Carjam TV." YouTube, http://www.youtube.com/watch?v=47ZZjEXcJ-U.

Index

Abernathy, Ralph, 24
Accuracy issue, 77–79
Aché tribe, 36
Ackerman, Josh, 166
Adaptive behavior
　accuracy and, 77–78
　biases and, 76
　exploiting, 185–186
　indicator of, 10
　and life history strategies, 119, 132,
　　135
　and loss aversion, 46, 47
　See also Evolutionary challenges, the
　　need to solve
Advertising
　and changing preferences, 27–30
　exploitation in, 188
　and marketing strategies, 190–194
　and stable preferences, 26
Advertising Age (magazine), 196
Affiliation subself
　ancestral problem of, 107–108
　and compatibility between subselves,
　　49
　described, 36–37, 212
　erasing errors by engaging, 113–114
　fulfilling the needs of, spending on,
　　189
　hierarchy of needs and, 43

mating effort and, 122
others exploiting, 186
parasites of, 199
and rules of the game, 60–64
somatic effort and, 122
Wason task and, 107, 108
See also specific aspects related to the
　affiliation subself
Age factors. *See* Childhood; Children;
　Men; Teenagers/young adults;
　Women
AIDS epidemic, 165
American culture, 144–145
Anderson, Siwan, 162, 163
Animals, people as, view focusing on. *See*
　Evolutionary psychologist
　perspective
Aniston, Jennifer, 169
Apple, Inc., 61, 64, 65, 93, 127
Assault, 17, 33, 134
Assumptions, avoiding, 209–210
Auditory looming, 78
Authority ranking, 64–65
Automobile culture, 149

Bachelor, The (television show), 180
Bachelorette, The (television show), 180
Bad judgment. *See* Errors/mistakes
Bankruptcy, 117–118, 119, 136, 138

Baumeister, Roy F., 163–164
Beal, Dan, 157
Beautiful young women, men's
    preference for, 167–169, 170, 171,
    173
Beauty products and regimes, women's
    spending on, 175–176
Becker, Vaughn, 34
Behavior
    mystery of, 215–216
    predicting, 16, 46
    See also Adaptive behavior
Behavioral economist perspective
    as both right and wrong, 9
    contributions of, and suggestions to
        improve upon, 214
    lesson about, 209–210
    of man as irrational, described, 4–7
    rational economists versus, 6, 7
    theory lacking in, 16
    See also specific ideas/concepts of
        behavioral economists
Behavioral immune system, 83–84
Belsky, Jay, 134
Bias
    assumptions about, avoiding, 209–210
    being born with, benefits of, 93–94
    calculated, 82
    clustering illusion, 6–7
    and the different subselves, 45, 73
    evolutionary view of, 10, 11
    false consensus, 76
    gambler's fallacy, 6, 7
    hindsight, 6, 7
    intentional, reason for, 76, 78
    loss aversion, 5, 9–11, 45–48
    overconfidence, 77, 91–93, 94, 123
    perceived as irrational, 5, 6–7, 9
    ultimate reasons for, perspective
        providing, 16, 20
    See also Errors/mistakes; Subselves
Bissoon, Lionel, 126

Bowerbird displays, 152–154, 155
Brain mass, 77
Brain programming, 31–32
Brain size, 40
Bride price, 162–163, 171, 182
Brin, Sergey, 127
Bringing Down the House (Mezrich), 167
Bryan, Angela, 83
Burrell, Stanley. See MC Hammer
Business
    aggressiveness in, 127
    market economics and, problem with,
        68–69
    See also Corporate economics; Family
        businesses
Buss, David, 178

Cameron, James, 92
Causes of behavior. See Proximate
    reasons; Ultimate reasons
Changing preferences, 27–29, 34, 39–40,
    46, 47–48
Charlson, John, 130
Cheater detection problem, 108–109
Chen, Keith, 9
Childhood
    environment during, influence of, on
        life history strategy, 134–137,
        138–140, 140–141
    imprints from, surfacing of, times
        most likely for, 138–139
Children
    birth of, and testosterone levels, 125
    equality matching and, 62
    fast versus slow strategies in, 128,
        136–137
    inclusive fitness and, 57
    somatic effort and, 122
    talking versus writing and, 99–100
    violent environments and, 134
Churchland, Patricia, 78
Cialdini, Robert "Bob," 28, 154, 196

Clinton, Bill, 65
Clooney, George, 89, 214–215
Clustering illusion, 6–7
Cognitive biases. *See* Bias
Commensalism, 187, 194
Communal sharing, 62
   See also Kinship game
Computer analogy, 31–32
Con men, 186, 188, 201–203, 204, 209
Conditional logic, testing, 106–107,
   108–109
Confidence
   bias involving, 77, 91, 92–93, 94, 123
   essentialness of, 91–92
Conflict, negotiating through, different
   approaches to, 51–53, 59
Consensus bias, false, 76
Conspicuous conservation, 149
Conspicuous consumption
   cultural explanation of, 144–145
   described, and examples of, 143–144
   different version of, 148–150
   fast versus slow strategies and,
     156–157
   human history of, 145–146
   mate-acquisition subself and,
     154–155, 156–157, 158, 159, 174
   multiple explanations for, 150–151
   people's own explanations for,
     146–148
   proximate reasons for, 158–159
   sex differences in, 154–155, 159,
     182–183
   status subself and, 143–144, 148–150,
     151
   ultimate reasons for, exploring,
     151–157, 158, 159
   utility explanation of, 146
Conspicuous displays, reasons for,
   152–154, 155, 157
Consumer Reports (magazine), 143, 149,
   150

Consumerism. *See* Conspicuous
   consumption
Corporate economics
   described, 55–56
   home economics versus, 59–60
   See also Market economics
Cosmetic surgery, 175
Cosmides, Leda, 107, 108, 109
Costello, Frank, 16
Counterfeit drugs, 201
Craig, Daniel, 215
Credit card debt, 179, 180–181
Curse of the Kennedys (Grady), 2, 4

Daly, Martin, 123, 124
Dangerous environments, influence of,
   on life history strategy, 134, 140
Dating guides, 89
Dating standards, 164
David, Larry, 147
Davis, Mike, 126
De Beers, 195–197, 198, 213
De Fraja, Gianni, 146
Death rates. *See* Mortality levels/rates
DeBruine, Lisa, 70–71
Debt, 117, 118, 138, 179, 180–181
   See also Bankruptcy
Deception, experts at, 203
   See also Parasitism
Decision making
   alternate view of, 2–3
   blinded by the modern world,
     114–115
   divisive debate over, 2, 7, 8
   exercising control over, 212–213
   most popular view of, 4, 209–210
   taking time for, to avoid exploitation,
     204–205
Deep rationality. *See* Evolutionary
   psychologist perspective
Defense and offense, importance of
   both, 86

Delaying gratification. *See* Slow strategy

Demand and supply, sexual, 179–182

Desire, manufactured, through
marketing, 196–197

Developmental pyramid, climbing the,
42–44, 122

Developmental stages, 121–125

"Diamond is forever" slogan, 196–197

Diamond rings, 163, 167, 195–199, 204,
213

Diaz, Cameron, 147

DiCaprio, Leonardo, 147, 149–150, 208

Dingley, Nicholas "Razzle," 138

Disease-avoidance subself
described, 34–36, 212
fulfilling the needs of, spending on,
189
hierarchy of needs and, 43
mating effort and, 123
parasites of, 199, 199–201, 201–203
parenting effort and, 125
pathogen detection system of, 83–84,
93
and the response to genetically
modified food, 85–86
somatic effort and, 122
*See also specific aspects related to the
disease-avoidance subself*

Disney, Roy E., 52, 59, 60, 73

Disney, Roy O., 51–52, 59, 60, 62, 72–73

Disney, Walt, 51–52, 59, 60, 62, 72–73,
208

Divorce, 94, 133, 172, 177, 178, 179

Doug E. Fresh (rapper), 126

Dowry, 162–163, 171–172

Drug companies, 199–201

Durante, Kristina, 13

Econs, people as, view focusing on. *See*
Rational economist perspective

Eisner, Michael, 52, 59, 60, 64, 65,
72–73, 208

Ellis, Bruce, 134

Emperor's Club, 161–162, 163, 167

Enemies, knowing your, 204
See also Parasitism

Entrepreneurism, age of, 125–128

Environment, childhood, influence of,
on life history strategy, 134–137,
138–140, 140–141

Equality matching, 62, 63, 64

Errors/mistakes
calculated, 88
costly, built-in mechanism to avoid,
79–81
due to bias, 6–7, 73, 76, 78
evolutionary view of, 11
financial, 81–82, 118–119
fundamentally different types of, 80
logic, 97, 99
math, 102, 103
medical, 97, 98, 102
perceived as irrational, 4
sexual, avoiding, 166
that are not random, reasons for, 82
ultimate reasons for, perspective
providing, 16, 20
and the way questions are presented,
99, 103, 114, 115
See also Bias

Evolutionary challenges, the need to
solve, 30–32, 46, 76, 93, 94, 172
See also Ultimate reasons

Evolutionary psychologist perspective
contributions to, recognition of,
213–214
of loss aversion, 9–11
of man, as deeply rational, described,
7–9
theory provided by, 16
three lessons from, 209–213
*See also specific ideas/concepts of
evolutionary psychologists*

Ewing, Patrick, 118

Exploitation
  beneficial, 187, 189, 203
  continuum of, 187–188, 194
  harmful, 187
  marketing strategies used in, 190–194
  pervasiveness of, 185–186
  See also Parasitism

Facebook, 36, 127
Fakes, spotting, 204
  See also Parasitism
False alarms, 79, 80, 81, 88
False consensus bias, 76
False positives, 102
Family businesses
  examples of, 51–52, 72–73
  running companies like, 71–72, 211,
    213
Family model. *See* Home economics
Fast strategy
  attitude in, example of, 140, 141
  and conspicuous consumption,
    156–157
  described, 118–119, 121
  environmental factors leading to,
    134–136, 137, 138, 139–140,
    140–141
  as a financial investment strategy,
    130–131
  genetic factor in, 133
  high variance of, 137–138
  mate-acquisition subself and, 154,
    155, 156, 157
  and sexual supply and demand, 181
  slow strategy versus, 128–129
  types of people following, 132–133
  unrestricted, 156, 157
Federal Trade Commission (FTC), 203
Fertility, indicator of, 168
Fessler, Dan, 36
Financial investments
  risk aversion and, 45, 82

smoke detector principle and, 81–82
  strategy in, types of, described,
    130–131
  testosterone levels and, 126
  unusual, 129, 130
Financial mistakes, 81–82, 118–119
  See also Bankruptcy; Debt;
    Exploitation; Gambling
Financial prospects, women's preference
    for men with, 170–171, 173
Financial spending
  dilemma over, 119
  excess, avoiding, by knowing your
    subselves and evolutionary needs,
    205
  to fulfill fundamental needs, 189–190
  See also Conspicuous consumption
Fiske, Alan, 61–62, 64
Fitness
  defined, 8
  enhancing, decisions leading to, 10,
    20
  inclusive, 56–58
Flashy/luxury items, reasons for
    purchasing. *See* Conspicuous
    consumption
Fluctuating environments, influence of,
    on life history strategy, 134–136,
    137, 139–140, 141
Followers and leaders, 64, 65, 66
Forbes (magazine), 117
Fortune (magazine), 71
Fowler, James, 92
Frank, Robert, 38
Friends, rules among, 62, 63
  See also Affiliation subself

Gambler's fallacy, 6, 7
Gambling, 124, 125–126, 129, 139, 182
  See also Lotteries
Game theory
  described, 53–56, 58

Game theory (*continued*)
  and home economics versus corporate
    economics, 59
  and rules for different subselves,
    60–67, 73
  trust and, 69
Gangestad, Steve, 156
Garfield, James, 66
Garrow, David, 24
Gates, Bill, 38, 127
Gazzaniga, Michael, 25
Gender factors. *See* Men; Women
Genetically modified food, responses to,
    75–76, 85–86
Gerety, Frances, 196
Giancana, Sam, 17
Gigerenzer, Gerd, 103–104
Gil-White, Francisco, 38
Goldstein, Noah, 28
Google, 127
Gordon Gecko (character), 3, 4
Gore, Al, 147, 150
Grady, Sandy, 4
Green products, status associated with,
    148, 149, 150, 151
Griskevicius, Vlad, 215
Guttentag, Marcia, 179–180

Harrelson, Woody, 147
Harry Potter series, 215
Harton, Robyn A., 199
Harvard students, 95–96, 108–109
Haselton, Martie, 80–81
Hawking, Stephen, 38
Hellmuth, Phil, 125, 126
Hendrix, Jimi, 138
Henrich, Joe, 38
Henry VIII, 168–169
Hershberger, Scott, 58
Hierarchy of needs, 42, *43*, 44
Hill, Kim, 36
Hill, Sarah, 176

Hindsight bias, 6, 7
Home economics
  bringing, into market economics,
    69–71
  versus corporate economics, 59–60
  described, 56–58
  family businesses and, 51–52, 71–73,
    211, 213
  lesson about, 211
  See also Kin-care subself
Homicides, 33, 57, 123–124, 134, 173,
    179, 180
Hurtado, Magdalena, 36
Hybrid cars, reason for buying,
    uncovering, 147–149, 150–151
Hypocrisy, 48, 49

Immune systems, 83–84
Impulsivity. *See* Fast strategy
Inclusive fitness, 56–58
Inconsistency, 21, 24, 25–26, 29–30, 48,
    49, 112–113
Infidelity, 179
Influence (Cialdini), 196
iPhones, 37
Irrational man. *See* Behavioral
    economist perspective
Irving, John, 6

Jealousy, 178–179
Jobs, Steve, 61, 62, 63–64, 65, 91, 93, 127
Johnson, Dominic, 91, 92
Johnson, Lyndon, 23–24
Jones, Brian, 138
Joplin, Janis, 138
Jordan, Brent, 14

Kahneman, Daniel, 5, 97, 111, 112, 113
Keefe, Rich, 168, 169
Kelleher, Herb, 71
Kennedy, David, 2
Kennedy, Jackie (Onassis), 155

Kennedy, John F., 2, 17, 66
Kennedy, John F., Jr., 2, 7
Kennedy, Joseph "Joe" Patrick, Jr., 2, 4, 7
Kennedy, Joseph "Joe" Patrick, Sr., 1–2, 3, 4, 7, 16–17, 19–20, 207
Kennedy, Michael, 2, 4, 17
Kennedy, Robert, 2
Kennedy, Teddy, 2, 4, 7, 17
Kenrick, Doug, 215
Khan, Genghis, 66–67
Killeen, Peter, 59
Kin-care subself
    activating, and shifting rules of the game, 71, 72
    and compatibility between subselves, 49
    described, 41–42, 212
    fulfilling the needs of, spending on, 190
    hierarchy of needs and, *43*, 44
    mate-acquisition subself versus, 42
    meeting needs of, without overspending, example of, 205
    parasites of, 199
    parenting effort and, 125
    and rules of the game, 56–58, 62, 70, 72
    and the trust game, 71
    voluntarily waking up your, 213
    See also specific aspects related to the kin-care subself
King, Larry, 118, 135–136, 138
King, Martin Luther, Jr., 21, 23–24, 48, 49, 72, 207–208
Kinship game, 56–58, 62, 70, 72
Kopechne, Mary Jo, 2, 17
Kurzban, Rob, 25, 26
Kwiat, 198

Labor relations, 69, 71
Lakshminarayanan, Venkat, 9

Large numbers paradox, 109–111, 113
Lautenberg, Frank, 186
Leaders and followers, 64, 65, 66
Lennon, John, 53, 61, 62, 63
Li, Jessica, 46
Li, Norm, 169–170
Life expectancy, 134, 138
    See also Risk taking
Life history theory
    described, 119–121
    and financial decisions, age factor in, 125–128
    stages in, 121–125, 141
    strategies in, 121, 132–133, 134–135, 137, 140, 141
    See also Fast strategy; Slow strategy
Life lessons, 209–213
Lifespan, 122, 129, 135
Limited resources, dilemma over, 119
Lincoln, Abraham, 66
LL Cool J (rapper), 126
Logic errors, 97, 99
Logic tests, 95–96, 97–98, 99, 106–107, 108–109
L'Oreal, 176
Loss aversion
    described, 5, 9–11
    reversing, 45–48
Lotteries, 129–130, 131, 136, 140, 141
Love, first professions of, sex differences in, 165–167
Luxury/flashy items, reasons for purchasing. *See* Conspicuous consumption

Madoff, Bernard "Bernie," 186, 188, 203, 204, 209
Maher, Bill, 147
Maner, Jon, 19, 34
Marcos, Imelda, 192
Market demand, strategy to increase, 192–193

Market economics
    bringing home economics into, 69–71, 72
    and business, problem with, 68–69
    corporations and, 55–56, 59
    described, 67
    lesson about, 211
    mate-retention and, 176–177
    and the rules of game theory, 55–56
    See also Game theory
Market pricing, 56, 61–62, 62–63, 67–68, 69, 190–192
Market segmentation, traditional, 27
Marketers, described, 188–189
Marketing strategies, 190–194
Marriage
    bride price for, 162–163, 171, 182
    diamond rings and, 196, 197
    and divorce, 94, 133, 172, 177, 178, 179
    dowry for, 162–163, 171–172
    jealousy in, 178–179
    parenting effort and, 124, 125
    standards for, 164, 167, 177–178
    television reality shows with the goal of, 180
    testosterone levels and, 125
Marsden, Michael, 149
Maslow, Abraham, 42
Mate preferences
    of men, 168–169, 170, 171
    of women, 170–171, 173
Mate-acquisition subself
    advertising preferences of, 29–30
    conspicuous consumption and, 154–155, 156–157, 158, 159, 174
    described, 39–40, 212
    fulfilling the needs of, spending on, 189–190
    hierarchy of needs and, 43, 44
    kin-care subself versus, 42
    and loss aversion, 47–48

mate-retention subself versus, 41
    mating effort and, 122, 123–124
    men's sex detectors and, 86–88, 93
    parasites of, 196–197, 204
    and rules of the game, 172–174
    sex differences in, 159
    and tension between subselves, 49
    women's sex detectors and, 88–90, 93
    See also specific aspects related to the mate-acquisition subself
Mate-retention subself
    described, 40–41, 212
    fulfilling the needs of, spending on, 190
    hierarchy of needs and, 43, 44
    mate-acquisition subself versus, 41
    parasites of, 198
    parenting effort and, 125
    and rules of the game, 176–178
    and tension between subselves, 49
    See also specific aspects related to the mate-retention subself
Materialism, cultural explanation of, 144–145
    See also Conspicuous consumption
Math errors, 102, 105
Math problems
    difficulty with, 97–98, 101–103
    and the large numbers paradox, 111
    and the way questions are presented, 99, 103–105, 111–114
Mating effort, 121, 122–124, 125, 132, 133, 152–153
Mating game, 40, 68, 172–174, 176–178
Mating Mind, The (Miller), 39
Mating opportunities/success
    conspicuous displays and, 153–154
    different tasks of, 121
    and the ovulatory cycle, 15
    and risk taking, 17, 18, 19
    sex detectors and, 86–88

See also Mating effort; Mating game; Parenting effort
Mating season, indicators of, 153, 154
Maximilian, Archduke, 195
MC Hammer (rapper), 117–118, 126, 133, 135–136, 138, 209
McCartney, Paul, 53, 61, 62, 63
McDonald's french fries, response to, 85–86
McKernan, Ron "Pigpen," 138
McKinley, William, 66
Mean Markets and Lizard Brains (Burnham), 81
Medical errors, 97, 98, 102
Men
    bride price paid by, 162–163, 171, 182
    and conspicuous consumption, 154–155, 159, 183
    dowry given to the bride for, 162–163, 171–172
    and first professions of love, 165–167
    generous tipping and, 173, 174
    homicide statistics and, 124
    jealousy and, 178, 179
    mate-acquisition game for, 173–174
    mate-retention game for, 177–178
    mating effort and, 122, 123
    parenting stage and, 124, 125
    paying for women escorts, 161–162, 167
    as playboys, 89, 90, 156–157
    preference of, for young beautiful women, 167–169, 170, 171, 173
    ratio of women to, and sexual supply and demand, 179–182
    risk taking and, 17–20, 173
    sex detectors of, and the mate-acquisition subself, 86–88, 93
    sexual economics and, 153, 163–164
    standards of, for partners, 164–165, 167–169, 177–178

testosterone levels of, 18–19, 123, 125, 126, 127, 183
    and their response to insults, 39
Menstruation, and age of onset, 134, 135
Mental errors. *See* Errors/mistakes
Mergers and acquisitions, 127
Mezrich, Ben, 167
Microeconomics, 120
Microsoft, 127
Miller, Geoffrey, 14, 39, 154
Miller, Saul, 19
Millionaire Next Door, The (Stanley and Danko), 118
Minimum parental investment, 163, 165, 173
Misses, 80, 88
Modern work, skills of, 101
Modern world, decision making blinded by, 114–115
Modern world, decision making blinded by the, 210
Money mistakes. *See* Financial mistakes
Moore, Demi, 169
Morons, people as, view focusing on. *See* Behavioral economist perspective
Morrison, Jim, 138
Mortality levels/rates
    from accidents/violence, 123, 173
    from drug adverse reactions, 200–201
    from medical errors, 97, 98
    of rock stars, 138
    and women's age of first birth, 134
Mortensen, Chad, 28
Mossi people, 61
Mr. T, 198
Mswati III, 169
Multiple personalities, having, 24–27
    See also Subselves
Murders. *See* Homicides
Murphy, Dwayne, 126
Mutualism, symbolic, 187, 189, 190, 194, 203

Mwanawasa, Levy, 75–76, 208
Mystery, 215–216

National Basketball Association, 118
National Football League, 118
Native Americans, 85
Natural frequencies, presenting
    statistical information in terms of,
    103–105
Navarrete, Carlos, 36
Needs
    fundamental, fulfilling our, spending
        on, 189–190
    hierarchy of, 42, *43*, 44
    See also Subselves
Negotiation
    in conflict, different approaches to,
        51–53, 59
    testosterone levels and, 127
Neil, Vince, 138
Nesse, Randy, 80–81
Neuberg, Steve, 46
Nisbett, Richard, 147
Nixon, Richard, 65
Nutrition for Life, 203

Offense and defense, importance of
    both, 86
On the Origin of Species (Darwin), 8
Onassis, Aristotle, 143–144, 155
Onassis, Jackie (Kennedy), 155
One-night stands, 89, 157, 164–165,
    167, 177
Oppenheimer, Ernest, 195, 196
Opportunities, so-called, taking a closer
    look at, 204
Optimism, 92
Otero, Ray, 129–130, 131, 140, 141
Overconfidence bias, 77, 91–93, 94,
    123
Ovulatory cycle, influence of the, 13–16,
    19, 89–90, 93, 182

Page, Larry, 127
Paradox, large numbers, 109–111, 113
Parasitism
    described, 187–188
    examples of, 185–186, 188,
        194–203
    lesson about, 210
    protection from, 203–205, 213
Parental investment, minimum, 163,
    165, 173
Parenting effort, 121, 122, 124–125
Parents, inclusive fitness and, 57
Paternal uncertainty, 178
Pathogen detector system, 83, 93
    See also Disease-avoidance subself
Personalities, having multiple, 24–27
    See also Subselves
Persuasion, primed for, 27–30
Pharmaceutical industry, 199–201
Pitt, Brad, 89
Playboys, 89, 90, 156–157
Predators, protection from. *See*
    Self-protection subself
Predictable environments, influence of,
    on life history strategy, 136, 139
Predicting behavior, 16, 46, 48
Preferences
    changing, 27–29, 34, 39–40, 46,
        47–48
    and inclusive fitness, 56–58
    mate, 167–169, 170–171, 173
    stable, 26, 46, 48
Prescription drug industry, 199–201
Prisoner's dilemma, 53–55, 56, 58, 59,
    62, 67, 69
Probability format, problem with, 97–98,
    101–102, 103–105
    See also Math problems
Promiscuity, 24, 156, 180
Proximate reasons
    awareness of, 158–159
    described, 11

focus on, 12
incomplete understanding of behavior
    provided by, 15–16
links between ultimate reasons and,
    being unaware of, 12–13, 150–151,
    158–159
for men's preference for young
    women, 168
and the ovulatory cycle, 14, 15
and ultimate reasons, as
    complementary, 15
Puberty, earlier onset of, 134
Pyramid schemes, 188, 203

Race relations, 72
Rags-to-riches-to-bankruptcy stories,
    117–118, 119, 136, 138
    See also Risk taking
Randazzo, Richie, 129, 130
Randeria, Shalini, 171–172
Rape, 17, 134, 138
Rational animals, people as,
    evolutionary view of. *See*
    Evolutionary psychologist
    perspective
Rational economist perspective
    behavioral economists versus, 6, 7
    as both right and wrong, 9
    contributions of, and suggestions to
        improve upon, 213–214
    examples of, 1–2, 3, 4
    lesson about, 210–211
    of man as rational, described, 3–4
    *See also specific ideas/concepts of rational
        economists*
Reproductive costs, 163, 165
Reproductive effort, 120, 121
    See also Mating effort; Parenting effort
Reproductive success, defined, 121
    See also Mating opportunities/success
Resource allocation. *See* Life history
    theory

Resources
    limited, dilemma over, 119
    uncertainty over, 135, 179
    willingness to provide, demonstrating,
        163, 172
Restricted strategists, 156, 157
Risk aversion
    as a calculated bias, 45, 82
    money mistakes and, 81–82
Risk taking
    described, 16–20
    inclusive fitness and, 56
    mate-acquisition game and, 173, 174,
        175
    mating effort and, 123, 125–127, 128,
        173
    types of, as financial strategies,
        130–131
    See also Fast strategy
Roberts, Julia, 147
Rock, Chris, 200
Rock stars, early death of, 138
Role-playing, presumption in, 48–49
Romantic subself. *See* Mate-acquisition
    subself
Ronay, Richard, 17
Roney, Jim, 154
Rowling, J. K., 214, 215

Saad, Gad, 157
Safe environments, influence of, on life
    history strategy, 136, 139
Sanabria, Federico, 59
Santos, Laurie, 9
Sapolsky, Robert, 37–38
Scarcity ploy, 196, 197, 203
Schaller, Mark, 35, 83, 84
Schmitt, David, 164
Science, appeal of, 215–216
Scientific management, principle of, 69
Secord, Paul, 179–180
Segal, Nancy, 56, 57–58

Self-actualization, 44
Self-interest
　described, 3–4
　lesson about, 210–211
　putting aside, 73
　See also Subselves
Self-protection subself
　advance warning system of, 78, 93
　advertising preferences of, 28–29,
　　30
　described, 33–34, 212
　fulfilling the needs of, spending on,
　　189
　hierarchy of needs and, 43
　and loss aversion, 47
　mating effort and, 123
　parasites of, 199
　parenting effort and, 125
　and rules of the game, 66–68
　somatic effort and, 122
　and tension between subselves, 49
　*See also specific aspects related to the
　　self-protection subself*
September 11, 2001, 140
Sex detector systems, 86–90, 93
Sex differences. *See* Men; Women
Sex ratios, 179–182, 183
Sexton, Alison, 149
Sexton, Steve, 149
Sexual economics
　conspicuous displays and, 153
　mate preference and, 170
　of reproduction, 163–164, 165
　See also Mate-acquisition subself;
　　Mate-retention subself; Men;
　　Women
Sexual mistakes, avoiding, 166
Sexual revolution, 180
Sharif, Ismael Ibn, 169
Sherman, William Tecumseh, 64
Shiwiar tribe, 95–96, 100, 104, 106,
　　108–109, 110–111

Siblings
　and inclusive fitness, 56–57, 57–58,
　　59–60
　twin, 56, 57–58, 62
Simpson, Jeff, 135, 156
Singh, Bhupinder, 64, 65
Singh, Rajinder, 169
Single parents, 117, 133, 136
Singles ads, 173
Sizemore, Chris, 25
Slow strategy
　attitude of people following the,
　　toward fast strategists, example of,
　　140
　and conspicuous consumption, 157
　described, 119, 121
　environmental factors leading to,
　　136–137, 138, 139
　fast strategy versus, 128–129
　as a financial investment strategy, 131
　genetic factor in, 133
　low variance of, 137
　mate-acquisition subself and, 156, 157
　restricted, 156, 157
　and sexual supply and demand, 181
　types of people following, 132–133
Smith, William Kennedy, 17
Smoke detector dilemma, 79–80
Smoke detector principle
　described, 80–81, 87
　flip side of the, 88
　money mistakes and the, 81–82
"Sociology of Bride Price and Dowry"
　　(Randeria and Visaria), 171–172
Sociopathy, indicator of, 68
Somatic effort, 120, 121, 122, 132
Southwest Airlines, 71–72, 213
Sperry, Roger W., 25
Spielberg, Steven, 186
Spitzer, Eliot, 161, 167, 209
Split-brain patients, 25
Sports Illustrated (magazine), 118

Stable preferences, 26, 46, 48
Statistical computations. *See* Math problems
Status subself
  conspicuous consumption and, 143–144, 148–150, 151
  described, 37–39, 212
  fulfilling the needs of, spending on, 189
  going green and, 148, 149, 150, 151
  hierarchy of needs and, 43
  mating effort and, 122, 123, 124
  overconfidence bias and, 91–93
  parasites of, 198
  and rules of the game, 64–66
  selling to, marketing strategy in, 191, 192
  See also specific aspects related to the status subself
Stepparents, inclusive fitness and, 57
Stress response, 138–140
Subselves
  compatibility between, 49
  different responses from, 26–27, 82–83
  game theory and rules for different, 60–67, 73
  knowing your evolutionary needs and, to avoid overspending, 205
  lesson about, 211–212
  making complex problems relevant to our, 105–106, 108, 109
  money and, 44–45
  multiple, existence of, 26
  number of, and how they work, 30–32
  others exploiting our, 186–187
  and persuasion, 27–30
  remembering, way of, 42–44
  versus roles, 48–49
  selling to, marketing strategies in, 190–194

  shut out of the decision-making process, 204
  tension between, 49
  types of, described, 32–42
  voluntarily waking up your own, 212–213
  See also Affiliation subself; Disease-avoidance subself; Kin-care subself; Mate-acquisition subself; Mate-retention subself; Self-protection subself; Status subself
Sugiyama, Larry, 95–96, 108, 109
Sundie, Jill, 28, 59, 154, 156–157
Supply and demand, sexual, 179–182
Swanson, Gloria, 1, 4, 17
Symbiotic mutualism, 187, 189, 190, 194, 203

Talking versus writing, 99–101
Taylor, Frederick Winslow, 69
Teenagers/young adults
  causes of death among, 123, 173
  equality matching and, 62
  fast versus slow strategies and, 128–129
  mating effort and, 122–123, 125–128, 173
  rating, as competent, 128
  status subself and, 38
Testosterone, 18, 19, 123, 125, 126, 127, 183
Theory of the Leisure Class, The (Veblen), 143
Theresa, Mother, 38
Three Faces of Eve, The (movie), 24–25
Tiffany & Co., 199
Time (magazine), 192
Tipping
  exploiting, 188
  sex differences in, 173, 174

Too Many Women? (Guttentag and Secord), 179–180

Topline Strategy Group, 147

Toyota Prius, reason for buying, uncovering, 147–149, 150–151

Trade-offs, making, 19, 119–120, 120–121

Trivers, Robert, 60

Trivial altercations, 123–124

Trudeau, Kevin, 201–203, 204

Trump, Donald, 168

Trust, 69, 186, 194, 195

Trust game, 70–71

Truth-seeking, accuracy and, 77–78

Tversky, Amos, 5, 97, 111, 112, 113

Twins, 56, 57–58, 62

Tybur, Josh, 14, 83, 148, 154, 157

Tyson, Mike, 118, 135–136, 138

Ultimate reasons
    as commonly overlooked, 12, 159
    described, 11–12
    exploring, for conspicuous consumption, 151–157, 158
    links between proximate reasons and, being unaware of, 12–13, 150–151, 158–159
    and the ovulatory cycle, 14, 15
    and proximate reasons, as complementary, 15
    valuable insight provided by, 16, 20
    See also Evolutionary challenges, the need to solve

Ultimatum game, 55, 66

Unpredictable environments, influence of, on life history strategy, 134–136, 137, 139–140, 141

Unrestricted strategists, 156, 157, 166

US presidents, expectations of, 64, 65–66

Utility, 12, 20, 146, 191

Van den Bergh, Bram, 148

Veblen, Thorstein, 143, 145, 151

Vigilant subself. *See* Self-protection subself

Violence, 17, 33, 57, 123–124, 134, 135, 138, 173, 179, 180

Virginity, 163

Visaria, Leela, 171–172

Vohs, Kathleen, 157, 163–164

von Hippel, William, 17

Vongas, John, 157

Wall Street game. *See* Game theory

Wall Street model. *See* Market economics

Wall Street (movie), 3

Wall Street traders, 1, 16, 45, 56, 67, 126

Walmart, 198

Walt Disney Company, 51–52, 72–73

Wang, X. T., 113, 114

Wason task, 106–107, 108–109

Wayne, Ronald "Ron," 93, 127

Why Everyone (Else) Is a Hypocrite (Kurzban), 25

Why Smart People Make Big Money Mistakes (Belsky and Gilovich), 81

Wiesel, Elie, 186

Wilson, Margo, 123, 124

Wilson, Tim, 147

Winehouse, Amy, 138

Women
    bride price paid for, 162–163, 171, 182
    and conspicuous consumption, 154–155, 159, 182
    dowry of, 162–163, 171–172
    as escorts, men paying for, 161–162, 163, 167
    and first professions of love, 165–167
    as first-time mothers, age of, 124, 132, 134
    generous tipping and, 173, 174

jealousy and, 178, 179
mate-acquisition game for, 173,
    174–176
mate-retention game for, 176–177
mating effort and, 122, 123, 132
and men's risk taking, 17, 19–20
and onset of menstruation, age of,
    134, 135
ovulatory cycle of, subconscious
    influence of, 13–16, 19, 89–90, 93,
    182
parenting stage and, 124, 125
preference of, for men with financial
    prospects, 170–171, 173
pregnant, and the disease-avoidance
    subself, 36
ratio of men to, and sexual supply and
    demand, 179–182
risk taking and, 175
sex detectors of, and the
    mate-acquisition subself, 88–90,
    93
sexual economics and, 153, 163, 164

standards of, for partners, 164–165,
    177
testosterone levels of, 123, 125
and their response to insults, 39
young and beautiful, men's preference
    for, 167–169, 170, 171, 173
World According to Garp, The (Irving), 6
World Health Organization, 35, 86
World Series of Poker, 125–126
Wozniak, Steve, 61, 62, 63–64, 91, 93,
    127
Writing, talking versus, 99–101

Young adults. See Teenagers/young
    adults
Young beautiful women, men's
    preference for, 167–169, 170, 171,
    173

Zambian aid fiasco, 75–76, 85–86
Zepter Luxury International, 199
Zuckerberg, Mark, 127
Zuckerman, Mort, 186